Korea's Developmental Alliance

South Korea is often cited as a case of miraculous transformation from poverty to prosperity. Korea's achievement of moving from one of the world's poorest countries as recently as the early 1960s to the ranks of the ten biggest economies only four decades later has rightly attracted interest from policymakers and scholars alike.

This book identifies the factors that shaped relations between the state and big business in Korea, the 'developmental alliance'. These factors offer a cogent framework in which to identify and predict changes in power relations between government and business. Rather than merely offering a means of explaining the rapid-growth phase of Korean development, the politics of the developmental alliance also help us understand how and why the Korean miracle turned to crisis in 1997 and why the subsequent recovery has been so uneven. In this way, the book highlights the political power of business, which is often underplayed in discussions of the development of Korea. It also sheds light on the constraints on policymakers during modernisation, and how power is shared among a small number of powerful parties.

Illustrating the tumultuous politics of the 'developmental alliance' between business and government during the rise and decline of South Korea's economic miracle, this book is an essential read for anyone interested in Korean politics, economics and development.

David Hundt is Lecturer in International Relations at Deakin University, Australia.

Routledge Advances in Korean Studies

Korea's Developmental Alliance

State, capital and the politics of rapid development

David Hundt

Routledge
Taylor & Francis Group

LONDON AND NEW YORK

First published 2009
by Routledge
2 Park Square, Milton Park, Abingdon, Oxon OX14 5RN

Simultaneously published in the USA and Canada
by Routledge
711 Third Avenue, New York, NY 10017

*Routledge is an imprint of the Taylor & Francis Group,
an informa business*

First issued in paperback 2012

© 2009 David Hundt

Typeset in Times New Roman by
Florence Production Ltd, Stoodleigh, Devon

British Library Cataloguing in Publication Data
A catalogue record for this book is available
from the British Library

Library of Congress Cataloging in Publication Data
Hundt, David.
  Korea's developmental alliance: state, capital and politics of
  rapid development/David Hundt.
      p.cm.
    Includes bibliographical references and index.
  1. Business and politics—Korea (South).   2. Korea (South)—
  Economic policy.   3. Economic development—Korea (South).
  4. Korea (South)—Economic conditions.   5. Korea (South)—
  Politics and government.   I. Title.
HC467.756.H86 2008
338.95195—dc22   2008017316

ISBN13: 978–0–415–54159–6 (pbk)
ISBN13: 978–0–415–46668–4 (hbk)
ISBN13: 978–0–203–88906–0 (ebk)

Contents

Acknowledgements

This book is the product of over fifteen years of involvement in the field of Korean Studies. The Korean staff at Griffith University – Professors Jung Jae-Hoon, Kim Chong-Woon and Nah Minjung – cultivated in me an enduring interest in this fascinating society. I am also grateful to Kim Yong-gi, Kim Hyeong-nam, Oh Mihwaja, Oh Kuija, Kim Hyeon-suk, Park Eun-sil, Chae Seong-il, Shin Seung-jun and Babak Bahmanzad. I thank Seoul National University's Professors Yoon Young-Kwan and Shin Wookhee for overseeing my masters thesis, and Kim Song-geon, Hur Gil-sang, Kim Joo Hwan, Dr Park Tae-gyun, and Dr Kim Joo Hwan for their assistance during my visit to Korea in 2004 for doctoral research. I would like to thank those people who agreed to interviews for my research. Officials from the Korean Democratic Labour Party, the National Assembly and the FKI offered valuable insights and information that assisted the writing of my thesis.

I would like to thank my supervisory team at the University of Queensland. Stephen Bell supported my research over a four-year period, and I am grateful for his patient encouragement and advice. Mark Beeson, Roland Bleiker and William Tow offered guidance at crucial stages of the thesis.

Since moving to Deakin University, I have been the recipient of much support and sagacious advice from colleagues such as Sally Totman and Geoff Stokes, and Helen Andrew in terms of administrative support. I also offer my thanks to Gary Smith, who ensured that the manuscript reached this final stage of production.

Among the Korean Studies community in Australia, special mention goes to Ruth Barraclough and Moon Kyoung-Hee. My doctoral candidature at the University of Queensland was made more enjoyable and enriching thanks to colleagues such as Greg Chaikin, Sarah Howe, John Mackenzie, Morgan Brigg and Paul Carnegie. I also thank Brooke Anderson, Michael Bissell, Jane Park, Mark Reed and Jack Saunders for their friendship. I am also most grateful to my family for their ongoing understanding at all times.

Finally, I would like to thank the people most directly involved in bringing this book to fruition. Stephanie Rogers, Sonja van Leeuwen and Leanne Hinves from Routledge not only provided valuable editorial direction but also did me a great service by sending the manuscript to two anonymous reviewers, who provided many suggestions about how to improve its quality. Furthermore I am indebted to the examiners of my doctoral thesis for incisive commentary and encouragement to publish in the first place. It would also be remiss of me to not comment on the sterling performance of Brendan Harris as copy editor and commentator in the final stages of the manuscript's production. Despite the substantial input of all these contributors, I take full responsibility for the final product.

Abbreviations

BOK	Bank of Korea
CEO	chief executive officer
DA	developmental alliance
D-E	debt-to-equity (ratio)
DLP	Democratic Liberal Party
DPRK	Democratic People's Republic of Korea
DRAM	dynamic random access memory
EOI	export-oriented industrialisation
EPB	Economic Planning Board
FKI	Federation of Korean Industries
FRUS	*Foreign Relations of the United States* (US government papers)
FSC	Financial Securities Commission
GNP	Grand National Party
HCI	Heavy and Chemical Industry (project)
HDTV	high-definition television
HMWU	Hyundai Motor Workers Union
IFIs	international financial institutions
IMF	International Monetary Fund
ISI	import-substitution industrialisation
KCIA	Korean Central Intelligence Agency
KCTU	Korean Council of Trade Unions
M&A	mergers and acquisitions
MCI	Ministry of Commerce and Industry
MITI	Ministry of International Trade and Industry (Japan)
MOF	Ministry of Finance
MOFE	Ministry of Finance and Economy
NBFI	non-bank financial institution
NGO	non-governmental organisation
NPL	non-performing loan
PSPD	People's Solidarity for Participatory Democracy
ROK	Republic of Korea

SMEs	small–medium enterprises
SOEs	state-owned enterprises
UN	United Nations
UNTCOK	United Nations Transitional Commission on Korea

Note on romanisation

This book follows the (South) Korean system of romanisation – refer to Ministry of Culture and Tourism proclamation 2000–8, available at: www.korea.net/korea/kor_loca.asp?code=A020303 (accessed 28 May 2008) – for transliterating Korean words. Proper nouns, such as '*chaebol*', may be romanised differently from the new system (which would render it '*jaebeol*') if such nouns are already widely used as to alter their romanisation now would only create unnecessary confusion. The new system is used almost uniformly for Korean place names: for instance, the south-eastern Kyongsang province is now known as 'Gyeongsang', its capital Pusan as 'Busan', and Cholla province as 'Jeolla'. Seoul is still spelt 'Seoul' under the new system. The book seeks to respect the wishes of individuals, such as the new president, who choose to transliterate their names in a manner inconsistent with the official system. It retains the transliteration of the names of former presidents Syngman Rhee, Park Chung Hee and Chang Myon, and also retains the Korean practice of placing surnames before given names, except when the author or figure seemingly prefers to adopt the Western style of placing the given names first. In the case of the former presidents listed above, Rhee, Park and Chang are surnames while Syngman, Chung Hee and Myon respectively are given names. Rhee chose to romanise his name in what might now be considered an unconventional manner; Park spelt his in the Korean style; Chang, confusingly, was sometimes also referred to by his English name of John, becoming variously John Chang, Chang Myon, Myon Chang or John M. Chang. There was confusion over the spelling of former president Park's name until the government revealed its preferred rendering of his name in the mid-1960s. In some American documents quoted in the book, his surname appears as 'Pak' instead of Park, and his given name as 'Chong-hui' rather than Chung Hee. Kim Jong-pil's given name also appears on occasion as 'Chong-pil'. When quoting directly from documents, the book retains the transliteration used in the original.

Introduction

The developmental alliance and Korean development

Prologue: a new beginning?

In late 2007, the conservative Grand National Party (GNP) won Korea's[1] presidential election in a landslide. It was the most comprehensive win by a presidential candidate in the period since Korea's transition to democracy two decades earlier. The victory of Lee Myung-bak[2] brought to an end ten years of progressive (centre-left) government, which had begun when Kim Dae-jung was elected amid the Asian financial crisis and continued with the presidency of Roh Moo-hyun from 2003. These leaders oversaw Korea's recovery from the financial crisis, the centrepiece of which was a rigorous programme of industrial and financial reform. In particular, the Kim and Roh administrations emphasised the reform of the *chaebols*, the ubiquitous industrial conglomerates that have for decades been the weightiest players in the Korean economy.

Unlike the previous two occupants of the Blue House, the GNP's candidate had brought his experience as CEO (chief executive officer) of Hyundai Construction to the mayoralty of Seoul in 2002. As mayor, Lee raised the quality of life of Seoul's citizens by improving the public transport system and restoring an ancient waterway through the middle of the city. While admirers attribute Lee's achievements to the managerial skills he acquired at Hyundai, opinion polls suggested that a substantial number of Koreans believed that serious ethical issues plagued their new president. Allegations of embezzlement and the fixing of stock prices dogged his election campaign for months, and for some time there were concerns that the president could be charged with a number of offences (Alford 2007: 22). Although the new president was not charged with impropriety, if he unduly favours either his

---

1 Although the official name of the country is the Republic of Korea (ROK), for the most part this volume uses the term Korea. When necessary – for instance when discussing North Korea (Democratic People's Republic of Korea, DPRK) – it reverts to South Korea or the ROK.
2 See page xi for note on romanisation.

former business associates or those of another of the *chaebols* during his term in office, he will only be the latest in a series of presidents who illustrate that political and economic power are closely entwined in Korea. A full ten years after Kim Dae-jung promised to reduce the dominance of the big business in political and economic life by resolving the '*chaebol* problem' (Haggard *et al*. 2003b), Korea's largest enterprises remain an integral element of the power elite. The election of a former CEO to the presidency only reinforces this sense of continuity.

This book explores the enduring and intimate relations between the state (government) and big business (*chaebols*) in the modernisation of South Korea. These relations, it is argued, have taken a form that is readily distinguishable from state–business collaboration in most other countries. In tracing a 'genealogy' of the East Asian developmental state, Bruce Cumings (1999) posits that Japan acted as a link between Germany statecraft of the late nineteenth century and the close relationship between political and corporate elites in Korean society since the 1960s. A common trait of the developmental state, Cumings tells us, is the simultaneous prioritisation of national security and economic development. Crucial here has been a shared belief among political leaders that the state should act as the primary agent of social transformation and, consequently, that it is *legitimate* for the state to mobilise societal resources to that end. While possessing substantial capacities with which to achieve its internal developmental agenda, Cumings argues (1998), the 'semi-sovereign' Korean state has struggled to resolve its external security dilemma.

The power of the state has thus been far from absolute, necessitating a collaborative relationship with business elites in order for political leaders to achieve goals of national importance. Influenced by notions of the centrality and proprietary of state leadership, and of the importance of acting in the 'national interest', a small group of Korean political and economic elites has jealously guarded its dominance of power via a *developmental alliance* (DA). The alliance, as will be explained in more detail below, incorporates a set of interlocking mutual interests but also sets the boundaries of disputes between the most influential actors in the Korean political economy. The existence of these interests has not, however, safeguarded the DA from tensions and even hostility, most notably when conflicts have arisen about the distribution of the costs and benefits of national development. Consequently this book draws on both primary and secondary materials – such as the author's interviews with government and business officials, memoirs of former politicians and policymakers, magazine and journal articles, statistical data and government reports – to illustrate the tense and yet close relations between big business and the state.

Given that the DA is a ubiquitous feature of Korean political economy that deserves attention in its own right, this book differs from the numerous publications that focus on the role of the state in Korean development. For instance the statist–institutionalist literature, responsible for 'bringing the state back in' to explanations about the locus of economic development, has dominated studies of Korean political economy since the 1980s (Amdsen 1992; Woo 1991). These scholars provide valuable insights about the ways in which the state creates an incentive structure that is conducive to capitalist development. An impressive stock of knowledge, drawing mainly on the related disciplines of political science, economics and sociology, has enhanced our understanding of the Korean state's *developmental project* – the economic component of nation-building efforts (see below). On the other hand a more recent innovation has been to 'bring capital back in' to the study of Korean development. Scholars such as Vivek Chibber (1999, 2005), Seok-Jin Lew (1992) and Timothy Lim (1998, 1999) note that the *structural power of capital* acts as a constraining force on the state's (self-appointed) prerogative to influence the pace, direction and content of economic development. This line of inquiry provides a valuable corrective to assumptions that it is only the state that contributes to a developmental project.

This book builds on these literatures by breaking the artificial binary between two varieties and sources of power. It focuses on the interaction between the state's power to productively contribute to capitalist development – also known as *infrastructural power* – and the structural power of capital. In this regard, the book acknowledges the output of scholars such as Eun Mee Kim (1997), and seeks to update and expand the study of state–business relations in Korea. Rather than seeing these two varieties of power being generated and exercised in separation from each other, this book instead analyses their interaction by presenting them in the context of the DA. Tracking the balance – or imbalance – of power in the developmental alliance offers a way to explain changes in economic policy. We do this by devising and consulting an analytical framework that plots and measures change in five major contextual variables – briefly outlined in the third section of this chapter – in each phase of Korean economic development.

In this way the book seeks to contribute to research on the modernisation of Korea since the 1960s. By any measure the achievements of South Korea in the post-war period – a consolidated albeit imperfect liberal democracy, a vibrant capitalist economy now among the world's dozen largest, a vigorous civil society and popular culture with regional if not global appeal – have been remarkable. And yet the central power relationship that has endured in this period, the developmental alliance, is still not well understood. Which factors have held the alliance together, and which have brought it under strain? Is it likely to retain such a central position in future? And has its legacy been – on the whole – beneficial or detrimental to Korean society? How do the vast majority of Koreans who have no involvement in the DA view this relationship that has so affected their lives?

More broadly, the book seeks to clarify the *specificity* of the Korean experience: Is there a 'unique' Korean mode of political economy? If so, to what degree has it survived the Asian financial crisis? If not, how readily can Korea reconcile itself to the dominant Anglo–American modes of production and regulation? Is Korea destined to adopt the features of the advanced industrialised countries, or at least move towards a hybrid model (Haggard *et al.* 2003a)? This in turn raises questions about the *legacy* of the Korean experience. As Peter Evans (1998) has asked, which lessons – if any – from Korea are transferable to other parts of the world? If other countries are to pursue developmental projects and join the ranks of the advanced nations, should they too expect power to accrue intensively to a small group of actors, as in Korea? Must those aspiring to prosperity rely on 'risk partnerships' (W. Lim 2003) like Korea's, whereby the state – and by implication, the public – guarantees private-sector investments? Or can a greater degree of democratic accountability accompany rapid development?[3] If the Republic of Korea (ROK) is to serve as an exemplar for other developing countries – and there is certainly no consensus about whether it can or should – the intricacies of the DA need to be fully appreciated. The crisis has been portrayed as the end of an era in state-led development, and if this were proven to be true, such a development would have significant impli- cations for the DA. Consequently, at this juncture it is worth reviewing the debate that emanated in the aftermath of the financial crisis, when the utility of the Korean model – and its very future application, even in Korea itself – came under intense scrutiny.

Power and political economy in Korea

The crisis of 1997–8 sparked robust debate about the *developmental state* in Korea. Chalmers Johnson – one of the concept's original proponents – considers the developmental state to be undeniably capitalist in nature, one that via 'conscious and consistent governmental policies' has actively sought to 'improve the outcomes of market forces' (Johnson 1999: 37, 49).

Most scholars, from a wide spectrum of normative perspectives, have been pessimistic about the continuing prospects for such state activism in Korea. First, liberals such as Ross Garnaut (1998) claim that the crisis represented the passing of Korea's dirigiste phase. These scholars argue that the substantial reforms demanded by the International Monetary Fund (IMF) ruled out a reversion to the style of state activism typical of the initial stages of Korean development. Consequently, Iain Pirie (2005a, 2005b) claims, a 'new' Korean state emerged in the wake of the financial crisis, one committed to the introduction of a market economy. What is more, he argues (2008) that the state's capacity to play such a facilitating role in national development was ever diminishing because of changes at the global level. Another variant of the liberal argument comes from Kanishka Jayasuriya (2005), who notes

---

3   Korea's 'corporatism without labour' has not gone unremarked or unchallenged. Refer for instance to Dennis McNamara's edited collection (1999) and also Hagen Koo (2001).

that East Asian states such as Korea are shifting from earlier developmental orientations to 'regulatory' ones, whereby state activism is heavily
circumscribed.

The statist–institutionalist school, meanwhile, argues that the basis for
effective state intervention had eroded in the years preceding the crisis. The
argument here is that the state had abandoned – either willingly or under
pressure from the US – its most effective forms of *industrial policy* (see
Johnson 1984), including those regulatory tools used to minimise irresponsible
behaviour on the part of business. Hence the crisis was the result of *too little*
regulation (J.-S. Shin and H.-J. Chang 2005). In the view of these scholars,
the reforms of 1997–8 expedited the process by which the state's capacity
to influence the growth trajectory of the Korean economy has been fatally
impaired. These scholars thus implicitly agree with the notion that the
crisis represented a fundamental change to the developmental state. A less
pessimistic variant of the statist argument sees the Korean developmental
state evolving into a 'transformative state' (Cherry 2005), one that relies less
on the traditional forms of industrial policy and more on indirect means of
influence. Linda Weiss (2005), furthermore, points to the 'state augmenting'
effects of globalisation, arguing that the objective of the state remains to
improve national outcomes, albeit under conditions of increasing integration
with the global economy.

Keeping broadly with the statist position, this volume agrees that there is
plentiful evidence to suggest that the Korean state retains the capacity to
contribute to the development of the capitalist economy since the financial
crisis. Nevertheless, these accounts tend to focus too exclusively on the
state. To focus solely – or primarily – on the state, as most studies have
done, is to neglect the *processes* through which the state interacts with society,
and especially the *chaebols*. This book thus emphasises the *structural power*
of capital, the power that business derives from its position in the economy,
and the ability that this grants business to protect its interests (Block 1992:
294). Consequently the primary unit of analysis for this book is the developmental alliance – that is, the interaction between the structural power of
capital and the *infrastructural power* of the state – rather than the state itself.

The key to understanding Korean developmentalism, this book argues, is
to focus on the changing dynamics of the relationship between the state and
the *chaebols* in the DA. As scholars such as Richard Luedde–Neurath (1986)
noted two decades ago, a distinguishing feature of the Korean developmental
state has been its concerted campaigns to regulate private capital. As discussed
in later chapters, the introduction of new regulatory mechanisms – even
those that the state does not control directly – signifies an ongoing commitment
to regulation on the part of the state. For instance, two of the most effective
regulatory tools introduced in order to induce an economic recovery were
state-sponsored 'Big Deals' (mergers) and the rationalisation of the banking
system (Mo and Moon 2003), which had the effect of reducing the capacity
of the *chaebols* to access finance free of state influence.

This transition from a top-down, state-centric mode of governance towards a new mode based on market-based disciplines and economic openness has encouraged the trend – noted above – for scholars to focus on what they perceive as a weakening of state power. However, attempts to measure the relative strength of the Korean state by observing its disciplinary mechanisms can lead to confusion between the *means* and *ends* of governance. This book, in contrast, treats the DA as not only a locus of governance but also a site of contestation over how governance should occur. That is, we focus on how the partners of the DA have directed the course of economic development and also on their competing visions for the economy.

The Korean experience with rapid development over the past four decades illustrates how the state has sought to harness societal resources (capital, labour, technology, raw materials) to a developmental project. Crucially, the state has induced cooperation from big business in this pursuit. Yet Korean capital, as Chibber (2005) reminds us, has in general possessed a higher degree of structural power than in most other countries. This has restricted the capacity of the state to formulate socially beneficial development policies. By 'bringing capital back in' (Lew 1992), we highlight the independent power resources of Korean capital. This fosters a focus on the DA, the long-lasting – albeit tense – relationship between state and capital.

The dynamics of the developmental alliance

Our methodological challenge is to construct a framework in which to analyse the two varieties of power discussed above. In this sense, the book concurs with the call by Richard Boyd and Tak-Wing Ngo (2005) for analysis of East Asia's experience with rapid growth to be conducted in a broader political economy framework. By widening the scope of analysis to encompass not only the state and capital but also the factors that shape their interaction, we seek to overcome the state–society dichotomy that characterises some studies of the developmental state (see Underhill and Zhang 2005: 4–6).

The study traces the dynamics of the relationship in light of five contextual variables: *bureaucracy*, *social pressures*, *national security*, *economic conditions* and *globalisation*. These variables add context to the political dynamics of economic development by illustrating how two forms of power – the structural power of capital and infrastructural power – interact in the developmental alliance.

Bureaucracy

A developmentalist, nationalist and competent bureaucracy has acted as a conduit through which the state has negotiated the terms of the developmental alliance. In particular, the bureaucracy has served as the direct and enabling force of the state, allowing the Korean government to exercise infrastructural power. Vivek Chibber (2002), for instance, reminds us that the emergence of the developmental orientation – and achievement of internal consensus on the prioritisation of the developmental project – sets the Korean bureaucracy apart from less successful developing countries.

As formulators and implementers of economic policy, senior policymakers who have enjoyed intimate access to political leaders – figures such as Kim Chung-yum, Kim Jae-ik and Lee Hun-jai in more recent times – have had a significant degree of input to the shaping of the developmental project. Consequently this book investigates the ideas and attitudes of the bureaucracy at each phase of Korean development and at each phase of the DA. Crucial to our study will be questions about the degree of insulation that the bureaucracy enjoys from the cut and thrust of mundane politics. We ask how well the bureaucracy protected its policymaking autonomy from populist political leaders, actors external to the DA – such as non-governmental organisations (NGOs) and trade unions – and also from the *chaebols*. Mindful of the observations of scholars such as Elizabeth Thurbon (2003), who notes that the policymaking elite includes both pro-state and pro-market elements, we also seek to avoid the assumption that the Korean bureaucracy is a unitary actor that enjoys internal cohesion and purpose.

Social pressures

When investigating the politics of the DA, a second consideration will be the responses of other actors to what is in essence a highly exclusive arrangement. As noted in respect to the role of bureaucracy, the democratisation of Korea from the 1980s has reduced the insulation of the DA from external scrutiny. Assessing precisely how what we term social pressures impacts on the DA is crucial not only in terms of its impact on policymakers but also on the responses of the *chaebols*, who have been exposed to both scrutiny and criticism for their business practices.

Negotiations between state and society are crucial for authoritarian regimes, which lack popular consent. As Vivek Chibber notes, 'While the Korean state in its developmentalist phase was by no means an exemplar of progressive governance, it does show the possibility of successfully "governing the market"' (2005: 124). The legitimacy of the Park Chung Hee regime, for instance, rested on economic development (see Chapter 4). This explains the Korean state's motivation for rapid, *sustained* economic growth, especially prior to the emergence of democratic politics in the late 1980s.[4] In what ways, if any, does the relationship between economic performance and legitimacy change under democratic governance? What does this imply for the top-down development model that Korea adopted in the 1960s?

---

4   Peter Evans (1989, 1995) compares the ways in which various Third World states – including Korea – have used different varieties of power.

National security

Given that the military alliance with the United States predated the developmental phase in Korea, analysis of the DA necessarily entails an investigation of the impact of national security. America's commitment to the ROK's survival has explicitly linked the military alliance to economic development. The attitude of American governments has varied from explicit support for Korean economic development to something approaching hostility in the face of large trade surpluses in the late 1980s, and during the financial crisis the US government – via the IMF – requested wholesale reform of the state-led development model and the '*chaebol* system'.

The Cold War context was crucial to the opportunities that the US afforded to Korea, so we need to investigate how the passing – or at least lessening – of Cold War tensions has impacted on American acquiescence to the state-led model. Crucial too are changes in the US economy and the country's standing in the world: how has the passing of the Cold War – and the emergence of an unbalanced American hegemony that is unchallenged in conventional military terms but in gradual decline in terms of economic power – impacted on the ways in which the US treats both friends and foes? In turn, how has the emergence of a more critical appraisal of American foreign policy by Korean governments affected the military and economic ties between the two long-term allies? And how have efforts by South Korea to improve ties with its northern counterpart, under the rubric of the Sunshine Policy, complicated the military alliance? What, in short, is the potential impact of a divergence in interests between the US and Korea?

Economic conditions

As the developmental alliance is primarily focused on improving the structure of the economy, we can confidently expect economic conditions to be a major influence on the power dynamics of state–business relations. The business power literature tells us that the state must not reduce the willingness of business to invest, because big business plays a disproportionately large role in helping to manage the economy. The 'privileged position of business', Charles Lindblom (1977) argues, makes the developmental project dependent on the willingness of large firms to invest.

When the economy is growing strongly, there is little incentive for government to make sudden policy changes, especially those of which business disapproves. It is at these times that we expect the implicit threat to withdraw or curtail to be most effective. The real issue is what happens when economic conditions change suddenly for the worse. If economic conditions are bad, the incentive for cooperation in the DA is greater. Given that the state often plays a crucial role in 'pump-priming' a moribund economy, business may be forced to acquiesce to greater oversight than it prefers. This is a pertinent issue for the Korean economy, whose four decades of rapid growth has been interspersed with a number of relatively short and yet tumultuous financial-economic crises. The financial crisis of 1997–8 was just the most recent of several calamitous crises, prompting Tat Yan Kong (2000: 18–19) to refer to Korea's period of rapid growth as a 'fragile miracle'. In order to engender a recovery from crisis, the emphasis in economic policy has switched from 'growth' to 'stabilisation', resulting in change to the incentive structures and regulatory approach of the state. It is worth noting that some critics blame the *chaebols'* purportedly reckless behaviour – especially in the form of duplicate investments and excessive borrowing – for Korea's intermittent financial crises, introducing a moral element to the exercise of power. For these reasons we will ascertain how the state of the economy impacts on the dynamics of the DA.

Globalisation

Discussion of the impact of general economic conditions encourages us to think about the specific role of the external environment on the DA, in the form of the forces of globalisation. This contextual variable, which we expect to partially correlate with national security (discussed above), describes the increasing integration of the Korean economy with the global economic system over the past two decades. Nick Bisley (2007) explains that the nature and extent of globalisation varies across time and space, and this book focuses on how it influences the DA in each phase of Korea's industrialisation.

An assumption from the neoclassical literature is that the liberalisation of markets will benefit firms by exposing them to competition, providing access to new markets, technologies, business practices and production methods. And yet, given the corporatist nature of the Korean model of development and its 'patient capital' model (Wade and Veneroso 1998), it is not readily apparent that the Korean *chaebols* would welcome market liberalisation. For instance, in the aftermath of the financial crisis, Korea implemented regulatory changes that have strengthened the powers of foreign investors and other external parties to oversee board-level decisions in *chaebol* enterprises (see Yun 2003). How have various forms of exposure to 'global standards' of business practice impacted on the *chaebols*, and the DA more broadly? Is globalisation necessarily detrimental to the state, or can its forces be somehow harnessed to the goals of state leaders?

The study thus poses a range of questions about each phase of Korean development, and seeks to trace state–business relations during each of these phases. Table 1.1 summarises the framework of the study, setting a research agenda that illustrates the Korean experience with rapid development and the place of the DA in it.

Overview of the book

The framework described in this chapter has the potential to provide a theoretical basis to Korean political economy. As noted above, one of the great unanswered questions is whether the Korean experience and 'model'

Table 1.1 Framework for analysis

Bureaucracy
- How have ideas and orientations changed over time?
- How well insulated has the pilot agency been from external penetration (and political interference)?
- Has the quality of the bureaucracy changed?

Social pressures
- How has democratisation affected the DA and the policy agenda?
- How important is it for the DA to be seen as legitimate in the eyes of civil society?
- To what degree have anti-capitalist measures been incorporated in the policy agenda?

National security
- How has the passing of the Cold War influenced the DA?
- What changes have ensued from the relative decline in American economic power?
- How has the US worldview changed since the 'war on terror', and how does this affect Korea's developmental trajectory?

Economic conditions
- What is the relationship between economic performance and business power?
- How do sudden economic declines and crises impact on the DA?
- How is both blame and kudos for economic performance apportioned? Who decides when and how this occurs?

Globalisation
- How has globalisation affected Korea's institutions, economic policies and business practices?
- How has globalisation influenced the capacity of the Korean state to direct the course of economic development?
- How has increasing competition impacted on the Korean political economy?

---

are unique products of the ROK's time and place in world history or whether they serve as a replicable model for other developing countries. How are we to assess the legacy of the DA? Prior to embarking on our analysis of the developmental alliance, it is worth reviewing the field of research into Korean political economy. For this reason Chapter 1 introduces the main approaches to the Korean state in the post-war era – neoclassical economics and the statist–institutionalist perspective – and explores the evolution of each framework and their main conceptual features. Given that both approaches are insufficient for analysing the DA, the book draws on the business power literature in order to formulate a historically focused, comprehensive explanatory framework. The framework is presented in Chapter 2, which examines state–business relations by considering the five contextual variables outlined briefly in the previous section.

Chapter 3 focuses on the patterns of political economy during the 'pre-take-off' stage of Korean development. Park Chung Hee and his fellow coup-makers were first-hand witnesses to a nationalist state-led development model during the Japanese colonial era. This 'demonstration effect' was twofold: the colonial era showcased the supposed virtues of state-led development and also the perils of relying on despotic power. In a similar manner, Rhee's government was not developmental; it instead relied on the ROK's close security ties with the US to focus on economic reconstruction via American aid projects, import substitution and land reform (Kong 2000: 24). Even though the DA did not come into being until the Park era, we focus on the gradual emergence of two crucial conditions for the developmental alliance – national security concerns and the rationale for a developmental state due to immature economic conditions – in the pre-take-off phase.

In Chapter 4, the book focuses on the Park era, the apotheosis of the developmental state. The developmental regime was founded on the premise of American support, and yet relations with the US deteriorated during the presidency of Richard Nixon. Consequently we expect the national security variable to figure prominently during this period. The role of the bureaucracy, the interface between the state and business, also became important to the DA in this period. The state could not achieve economic development without business, and the bureaucracy would be crucial to how closely the alliance partners would collaborate. At the same time, the state was cognisant of the need to involve the wider public in the developmental project while maximising the capacity of the DA partners to formulate economic policy. For this reason, we would expect that social pressures would increase in importance in the DA, especially given the imperative for the state to create an urban workforce to meet the needs of an industrial economy (see Koo 1990). A further consideration is to investigate the role of economic conditions, especially in terms of the Heavy and Chemical Industry (HCI) programme. In addition, the chapter focuses on the growing importance of globalisation due to Korea's reliance on export revenues, technology transfers and inflows of foreign capital.

Chapter 5 explains how Chun Doo-hwan liberalised the economy and dispensed with dirigiste policy tools such as preferential access to credit in the early 1980s. The relative importance of the bureaucracy rose substantially, increasing the impact of globalisation on the state–business alliance. The study also considers the role of economic conditions, as policy reflected a renewed emphasis on stabilisation rather than growth in the wake of the slowdown in 1979–80. Chang Ha-Joon (1993), for instance, notes that the perceived need to stabilise the economy strengthened the hand of the state in rationalising those industrial sectors that were deemed to be overcrowded following the substantial investments during the HCI period. We expect the salience of national security to decline relative to the Park period, but American influence was still apparent given the neoliberal shift encouraged by US-trained bureaucrats such as Kim Jae-ik. The government's adoption of more socially inclusive and populist policies during the presidency of Roh Tae-woo (1988–93) highlighted the growing importance of social pressures. This encouraged the government to adopt a neutral or anti-*chaebol* stance on some issues, with implications for the DA. Also of relevance was the ongoing globalisation of the Korean economy, especially during the presidency of Kim Young-sam.

Chapter 6 argues that during the post-crisis period the state gained influence over the policymaking agenda by drawing on support from domestic and international actors. This entailed appeals to populism, the adoption of neoliberal reform and a renewed emphasis on stabilisation. These policy shifts underline the role of the bureaucracy, raising questions about precisely what role civil servants play in the DA. The state's success in re-legitimating itself was at least in part due to social pressures. The book will measure the impact of anti-*chaebol* sentiment of the government and the public. The chapter notes that globalisation reached its greatest level yet in this period, a time when economic conditions swung from decades of relatively strong growth to crisis. That the impetus for reform came from Korean political and economic elites rather than external actors such as the IMF and the US Treasury raises issues of national security and American imperatives in the post-Cold War era.

The conclusions of the book, presented in Chapter 7, review the questions raised at the outset. Here the book highlights the most important trends, such as the correlation among certain variables. What implications do recent developments have for the military alliance, for democracy – and democratic governance – and for the Korean manufacturing base? Is it possible for a post-nationalist developmental state to emerge, or is the developmental state inherently a creature of the nation–state? We explore the implications of the book for state autonomy and state–society relations, and the prospects for state-led development.

1 Korea in the political economy literature

Introduction

The developmental alliance (DA) has underpinned Korean industrialisation over the past four decades. Central to the DA has been an ongoing process of collaboration as well as conflict, of shared priorities as well as divergences of interests. And yet, as this chapter will illustrate, the relationship between the state and capital, the two partners of Korea's modernisation, has been insufficiently appreciated and theorised in the existing literature on the East Asian model.

Before detailing the framework that this book proposes for studying the power relations of the DA, it is worth reviewing the literature on East Asian political economy. The chapter begins by outlining neoclassical (liberal) views of economic development, which focus on the centrality of the market. Liberals tend to dismiss state-led development projects on the grounds that economic actors are vulnerable to inefficient and costly 'rent-seeking' activities. While the neoclassical interpretation of interaction between market-based economic agents is useful for describing capitalistic behaviour, it underplays economic history itself, which is replete with cases where state intervention has proven highly effective. Some of the most celebrated examples is the dirigisme showcased in Korea and other rapidly developing East Asian economies.

The chapter next examines the statist–institutionalist approach to the developmental state. The thrust of this approach is to legitimise the role of an activist state in national development. Statists argue that while the market may be the venue for development, it is the state that is best placed to oversee the project. While East Asia's experience of spectacular growth since the 1960s appears to validate much of the statist paradigm, it relies on the assumption of state autonomy. In a similar fashion to liberal analysis, statists underestimate the structural power that capital accrues from its position in the economy.

Nonetheless, these two perspectives provide useful points of reference for a study of the DA. To this end, the chapter concludes by illustrating the utility of the *business power* literature, which, combined with elements of the statist paradigm, informs this study's approach to state–business relations in Korea. The concept of business power – also known as the structural power of capital – allows us to analyse the two varieties of power that feature in the DA.

Appraising the neoclassical approach

Until the 1980s the dominant paradigm in studies of East Asian development was the neoclassical (liberal) approach to economics. Drawing on rational choice theory, the neoclassical approach posits that the market is an arena for interaction between self-interested economic actors. It is also the market that provides the impetus for economic growth. Through a series of rational choices, individuals maximise their 'utility' in a given situation. The neoclassical approach posits that the net outcome of rational choices is the maximisation of profitable economic activity (Cumings and Jacobsen 2006: 57).

This approach assumes that via competition each actor serves as a countervailing check on the power of other actors or groups. Even if all actors are not equal, the market provides a venue for the strongest to survive and prosper. The neoclassical conception of interest group behaviour produces a policy prescription that calls for minimal state intervention. The appropriate role for the state is to maintain the 'rules of the game' that allow market forces to operate smoothly. Society achieves sub-optimal outcomes in terms of income and production if the state intervenes and 'distorts' the operation of market forces (Grant and Sargent 1987). For this reason liberals highlight failed attempts at import-substitution industrialisation in regions such as Latin America, where governments subsidised the establishment of industries that did not possess economies of scale. Furthermore, liberals claim, even if state intervention has succeeded in the past, the changed context of globalisation means that such intervention is no longer possible.

While the criticisms of Latin America may be valid, overall the neoclassical approach tends to conduct a selective reading of economic history. Evidence from other regions refutes the claim that intervention is bound to be detrimental to economic development. For instance, scholars such as Chang Ha-Joon (2002) argue that state intervention was common in the initial phases of development in all industrialised countries, especially the United States and Great Britain. Proponents of an activist state claim that the state can aid economic development through the resolution of information problems. That is, the state can set an industrial sector's level of competition to the optimal level (Shaw and Hughes 2002: 200–2).

Nowhere is the evidence for the benefits of intervention stronger than in East Asia. Whereas Chang notes the activist role of the state in establishing infrastructure such as canals and railways in the US and the UK, intervention on the part of the Korean developmental state has taken a variety of forms that neoclassical accounts fail to acknowledge. For instance Richard

Luedde–Neurath (1986) argues that 'directive' forms of intervention are just as important – if not more so – than the more readily identifiable 'promotional' varieties (subsidies and other incentives) that neoclassical accounts criticise. Luedde–Neurath calculates that a thicket of import restrictions (licences, duties, anti-import campaigns) overstated the openness of the Korean economy in the early stages of rapid development, refuting the neoclassical rendition of this phase.

The success of the East Asian economies during the 1980s forced the World Bank to partially re-evaluate its stance on the most efficacious model of development. While the Bank's report on the 'Asian miracle' defined industrial policy as 'government efforts to alter industrial structure to promote productivity based growth' (1993: 104), it claimed that intervention in East Asia was consistent with market principles. The report conceded that the East Asian states promoted high levels of savings and investment, and devoted sufficient resources to education so that there was a plentiful supply of well-trained labour available to the private sector. They also facilitated development by sponsoring the importation of high-quality technology and foreign capital. The Bank thus acknowledged that *some* forms of intervention were consistent with rapid growth (Jessop 2005: 22; Kong 2000: 2–3).

A further issue where critics take the neoclassical literature to task involves the artificial divide that the approach erects between the political and economic realms. Such a divide is a product of liberalism's normative critique of intervention, but this creates a false dichotomy between polity and economy, one that cannot withstand an analysis of contemporary East Asian history. In short, the neoclassical literature seriously underplays the *politics* of development. The rational choice framework tends to view relations between the state and business as improper and collusive. It treats these relations in a purely economistic manner despite development being an inherently *political* process. Richard Higgott argues that liberalism's 'concentration on openness and growth at the expense of non-economic factors' causes it to 'minimise the salience of all other factors and make economics analytically insensitive to much of . . . complex and combative politics' (1999: 6).

A consequence of liberalism's dismissal of non-economic factors is its lack of analysis of the power that emanates from economic actors' holding influential positions in the economy. According to Stephen Gill and David Law, 'businesspeople are able to claim an expertise of public value, partly because there is widespread acceptance of the view that economic growth is fundamentally dependent on investment and innovation by private enterprise' (1989: 480). In countries such as Japan and Korea, the active and purposeful collaboration between the state and capital, largely with the exclusion of labour, has taken the shape of a *developmental alliance*. A developmental alliance is more than just an ongoing collaboration between the state and business. The alliance is geared towards the modernisation of the national economy along advanced capitalist lines. In this sense a DA stands at odds with the neoclassical approach to interest-group politics. Liberals strongly oppose 'nation building' projects, which are ostensibly political in nature and thus difficult to quantify in cost. Liberalism is thus deficient in its analysis of both politics and power, making problematic the use of the neoclassical approach to analyse economic development.

Power can be ranged in a variety of forms across society, and between the state and capital. This points to the importance of *structural* relations to the analysis of a developmental alliance. The success or failure of such an alliance will depend on each party's possession of power resources. It also depends on their capacities to employ those resources, and the degree to which conflict can be avoided. These conditions in turn depend in large part on the structural position of capital. If big business is structurally well positioned in the political economy, it has the wherewithal to forge an alliance with the state that privileges business interests. This requires business to have the capacity to credibly threaten to take action that would be detrimental to the interests of the state.

The three decades of sustained economic growth via the state-led development model generally vindicated 'revisionist' accounts – explained in detail in the following section – rather than neoclassical renditions of East Asia. Nonetheless, liberals were quick to seize upon the chaos of the Asian financial crisis as evidence of the pitfalls inherent in the dirigiste model. In the case of Korea, the liberal prognosis was that the *chaebols* had 'concentrated economic and political power, the ability to distort government policies and associated moral hazard problems' (East Asia Analytical Unit 1999: 23). The liberals further argued that the state's close ties with the *chaebols* compromised its supervisory role. This absence of a system of checks and balances encouraged moral hazard, corruption and rent seeking (H.-R. Kim 2000: 559). Most damningly, liberals such as Heather Smith concluded that Korea's experience with development 'would seem to offer little in the way of positive lessons for developing countries' (2000: 79). For Iain Pirie, the financial crisis symbolised the end of not only the dirigiste phase of Korean development but also – more importantly – the global economic conditions and opportunities that made state-led development viable in the first place. Pirie argued that the way was open for a fully fledged neoliberal economy to emerge in Korea (2008: 10–13).

Neoclassical accounts of the Asian crisis and its aftermath, in short, were highly pessimistic about the potential for the state to contribute to economic development, on both theoretical and empirical grounds. However, just as the neoclassical framework had problems accounting for the successes enjoyed by the Korean developmental state prior to the crisis, so its capacity to predict the next phase of state–business relations would appear to be limited. Instead of the liberal framework's narrow understanding of interest-group behaviour, we need to concentrate more on the state and also business power. For this reason we now turn to the statist school of Korean political economy.

The developmental state and Korea

In light of the deficiencies of the neoclassical interpretation of the East Asian experience, a 'revisionist' school emerged from the early 1980s. These scholars lauded the state's role in national development. One of the initial proponents of the East Asian model was Chalmers Johnson, who criticised the neoclassical reading of East Asia's development for attributing the region's growth to market forces and assistance from the United States. Johnson instead argued that the Japanese *developmental state* operated according to a 'political and not an economic basis' (1982: 24). This system of political economy, which Richard Samuels (1994) described as 'techno-nationalist', was designed to help Japan catch up with the West. Adrian Leftwich added that the developmental state represents a transitional form of the nation–state; it 'must first and foremost be understood politically, for its provenance lay in the essentially political and nationalist objectives of the late developer, concerned to protect and promote itself in a hostile world' (2000: 158).

The developmental state was thus conceived as complementing the more traditionally accepted monetary and fiscal policies with *industrial policy*. This 'third side of the economic triangle' entailed the formulation and implementation of policies that improve the economic structure at a given stage of development (Johnson 1984: 5). Industrial policy was not 'an alternative to the market but what the state does when it intentionally alters incentives within markets to influence the behaviour of civilian producers, consumers and investors' (Johnson 1999: 48). For instance, in the case of Korea the state sponsored the importation of technology and capital for national development from the 1960s. Given the limited capacities of the private sector, it was incumbent on the state to provide access to these key inputs. The state bore risks on behalf of big business; in return, it sought assurances that resources were used well (Amsden 1992: 146–7; W. Lim 2003).

A defining feature of the statist perspective is the assumption that the *state can intervene effectively* and allocate resources in a way that benefits the national economy to a greater extent than if it relied solely on market forces. The Korean state deliberately 'got the prices wrong' for credit and other key economic resources, and intervened 'with subsidies deliberately to distort relative prices in order to stimulate economic activity' (Amsden 1992: 8). That is, the state 'governed' the market (Wade 1993) rather than letting market forces operate and set the prices of wages and money. State intervention, it is argued, augments market forces and thus creates economies of scale (E. M. Kim 1997: 9–10).

In a general sense it is difficult to dispute the thrust of the statists' evidence for effective state intervention in East Asia. However, the application of certain caveats is necessary to present a more qualified depiction of the state's role in economic development. How should we define and measure 'effective' intervention? Without benchmarks, the statist position is open to contestation from critics. For instance, a caveat concerns the longevity of the state's capacity to intervene. While the developmental state was effective in the initial stages of economic development in Japan and other Asian countries, it appears that the quality of intervention declined as the economy reached higher stages of development. Kim Eun Mee (1997: 12–13) argues that the Korean state became less effective from the 1980s. The 'transformationalist' variant of the statist school (for instance S. Kim 2006; Weiss 2003) addresses these concerns by noting that the means of intervention change as an economy's level of development increases, and thus measures of effectiveness change commensurately.

Statists further argue that a cadre of *competent policymakers enhanced the quality of intervention*. Peter Evans (1989) claims that East Asian states were 'developmental' precisely because they contributed to economic development; this stood in contrast to the 'predatory' nature of other Third World states. Edward Mason *et al.* claim that the Korean state was 'highly pragmatic in the sense that it shows no hesitation in devising means most appropriate to the end in view without significant ideological bias' (1980: 261). While civil servants in the West might be as adept, talented and loyal as their Asian counterparts, they were not considered to be *developmental* in the same sense as in countries such as Korea. Unlike in Western societies, the bureaucratic elite in the developmental state enjoyed a higher status than civilian politicians. While there was substantial debate within this elite, statists argued that policy was focused clearly on the task of national development (Leftwich 2000: 158–61).

The main problem here is the assumption of common purpose within the bureaucratic apparatus. Fred Block (1992) warns that reductionist assumptions of the state as a unified, rational actor obviate questions about what occurs within the 'black box' of the state apparatus. In this sense, Vivek Chibber's contributions (2003, 2005), as well as the work of Chung-In Moon and Rashemi Prasad (1994), are valuable insofar as they account for the battles over ideas within bureaucracies and the creation of a developmental consensus in Korea. Unlike statists, these scholars do not assume that the state is unified in purposes. By assuming that the developmental state enjoys internal consensus, statists negate the possibility that factions within the state seek to influence the direction and content of policy. For instance, even the Korean economic *bureaucracy* has been divided between conservative and liberal elements, and they have considerably different views on the appropriate role of the state in the economy and the degree to which big business needs to be accommodated (J.-H. Kim 2000; Pempel 1999: 144–5; Polidano 2001: 520). This again hints at the importance of analysing the politics of the alliance between the state and capital in Korean economic development. Once the assumption of unitary purpose is relaxed, the way is open to analyse the divergent interests and policy prescriptions of various elements of the bureaucracy – for instance, between the more liberal Economic Planning Board (EPB) and the comparatively statist ministries of finance and industry (see Thurbon 2003) – and to focus on their competition for primacy within the state apparatus.

In addition to emphasising the role of the bureaucracy, statists argued that another crucial component of the developmental state was that *pilot agencies guide the overall process of intervention*. In particular, pilot agencies coordinate investment decisions and set priorities for targeted industries. The most famous of these agencies was the Ministry of Trade and Industry (MITI) in Japan (Onïs 1991: 114–16; Wilson 1990: 90–2). In a Korean context, it was the EPB that for three decades steered the course of national development. For instance the EPB orchestrated the upgrading of the industrial base by promoting labour-intensive manufactures in the 1960s, heavy industries in the 1970s, and then technology and services from the 1980s (H. Yoon 2001: 221–3).

Despite the presence of pilot agencies, some scholars question the degree to which the state guided the process of development. For instance, Richard Samuels' notion of 'reciprocal consent' (1987) highlights the way in which the state elicited cooperation from firms in Japan's energy-generation sector. For Samuels, the bureaucracy was not a dominant force; rather, it *negotiated* with business. Likewise, Friedman (1988) argues that firms could survive and also prosper even if they were not favoured by the state. And not all the state's favoured projects went to plan, as Scott Callon (1995) shows in the high-definition television sector. Daniel Okimoto (1989), meanwhile, notes that Japan's success in the IT industry depended on both public policy *and* market forces. It was the combined effort of the state and big business that facilitated the industry's development.

Moving beyond the case of Japan, Robert Wade (1990) investigated state intervention in Taiwan and South Korea. While agreeing in principle with the centrality of the state to economic development, he noted that in addition to 'leading' the market, the state could also be a 'follower' that augments the success of private enterprise. Eun Mee Kim (1997) and Timothy Lim (1999) raised further questions about the state's instigation of specific policies. Rather than the state *pushing* firms into certain sectors, it was the private sector that successfully lobbied for assistance in – or *pulled* the state in the direction of – certain sectors. For instance Vivek Chibber (2005: 128–9) typified the relationship between pilot agencies and the private sector as one where firms unilaterally decided to enter certain industries rather than acting at the behest of the state. Once a substantial number of producers had entered an industry, Chibber argues, it became possible – and rational – for pilot agencies to exercise overall regulation. It is thus useful to consider the roles of *all* actors in the process of development rather than conceptualise it as a static process that the state dominates.

This leads to a related assumption: that *policy levers are linked to private sector performance* through a structure of incentives. According to Alice Amsden's 'support–discipline' thesis, the Korean state set strict performance criteria for firms participating in priority sectors. The state offered incentives to firms to participate in target sectors, but attached stringent conditions to these incentives: 'Subsidies have not been giveaways, but instead have been dispensed on the principle of reciprocity' (Amsden 1992: 8). For instance, export success was one of the main criteria for continued assistance. According to Jeff Frieden, the state 'has played a major role in spurring industrial development ... The conglomerates and their affiliated trading companies are enticed and persecuted into continually increasing exports' (1981: 427). And as Yoon Heo notes, the 'targeted' nature of its planning 'dispels the myth that Korea succeeded by allowing the free market to work' (2001: 220). In other words, statists assume that the developmental state has the capacity to regulate the behaviour of economic agents, through, for instance, access to finance (Woo 1991).

While the intention of state elites has been to create a clear link between the private sector's access to subsidies and its performance, some scholars have noted that the capacity of the state to effectively discipline non-performers is somewhat limited. That is, while the developmental state has rewarded *good* performances, it has not always punished *bad* ones. For instance, in a study of the Korean shipbuilding industry, Kim Joo-Hwan (1999) shows that the pervasive influence of the *chaebols* across numerous industrial sectors, coupled with the high sunk costs of heavy industries, limit the capacity of the state to withdraw support for some firms. David Friedman challenges statist assumptions through counterfactual cases of 'failed' state planning. In the case of the Japanese machine tools sector, the industry 'grew in a pattern the reverse of what the bureaucracy sought' (1988: 33). The state sought to develop a small number of national champions in the sector, but existing firms refused to coordinate their activities and new entrants appeared. Timothy Lim (1998) notes also that the political survival of state elites is often linked to the success of developmental projects, granting big business a position of influence. Consequently, it may be politically unfeasible for the state to withdraw support from firms whose performance fails to meet expectations. Furthermore the liberalisation of the Korean economy has robbed the developmental state of some of its most potent disciplinary tools. Most notably, the state has lost control of credit rationing, a form of discipline that had allowed the state to limit speculative investment on the part of the *chaebols* (Y. T. Kim 1999: 443–4).

A further assumption is that the state had *adequate access to information* to guide a developmental project. In the view of statists, the developmental state proved highly adept at solving informational problems. They argue that the East Asian state managed to minimise (if not eliminate) this problem by identifying the long-term structural needs of the national economy and altering its incentive structure accordingly (H.-J. Chang 1993; Wade 1990: 142; Wilson 1990: 96). This is a crucial assumption, given the neoclassical opposition to intervention rests on the premise that only economic agents can access information adequately.

Nonetheless, there is some evidence that statists overplay the capacity of the state to resolve informational problems alone. Instead, argues Richard Doner (1992: 415), it is the input of the private sector to regular consultations with government that allows planning to proceed. Cooperation rather than domination, Doner argues, is the hallmark of rapidly developing Asian states such as Korea. Similar findings have appeared in relation to the development of Japan's high-definition television (HDTV) sector. In the 1980s, Scott Callon argues, MITI's efforts to promote the development of HDTVs failed to produce the desired results. While unwilling to incur the wrath of the state by not participating in the project, leading Japanese firms participated in only a formulaic manner: they were unwilling to invest resources and share information in a way that statists would predict (Callon 1995: 186).

The Asian financial crisis illustrated that insufficient regulation can deny the developmental state of information vital to prudent economic management. Korea deregulated its financial markets during the 1980s and 1990s, reducing its capacity to ward off financial crises. Not only did the state have insufficient information about the potential for speculators to attack the Korean currency and stock market; it also had little information about how much debt the *chaebols* were amassing. In the case of the Dongbang group, a downturn in the fortunes of its Hong Kong-based affiliate in 1997 adversely impacted upon the group's overall operations. Korean supervisory agencies were unaware of the extent of the problem until the crisis had engulfed the economy (U.-C. Chung 1998: 80).

Perhaps the most important component of the statist approach is the assumption that the *state is autonomous and insulated from external pressures*. If this insulation is ensured, the state can focus on the goal of economic development rather than the partisan demands of private interests. Hagen Koo and Eun Mee Kim for instance argue that the state 'has a *considerable amount* of autonomy to adopt policies without interference from class interests and a capacity to implement these policies effectively' (1992: 126, emphasis added). Determining the degree to which the state is autonomous from societal pressures – including business – goes to the heart of the debate about the efficacy of developmentalism. It raises questions about the degree to which class interests, especially business, could influence policymakers. For instance, Peter Evans emphasises the principle of reciprocity between the state and capital via the notion of *embedded autonomy*. That is, state autonomy was predicated upon a strong connection with society. For Evans:

> Mutual reinforcement . . . lies at the core of the developmental state's success. A robust and coherent state apparatus facilitates the organisation of industrial capital; an organized class of industrialists facilitates a joint project of industrialization, which in turn legitimates both the state and industrialists.
>
> (1995: 228)

For Linda Weiss (1998), the problem is one of *governed interdependence*. Weiss also emphasises the state's connection with – or embeddedness in – society, arguing that close working relations with business provides the state with sufficient information to set broad parameters for development. In turn, the state bears much of the risk of development and grants business leaders a privileged position in the political economy. This depiction accords with that of James West, who describes the Korean state's relations with business as 'a practical dialectic of power and profit in which the senior partner is power' (1987: 63).

While conceding that big business can shape the policy agenda, statists also presume that the developmental state operates in an environment where civil society is weak and subordinated. The political basis for a strong developmental state is assumed to be a coalition with industry and the destruction of leftist elements. This depiction is problematic given the emergence of well-organised trade unions in Korea in the 1980s (Kong 1995; Leftwich 2000: 163–4; Onïs 1991: 114; Polidano 2001: 515). If the state was dominant until the 1970s, statists need to account adequately for the great changes that took place in the 1980s and beyond. Tat Yan Kong, for instance, refers to the 'dual transition' that occurred in this period – the liberalisation of the economy and the democratisation of the polity – as substantial changes that undermine assumptions of state autonomy (2000: 3–7). How can we account for this greatly increased degree of contestation in Korean political economy? How can we account for both the continuity of the developmental elements of the Korean state and also its declining authority? What implication does this hold for the revisionist canon, with its assumptions of a dominant role for the state?

A potential lacuna in the statist literature revealed here is the presumption, either explicit or implicit, that the state dominates – or at least directs – the process of development. By portraying the market – and business – as an object that state elites can manage, the state is seen to be not only separate from the market but also capable of dominating it. Bob Jessop (2005: 24) cautions that this creates a false dichotomy between the economy and the state. The state should instead be considered an economic actor that operates within the market, albeit in an authoritative manner. Chibber also warns against the presumption of state autonomy, arguing that:

> [a] neo-Weberian strand of theorizing has become quite prominent among political scientists and sociologists, which views the state in capitalism as far more autonomous from class constraints than Marxist theory . . . the basic claims of Marxian theory – for the constrained position of state in capitalist economies – are valid for the Korean case.
>
> (Chibber 2005: 124)

In short, the statist literature has proven to be a valuable corrective to the view of East Asian development as solely – or primarily – attributable to market forces. Nonetheless it appears clear that revisionist accounts have overestimated both the degree of autonomy of the developmental state and its longevity. They have also overlooked the countervailing forces that the phase of rapid development in Korea and other Asian states has generated. Consequently it is necessary to explore alternative sources – and the exercise – of power.

The structural power of business

To date this chapter has examined the two main approaches to the political economy of Korean development. The neoclassical approach views political economy in doctrinaire terms, affording the state no place in economic decision-making. It thus has limited value in analysing changes in the developmental alliance over time because it assumes that an 'activist' state is harmful to the economy and that collaboration between the state and capital will devolve into corruption and waste. Although providing evidence of successful state-led development in East Asia, the statist thesis also involves a degree of reification. Whereas liberals assert that the market should be the ultimate allocator of economic resources (and thus the engine of development), state-centric theories assign that role to an omnipresent and omnipotent state. In addition, this approach encounters empirical difficulties, as is evident in the problems that the Korean developmental state experienced in the 1990s, especially its inability to prevent speculative investments by the *chaebols*.

A third field of research concentrates on the autonomous power that business (capital) accrues by dint of its structural position in the economy. In part inspired by Marxist- and class-based analytical assumptions, this literature adds valuable context to discussions of the developmental state. It highlights the challenges that a dirigiste state faces in seeking to induce business – and other societal forces – into a developmental alliance. In particular, the business power literature provides explanatory tools for analysing the politics of the DA. The starting point for the business power literature is the assumption that business is no ordinary actor. Charles Lindblom claims that business leaders in the United States have a 'privileged position' in public life deriving from the role that they play in the economy. He argues that the state faces pressure to formulate policies amenable to the interests of business. An unwillingness to do so risks a backlash from business: 'even the unspoken possibility of adversity for business operates as an all-pervasive constraint on government authority' (Lindblom 1977: 178). Over time the broad interests of capital become embedded in the considerations of policy elites, ruling out radical policy options. Consequently policy remains within a predetermined set of parameters: 'This threat is implicit ... Government anticipates the interests and reaction of capital without the need for interest group representations' (Marsh 1983: 4).

In other words, their role in the economy endows business leaders with a specific variety of power – the *structural power of capital*. Fred Block defines structural power as 'the ability to resist changes that conflict with the broad interests of wealth-holders' (1992: 284). He argues that firms can prevent changes that they view as deleterious to their interests by threatening to withdraw their resources from the economy. This is especially the case if capital is mobile and not limited to a territorially defined space. How precisely does business articulate that variety of threat, and how effective is it? What factors will influence the exercise of such a threat? David Vogel, one of the foremost proponents of theories of business power, notes that the 'political power of business can and does vary over time. Furthermore, these variations follow a discernible pattern' (1989: 6). The power of business, Vogel tells us, varies in accordance with: i) the *position of capital* in the economy; ii) *expectations of society*; and iii) the *dynamics of the political system*.

The position of capital can be divided into its temporal, structural and competitive elements. For instance, business has relatively *less* power in the early stages of industrialisation, when the state is required to play a more expansive role in creating the conditions for capitalist development. Richard Samuels notes that a relatively powerful state may emerge if 'the economy is undergoing late development or reconstruction, especially when this involves a concentration of financial resources' or if an industry 'is vulnerable in world markets' (1987: 17). Given that the state is playing a legitimate and beneficial role, these conditions may constrain the structural power of capital by making business relatively more reliant on the state. In contrast, we would intuitively expect that in a mature capitalist economy, the responsibility for stimulating economic growth will increasingly fall to the private sector.

The position of capital can also be analysed in terms of industry (or market) structures. If an industry 'is fragmented vertically or isolated horizontally from other sectors' (Samuels 1987: 17), the cohesion of the business community is impaired. This is generally the case in highly competitive sectors. Larger firms are less vulnerable to state pressure than smaller producers. Stephen Gill and David Law note that 'large firms possess some market power over prices and perhaps wages' (1989: 480) in oligopolistic industries. These references to *large* firms are apt, given that 'any remarks about business privilege really only apply to big business. Small businesses operate in a completely different environment' (Grant and Sargent 1987: 27). In other words, business power applies primarily to actions taken to further the interests of an economy's largest firms.

This is pertinent to discussion of the Korean developmental alliance, given that the *chaebols* have such a weighty role in the economy. As a ruling party legislator on the National Assembly's Political Affairs Committee commented, 'the monopoly power of a small number of *chaebols* is hard to control, but it has had a significant influence on Korea's growth strategy' (author interview 2004). In keeping with Fred Block's notion of a 'capital strike' (1992), for example, there is evidence from the Korean case that the *chaebols'* dominance of key sectors of the economy endows them with a unique form of influence over the state.

In a Korean context, big business has not invested too little. The *chaebols* have instead *over*-invested and thus created problems of excess capacity. It is the *quality* rather than the quantity of investment that is of concern to the

Korean state. The challenge for the state, especially since the loss of its most potent disciplinary tools, has been to prevent irresponsible behaviour on the part of the *chaebols* in the form of redundant or speculative investments. The excessive investments and indebtedness have more firmly entrenched the *chaebols* in the structure of the national economy, and thus more closely linked the fortunes of the *chaebols* to the developmental alliance (Oh and Varcin 2002: 713).

A third element of the position of capital relates to competition between firms to attain the most influential or lucrative positions in the economy. For instance, firms recognise the benefits that accrue from being a market leader, both in terms of achieving economies of scale and also in wielding influence over policymaking. If a market is populated by a small number of powerful producers – akin to oligopoly conditions – competition between producers may give way to collusion, raising the possibility that structural power will be abused to induce policy changes amenable to corporate interests. For instance, in Korea the *chaebol* enterprises have tended to dominate globally competitive industries such as automobiles, electronics and shipbuilding, at the same time creating a strong economic concentration that readily translates into market power. At its worst, firms may offer inducements to state officials to grant them permission to enter lucrative industries.

At the same time, we cannot assume that even big business will *always* act in unison to further its interests. 'When business is both mobilized and unified', Vogel argues of the American context, 'its political power can be formidable. But while the former is now the norm, the latter occurs infrequently' (1989: 291). It has been specific fractions of big business that have taken collective action to protect their interests.

Partaking in economic activity grants the *chaebols* leverage over the Korean state. As Michael Mann notes, 'once a form of exchange emerges, it is a social fact, potentially powerful. Traders can react to opportunity at their end of the economic chain and then act back upon the organisation of production that originally spawned them' (1986: 24). The degree of this leverage is significant, as witnessed by the fact that the thirty biggest *chaebols* accounted for roughly half of national assets, debt and sales in 1998. They also accounted for about 70 per cent of profits and exports, and almost 5 per cent of employment. The five biggest *chaebols* controlled about one-quarter of assets debts and sales, and over half of exports (E. M. Lim 2002: 3). In short, the position of the *chaebols* has, during the life of the DA, enhanced their capacity to exercise structural power. Nonetheless, as noted below, this form of power has been partially constrained in unexpected ways, setting in train a tense but close relationship with the state.

The second determinant of business power is the issue of public expectations. Vogel (1989: 290) notes that public perceptions of the strength of the economy are crucial to the interests of business in advanced capitalist economies such as the US. He argues that there is an inverse relationship between business power and economic performance:

business had tended to lose political influence when the economy was performing relatively well and has become more influential when the performance of the economy deteriorated. The relative political power of business is *not* a function of the business cycle. Otherwise, the political power of business would be more unstable than it actually has been. Rather, what *is* critical is the public's perception of the long-term strength of the American economy.

(Vogel 1989: 8, emphasis in original)

That is, business receives kudos in the eyes of the public not for the relative strength of the economy at a specific point in time but instead for performance over the longer term. This insight is crucial to an analysis of the developmental alliance, because it implies that – at best – there is a lag between strong economic performance, its translation into political influence and its manifestation in policy outcomes. Vogel reminds us of the cyclical nature of business power, and the potential for critics of capitalism to demand reform of capitalistic practices. For instance, in the 1960s consumer advocates, the environmental movement and labour activists succeeded in lobbying for new regulations on business activity in the US. Business lobbies, in turn, sought to regain influence over the public policy agenda in order to ensure that it reflected corporate interests rather than those associated with advocacy groups (Vogel 1989: 40–1).

Even in Korea, where the DA has been largely closed to outside scrutiny, public expectations have – to some extent – constrained the structural power of business. For instance, the *chaebols* are sensitive to accusations that they benefited from the authoritarian period. Subsequently they have sought to document what they argue has been a substantial contribution to the developmental alliance (C. Song 2003). The sensitivity of the *chaebols* to their perception in society stems from the traditional conception of the various occupations in East Asian society (*sanonggongsang*) whereby public officials hold the most prestigious positions and the merchant class the least. This has endowed the state with a degree of authority that may appear to be unwarranted in a Western context. Jongwoo Han and L. H. M. Ling, for instance, argue that a 'hyper masculinized' developmental state in East Asia 'assumes all the rights and privileges of classical Confucian patriarchy' while 'assigning to society the characteristics of classical Confucian womanhood: diligence, discipline and deference' (1998: 53).

East Asian state elites are also required to observe and respond to public expectations, and have thus emphasised the *legitimacy* of their leadership role in social life, including the economy. This contrasts with the state's relatively precarious role in the economy in the West, where activist states are often viewed as illegitimate. This contrast is apparent, given that the Korean state has at times adopted a dictatorial tone in its dealings with business. The state has appealed to the *chaebols* to meet their (vaguely defined) obligations to society in order to ameliorate the worst aspects of the *chaebols'* behaviour.

The developmental alliance requires key economic actors, including the state, to to prioritise development over other objectives. This ensures that society also has some way of measuring the performance of the state and business, even if the somewhat authoritarian nature of the polity has limited the public's capacity to punish inadequate performances. Japan's MITI, for instance, had the capacity to coerce firms to participate in collaborative research, even if firms were sceptical about the utility of such projects. The public *expected* firms such as Sony to contribute to Japanese economic development. In turn, business recognised the importance of being *seen* to fulfil its legitimate obligations to society (Polidano 2001: 521–2). Social expectations of the appropriate role of business thus constrained business activity and strengthened the authority of the state. Likewise, Leonard Seabrooke argues that the state in Japan did not lose legitimacy because of the economic slowdown and subsequent financial difficulties of the 1990s. Rather the state lost legitimacy for its *'failure to justify* financial reforms according to Japanese social norms concerning the responsible, responsive, role of government' (Seabrooke 2002: 37, emphasis in original).

Both the state and business, it is argued in this book, acknowledge the importance of retaining the approval of the public. Public expectations influence the degree of structural power that business is willing and able to exercise. Pressure from society thus acts as a form of sanction on business – and the state – despite its being external to the developmental alliance. The morality (or lack thereof) of the *chaebols* has been a trope since the launch of the DA. Actors other than the *chaebols* – the state, small–medium enterprises, labour, civil society and even external actors such as the US – have raised the issue to criticise business at different points in time. Such public criticism has necessarily limited the power of business.

Following on from the notion that social pressures can ameliorate some potential abuse of the privileged position of business in public life, the third determinant of the capacity of firms to accumulate and exercise structural power lies in the dynamics of the political system. Given that the expectations of society can hamstring business power, populist politicians can capitalise on anti-business sentiment and thus champion policies unfavourable to corporate interests (Vogel 1989: 292).

Political dynamics can influence the degree to which the state intervenes in the economy. The likelihood of intervention rises when 'the state is highly centralized either vertically, vis-à-vis local and regional governments, or horizontally, with a consolidated national bureaucracy', when ruling coalitions are 'narrow and unstable' and when 'there is an "administrative tradition" of state interventionism' (Samuels 1987: 17). This generally results in greater willingness on the part of the state to intervene through infrastructural power.

As long as conditions are conducive to investment, business does not appear to be overly concerned about the nature of the regime in power (Block 1977: 16–17). East Asia's development during the past few decades suggests that business is willing to coexist with authoritarian regimes. Indeed, business tends to favour 'strong' states that create conditions conducive to business interests during the initial stages of development. As Vivek Chibber argues:

> the Korean state's ability to discipline local firms issued from its general domination of the capitalist class as a whole. In other words, Korean planners were ensconced in a state that, because of its dominance over local capital, was free from the pressures that normally issue from powerful capitalists.
>
> (2005: 123)

As long as both partners to a developmental project remain committed to the shared goal of rapid growth, the compact can hold. Indeed, a defining feature of the Korean route to industrialisation has been the highly corporatist nature of state–business relations, and the concomitant efforts to protect it from external scrutiny. In contrast, political dynamics may, in response to calls from trade unions or NGOs, encourage a government to adopt measures that antagonise business. For instance, in Korea the state's approach to industrial disputes has changed markedly since the 1980s, as Chapter 5 will note. Instead of invariably intervening on the side of the *chaebols*, the state in the 1980s responded to electoral dynamics by adopting a more neutral approach to wage claims. This paved the way for substantial wage increases in sectors – such as steel and shipbuilding – with relatively high rates of union density. A more recent example of political dynamics impacting on state–business relations came in the wake of the financial crisis of 1997–8, when the state explicitly blamed the *chaebols* for the crisis. Making a scapegoat of the *chaebols* gave the government the political capital with which to enact a reform agenda.

Consequently, the degree to which firms can exercise structural power is dependent on the attitudes of state leaders to business, and their responses to calls to reduce anti-social aspects of business activity. Given the potential for their activities to become politicised, it is in the interests of the *chaebols* to protect their interests through institutional links to the state such as the DA.

Conclusions

Korean economic development certainly did not unfold free of contestation. While the state was largely responsible for shaping economic policy, the *chaebols* were also intimately involved in its formation. Policy is better thought of as the *final* outcome of a process of bargaining between various actors. It is not a pre-ordained set of preferences that state elites take to the negotiating table. A fuller analysis of power relations thus sheds light on policy changes, as well as the preferences that each party to the developmental alliance has in regard to policy content and direction. In addition to overplaying the value of 'autonomy' in granting the state freedom from social pressures, the statist analysis exaggerates the capacity of the state to direct economic development. Yet the state needed to cooperate with business in order to achieve its economic goals within the context of the DA. In this sense we view state power as a relational or 'network' concept, wherein 'negotiated consent' is the means by which the state and business agree on the terms by which to manage the economy (Bell 1994: 300–1).

The insights about the tendentious nature of business power suggest that a more fruitful project is to examine the historical process by which state *authority* changes within the developmental alliance. Such an approach would also examine how the structural power of business has accrued and how the power dynamics between the state and business have shifted in historical terms. A change in the focus of analysis from autonomy to authority encourages a renewed interest in the politics of policymaking. The state's political ties with the *chaebols* will determine the degree to which its preferences are reflected in policy outcomes. If the state can exercise authority over business without adversely affecting investment sentiment, policy – and the DA – can follow the path that the state prefers.

On the other hand we also need to be more sensitive to the overt and covert campaigns by business to protect its interests. Given the nature of business power, it may not be even necessary for business to actively lobby for a public policy agenda that is amenable to corporate interests. Crucially, from the perspective of this book, it has been their *structural power* that has allowed the *chaebols* to lobby for policies that they preferred. Unlike other economic actors, the *chaebols* have enjoyed unique access to policymakers by virtue of their status in the DA. This capacity to act as agent of change has ensured that policy output has reflected the influence of the *chaebols* on the policymaking process.

Drawing on the discussion of the determinants of business power above, we now proceed to a new framework for analysing state–business relations. The insights from the business power literature form the basis for the five-variable model discussed in the next chapter.

2 The dynamics of the developmental alliance

Introduction

As argued in Chapter 1, state–business relations in Korea need to be characterised as interaction between two different forms of power – the infrastructural power of the state and the structural power of capital. This chapter constructs a five-variable model that considers contextual factors such as national security, globalisation and social pressures to explain power relativities within the Korean developmental alliance. These variables, which *condition* the exercise of state infrastructural power and the *chaebols'* structural power, illustrate the process of economic development. In this chapter, we seek to conceptualise the variables in order to explain the politics of Korean economic development. Each variable raises a line of inquiry into the shifting relations within the DA on the one hand and between the developmental alliance and external actors on the other.

The book divides the process of development in Korea into four phases. The pre-DA phase consists of the colonial period and the Syngman Rhee and Chang Myon governments, which ended in 1961. Next, the study examines the authoritarian rule of Park Chung Hee from the military coup until his assassination in 1979. The third period encompasses the presidencies of Chun Doo-hwan, Roh Tae-woo and Kim Young-sam (1979–97). Finally, the post-crisis period encapsulates Kim Dae-jung's and Roh Moo-hyun's terms as president. The study will look for correlations between the five contextual variables as they impact on the DA in each of these periods.

From developmental state to developmental alliance

A number of scholars have attempted to conceptualise state–business alliances in East Asia in a more nuanced manner than the statist literature in the previous chapter. For instance, Kim Joo Hwan refers to state–business relations as a process of 'guided strategic interaction' (1999: 213) whereby the state sets the agenda for industrialisation. He argues that the state's interaction with business determines the success or failure of specific industries as well as the degree of discipline the state exercises. Meredith Woo–Cumings similarly argues that the developmental state 'is not an imperious entity lording it over society but a partner with the business sector in a historical compact of industrial transformation' (1999: 16). Linda Weiss claims that the early stages of development accord with the notion of 'governed inter-dependence', whereby an autonomous state and capital enter 'a negotiated relationship ... which is nevertheless governed by broader goals set and monitored by the state' (1999: 38).

Other scholars are more explicit in their depiction of the institutionalised nature of public–private collaboration. For instance Richard Doner presents a 'broader institutionalism' – one that overcomes the narrower focus of the statist paradigm – that incorporates the coalitional basis of the resolution of collective action problems in East Asian industrialisation (1992: 401). Geoffrey Underhill and Xiaoke Zhang, meanwhile, argue that the state is the leader in any collaborative project with capital in a 'state–market condominium' (2005). Given that 'the state thinks like a public–private condominium, it internalises many of the antagonisms of the society it reflects' (2005: 2).

In relation to Japan, Richard Samuels has provided perhaps the most elaborate discussion of state–business interaction. Samuels' concept of 'reciprocal consent' seeks to challenge the notion of state dominance in the process of Japanese economic development. He argues that the Japanese state 'often helps structure market choices, but public/private negotiations invariably structure state and market choices alike ... For the politics of reciprocal consent, negotiation and compact are the core of business–state relations' (Samuels 1987: 2). Samuels assumes that there are no barriers or permanent balances of power between state and society. Reciprocal consent 'is the mutual accommodation of state and market. It is an iterative process of reassurance among market players and public officials' (1987: 8). Samuels argues that six factors – market structures, centralisation, developmental timing, openness, ruling coalitions and administrative tradition – explain the *nature* and *extent* of state intervention. Although the focus is on *state* action – the conditions in which the state intervenes in a given industry – rather than state–business relations, this schema can be incorporated fruitfully into a broader analysis of the DA.

These renditions of the developmental alliance treat the *chaebols* as a tool with which the state pursues economic development. They do not treat the *chaebols* as independent actors, or a group thereof, in their own right. Such a depiction does not grant a high degree of agency to the *chaebols*, rendering them as largely adjuncts of the state. The process of development is unpredictable, risky and inherently political. It is a process over which no single party has substantial control (T. C. Lim 1996).

The 1980s, for instance, was a period of notable change in Korea's political economy. The most common reading of this period is that the balance of power in the developmental alliance underwent an irreversible change, with the *chaebols* gaining at the expense of the state. Tat Yan Kong describes this as a transition from 'state dominance to interdependence' (2000: 108).

He argues that the *chaebols* could resist reform because of their place in the developmental alliance. Eun Mee Kim likewise calls the 1980s a period of transition 'from dominance to symbiosis' (1997: 45–6). She argues that the very success of the state's developmental capacities sowed the seeds for its own decline as civil society and the *chaebols* grew in strength. Peter Evans makes a similar argument, recalling Karl Marx's analogy of the capitalist state 'acting as its own gravedigger' (1995: 229–30). Oh Ingyu and Recep Varcin (2002) meanwhile argue that the *chaebols* attempted to reduce their vulnerability to the caprices of the state by exercising structural power. When conditions became more precipitous to the *chaebols* in the 1980s, they accumulated sufficient structural power to reduce the ability of the state to intervene in their affairs. In a similar vein, Eun Mie Lim (2002) argues that the state's degree of control over the *chaebols* is questionable, especially in terms of internal organisation.

These accounts all assume that the state irretrievably lost the capacity to discipline the *chaebols* in the 1980s. Yet this claim lacks validity in light of events that followed the Asian crisis. Most notably, the state oversaw a wide-ranging industrial and financial restructuring program in order to comply with the conditions of the IMF's bailout. When it saw fit, the state took action against the *chaebols* that clearly ran counter to their interests. The seemingly impregnable *chaebols* became decidedly vulnerable to dismantlement, as witnessed by the collapse of the Daewoo Group.

A theory of the developmental alliance cannot assume that the balance of power will rest indefinitely with one party or the other. This study instead assumes that power is contested on an ongoing basis within the DA. Identifying the contextual factors that influence the relative levels of each party's power resources helps explain their capacity to promote their interests at a given point of time.

In addition to aggregate power resources, the DA can be analysed in terms of influence over policy content and direction. It is not sufficient to assume that shifts in policy direction and substantive content derive solely from the changing preferences and strength of state elites. For this reason the insights of Cho Yeong-cheol (2003) are useful. Cho claims that the state rewarded the *chaebols* for assenting to its economic policies, so state–business relations were both cooperative *and* collusive. Other scholars argue that this was certainly the case in the initial stages of the DA. Seok-Jin Lew (1992), for instance, argues that the notion of 'state-led industrialisation' has limited applicability for analysis of the Korean automobile industry. He argues that the willingness and capacity of domestic capital were more influential to the pattern and direction of industrial development than state power. Kwon-Hyung Lee's (1998) study of the Korean automobile industry, meanwhile, argues that the extant literature has paid insufficient attention to the underlying interests of economic agents in the developmental alliance.

Cho's aforementioned argument is also pertinent to the analysis of the latter phases of the DA, during which 'the interests of the *chaebols* already lay in the retreat of the state, which dismantled powerful policy tools, rather than state intervention . . . the basic direction of economic policy that accorded with the interests of the *chaebols* was liberalization' (Cho 2003: 158). That is, the *chaebols* used the more open political environment of the 1980s to lobby for policies that they preferred, chiefly liberalisation. In keeping with the insights from the business power literature that were noted in the previous chapter, the *chaebols* took umbrage at the state's adoption of populist policies. The clearest manifestation of the *chaebols'* discontent occurred, as Chapter 5 will outline, when Hyundai chairman Chung Ju-yong stood against the government's candidate at the 1992 election (Y. T. Kim 1999: 448–9). The *chaebols* pursued more liberal policies in order to reduce the state's oversight of their activities. They also favoured greater competition in the financial sector because this would provide new resources for their industrial expansion. Further, it would be erroneous to attribute the neoliberal shift of the 1980s and beyond solely to the ascension of liberal policymakers during that period. Instead, the neoliberal shift was a coalescence of sometimes contradictory and sometimes complementary interests between the state and the *chaebols*. It is thus fruitful to bring the preferences of capital back into an analysis of policymaking as it relates to Korean development.

Studies that emphasise the role of business power contribute to a more complete account of the developmental state. Coupled with the insights from the business power literature reviewed in the previous chapter, they draw attention to the *dynamics* of the developmental alliance. Timothy Lim notes that development is part of a larger socio-political process. Therein, power is structurally dispersed among various actors. By treating power in a structural manner, Lim (1998: 457–8) depicts the state and other actors as engaged in a mutually dependent relationship. The state does not dominate society, but negotiates with it.

The reconstituted framework traces the power dynamics of the DA by considering the following contextual variables: bureaucracy, social pressures, national security, economic conditions and globalisation. These variables help illustrate the power dynamics of the developmental alliance because they impact on the entire process of economic development rather than merely on the state. In addition, as explained below, they describe and record change in power relations at all significant levels of analysis.

Bureaucracy

The Korean economic *bureaucracy*, by operating at the intra-state and DA level, has been a central force shaping the developmental alliance. Samuels argues that state intervention is effective when 'the state is highly centralized either vertically, vis-à-vis local and regional governments, or horizontally, with a consolidated national bureaucracy', and when 'there is an "administrative tradition" of state interventionism' (1987: 17). The bureaucracy, or sections of it, may adopt reformist notions that are inimical to the narrow interests of state elites. The study seeks to identify the degree to which a developmental ideology has guided the bureaucracy in each stage of the process, starting with the nationalist and state-led model of the 1960s and going on to the gradual rise of neoliberal thought from the 1980s.

These ideational factors necessarily impact on the developmental alliance because bureaucrats act as the interface between the state and the *chaebols*. While the *chaebols* can directly consult the political elite and convey business concerns to them, the bureaucracy informs the political elite about issues that the *chaebols* see as vital, and suggest appropriate responses. The policymaking elite have also on occasion taken advantage of the relative paucity of economic vision among the political elite to put their own stamp on the developmental alliance – the clearest case being the Chun and Roh presidencies. Accordingly, bureaucrats in the economic ministries help define the goals of the alliance. The bureaucracy thus has a significant influence on the power dynamics of the developmental alliance.

In the early stages of the DA, civil servants in the pilot agency (the EPB) enjoyed a high degree of insulation from external scrutiny, but in latter stages this has not been the case. How and in what ways has the democratisation of Korea affected the capacity of the bureaucracy to formulate sound public policy? Have bureaucrats reacted negatively to this new form of accountability, or do they see it as checking the excesses of what might be perceived as a populist political leadership? What divergences – if any – exist between the political leadership and career civil servants?

In addition to the internal components of the bureaucracy's dealings with government, we also investigate how civil servants interact with external parties. Has the bureaucracy come under other forms of pressure, and if so, how has this affected their influence on the DA? In particular, it is important to track relations between civil servants and *chaebol* leaders. Finally, is the capacity of the bureaucracy being dulled by recruitment problems? That is, has the prestige attached to the bureaucracy – and its capacity to attract the 'best and brightest' to national service – been debased over time? Addressing these questions will offer insights into the pressures on the bureaucracy and its impact on the DA.

Social pressures

The second contextual variable that this study considers is the *social pressures* to which the developmental alliance is subjected, or the national–domestic level of analysis. Part of the rationale of the developmental alliance is to inoculate the policymaking process from the scrutiny of society. The alliance is thus by its very nature a corporatist and elitist arrangement. Samuels argues that state intervention is more effective when 'the ruling coalition is narrow and unstable', implying that corporatist arrangements will enhance state action (1987: 17). This makes problematic the study of transition societies such as Korea, which has moved from authoritarianism to democracy during its modernisation. Social pressures have increasingly constrained the developmental alliance. This study argues that even if the state and business adhere to their compact, social pressures matter to the extent that the developmental alliance needs a degree of assent and thus cooperation from society. Social pressures thus work in the favour of business.

At the same time, if the state adopts a populist stance and draws on public support to attack business, social pressures can serve the state rather than capital. They also offer the possibility of the state enacting reforms that are unfavourable to business. Consequently we seek to ascertain if and how civilian governments, eager to distance themselves from their authoritarian predecessors, have harnessed anti-*chaebol* sentiment to their own ends. To what degree, if any, can social pressures constrain the structural power of capital? To what extent have the labour movement and reformist NGOs succeeded in their quests to monitor the DA, especially in terms of ensuring deliverance on its promise of improvements in economic and social welfare conditions?

By its very nature, the DA denies small–medium enterprises, as well as labour, the privileges enjoyed by big business. The business power literature suggests that structural power will both shield capital from the despotic variety of state power and also ensure that the state formulates policies that tend to favour big business and promote economic development. So this study will assess the degree to which the DA has remained closed to other parties. What happens when there is pressure to open the developmental alliance or to expand its agenda? Is a leftist–nationalist variant of the DA possible, or must the political persuasion of the governing party or clique be conservative? If so, could the inauguration of Lee Myung-bak signal a renewed phase of developmentalism?

National security

The prioritisation of *national security* is a defining feature of the developmental state. Along with Japan and Taiwan, Korea received American support due to its position in the frontline of the Cold War. Security considerations heavily influenced state formation during this phase, bringing the international level of analysis to attention. The support of the United States thus helped launch the developmental alliance, providing material resources and political support. Korea also relied on the openness of the American market to generate export revenues during the early phases of its industrialisation. This reliance has persisted until recently, but access to the US market has become more difficult in the post-Cold War period, during which America's 'benign neglect' has appeared limited (Strange 1994: 6–7; Woo–Cumings 1994: 415).

Support from the US has not been unconditional. Korea has had to satisfy conditions to ensure ongoing support, with the US pressuring its ally to pursue policies conducive to the DA. So this study expects national security to act in favour of the alliance but not necessarily domestic capital (*chaebols*).

Subsequently this study draws on the insights of Hee-Yeon Cho and Bob Jessop, who argue that the early stages of the alliance featured a 'Listian warfare national state', which later evolved into a 'Listian workfare national state' (2001). In this way, the study acknowledges the impact of national security concerns on the developmental alliance.

We seek to ascertain the ways in which changes in the US political economy and its global standing – in both its economic and political dimensions – have, through national security, impacted on the DA. As the world's only superpower, the US enjoys an asymmetric power relationship with not only Korea but also its other alliance partners. While more amenable to the preferences of allies than of enemies, the US has the capacity to severely disrupt the foreign policy and developmental objectives of smaller countries such as Korea. So we will focus on how changes in US foreign policy have affected Korea's developmental project, and its chief mode of delivery, the DA.

Economic conditions

A crucial factor in state–business relations is the link between general *economic conditions* and the power of capital. Structural power can be most effectively wielded when key sectors of the industrial economy are in poor condition, because the state needs private sector investment to deliver an economic recovery. In particular, it is the needs of sectors such as the steel, automobile, electronics and semiconductor sectors that the state must be cognisant of, which underscores the salience of the market–institutional level of analysis. This concurs with Samuels' argument that market structures are a determinant of the state's capacity to intervene. He notes that intervention is effective when 'the targeted industry is fragmented vertically or isolated horizontally from other sectors' (Samuels 1987: 17).

This book agrees with Samuels' argument about the relevance of 'developmental timing' (1987: 17). That is, conditions in the initial stages of development are relatively more conducive to state intervention. We incorporate Samuels' insights into a broader argument that the state needs to justify intervention in terms of the developmental alliance. For instance, the Korean state regained a degree of balance in its power relations with the *chaebols* in the post-crisis period. This was because it won a rhetorical battle with the *chaebols* during that period. The state argued that it had a crucial and legitimate role to play in industrial and financial restructuring.

As the business power literature reminds us, key industrial sectors are largely immune from the exercise of the despotic variety of state power. Sectors such as heavy manufacturing, which the *chaebols* dominate, are crucial to the success of Korean economic development. The political imperative for rapid growth is thus relatively low when the economy is strong, reducing the influence of structural power. Good economic performances are 'taken as given', and business does not gain any specific kudos for this.

If anything, it is the government of the day that gains credit for a flourishing economy.

On the other hand, when there is a sudden downturn, business 'excesses' – which in the case of Korea include duplicate and reckless investments – are cited as prime causes of economic crisis. This may provide political cover for intervention. Such activism may well be welcome by business in the short term, but it has the effect of reducing the structural power of capital. At the same time it reflects a sense on the part of the government that large firms are of such importance to the economy's long-term growth prospects that firms need to be supported in times of crisis. The injection of funds into the US and global financial markets in the second half of 2007, in response to the 'sub-prime' mortgage crisis, is only the most recent example of this phenomenon. Tracing how economic conditions impact on the state–business relations is expected to reveal much about how closely the DA partners are collaborating.

Globalisation

During the past two decades the Korean economy has become increasingly exposed to the forces of *globalisation*. The term refers to the integration of the national economy with the international economic system (see Bisley 2007), bringing in to play the systemic level of analysis. Intuitively at least, a higher degree of globalisation will favour business in the developmental alliance because of the state's inherently *national* focus. In contrast, capital operates at both the national level and the international level. Integration with global markets thus decreases the dependence of domestic capital on the state. To what extent has increasing exposure to the forces of globalisation debased the policy agenda and political logic of the DA? Given that globalisation is an intensifying but not necessarily new phenomenon, does the DA have the capacity to further adapt to even greater challenges to its insularity?

Globalisation should in and of itself work in favour of capital. However, when capital is disaggregated, some sectors may gain more than most. And the disciplinary powers of global markets may penalise under-performers. Globalisation can thus assist the state in a DA, especially if the state promotes policies of which markets approve. The study thus concurs with Samuels' argument about the salience of 'openness' to state intervention (1987: 17). As Russell Mardon (1990) has noted, the Korean state – at least in the early phases of the DA – acted as a mediating force between the global and national economies, and was able to maximise national autonomy by placing conditions on the involvement of foreign capital in some industrial sectors. In this sense it is possible to say that globalisation can be harnessed to the objectives of state – although these may be shared with the *chaebols* through the DA. If this is the case, to what extent has globalisation acted solely in favour of business, and to what extent has it served shared interests?

Conclusions: a new understanding of Korean development

The five variables outlined in this chapter have incorporated the existing literature into a broader analytical framework. Seen in the light of these variables, the developmental alliance appears as a highly dynamic and interactive process. It is subject to periodic tension and crisis, and a highly contingent process. Relations between the state and business in Korea thus offer great potential for insights into the politics of development.

Collectively the variables constitute an explanatory model of Korea's political economy. More broadly, they inform us of the tensions, risks and travails of late development. For instance, they illustrate how the *bureaucracy* informs Korean political leaders of policy options that may undermine state power. This ideational aspect is central to a definition of the developmental alliance as it captures the tension emanating from the simultaneous pursuit of maximal state autonomy and socio-economic development. The study reflects the importance of 'ruling coalitions' in terms of *social pressures*. It illustrates how civil society can aid the state in its power relations with business, but also how the inherently exclusive nature of the DA creates resentment on the part of civil society. In fact, the very success of the developmental alliance helps strengthen those parties who the DA partners seek to exclude from policymaking. The book infuses its analysis of Korean economic development with a broad appreciation of *national security*. Not only do the roots of the DA lie firmly in the state-led development tradition of Japan's imperial expansion of the early twentieth century but the scale of American military, political and economic aid in the post-war period is simply too important to ignore in the story of Korea's modernisation. The study includes Samuels' notions of 'market structures' and 'developmental timing' in the *economic conditions* variable in order to consider the economy's level of development and the structural position of capital. This variable also explicitly considers the state and its role in the DA. Finally, the *globalisation* variable incorporates Samuels' arguments about the relevance of 'openness' to the power relations between the state and business. The pressures of the global economic system necessarily affect both the state and capital, and the model presented here has the capacity to trace and measure its effects.

3 Priming for take-off

Introduction

A developmental alliance, as previous chapters have argued, results from the interaction between state infrastructural power and the structural power of capital. In this chapter we sketch the background to the emergence of the DA under Park Chung Hee. For the Korean state, the DA was a means of modernising Korean society and partaking in the Western-dominated international system. The key members of the junta that seized power in 1961 witnessed the nationalist state-led development model of the Japanese colonial era. This 'demonstration effect' would be twofold for Park and his coterie. The pre-1945 period showcased the supposed virtues of state-led development. Further, the instability and poverty that plagued Korea during the presidency of Syngman Rhee only confirmed Park's belief that an activist state needed to lead the process of modernisation. Park's motivation for intervening in 1961 was that Rhee had neglected the national interest.

During the integration of Korea into the Japanese empire in the early twentieth century, Japan strengthened its grip on colonial society by incorporating state, corporate and financial institutions into the imperial enterprise. The growth-oriented authoritarian state centralised control of finance, allowed economic power to be concentrated in a small number of industrial conglomerates, and repressed labour. While these patterns of political economy were also broadly evident during the Park era, we seek to identify the differences between these eras. For instance, the *globalisation* variable had a differentiated effect given that the colonial state, as a direct extension of the Japanese empire, consciously sought to minimise all interaction with regions outside the imperial realm. While the developmental state under Park and his successors also had strong mercantilist tendencies, Korean leaders have been less hostile than the colonial state to international trade. Another difference we will seek to quantify relates to the state's interaction with society. Without a patron for whom democratic reform was a prominent foreign policy goal, the Park-era state had less scope for ignoring *social pressures* than the colonial enterprise.

The third part of the chapter examines America's role in facilitating the transition of the state-centred, authoritarian development paradigm to the post-liberation period in Korea. The US would intensify the impact of *national security* on the developmental alliance. As part of its efforts to prevent the proliferation of communism in East Asia, the United States enmeshed Japan, Korea and Taiwan in a regional security network. America's commitment to its allies included its tolerance of mercantilist, state-centred development. This raises the issue of *bureaucracy*, whose developmental orientation would form the basis of the DA following the war.

The chapter next turns to the post-liberation political economy. It notes how the pre-developmental alliance period did not allow for productive and strategic interaction between the state and capital. Syngman Rhee attained the support of the US for his staunch anti-communism. Equally important to the maintenance of his rule was the support he received from domestic capital, with whom the government was mutually dependent for survival. We ask how the economic policy mix under Rhee – such as it was – affected *economic conditions*, what implications this had for relations between the state and business.

Learning the lessons of Japan

The outline of the institutional template that the Japanese colonial state passed on to Korea had its roots in the Prussian bureaucratic tradition of the late nineteenth century. With memories of Commodore William Perry's 'black ships' still fresh in the national psyche, Japan embarked on a programme of 'self-strengthening'. Japan sought to avoid having the Western imperialist powers infringe upon its sovereignty. This was the fate that its East Asian neighbours endured (Woo–Cumings 1999: 1). In light of the Western powers' repeated infringement of Chinese sovereignty, Japan strove to build a modern navy and army that could keep the Western powers at bay.

Japan's imperial ambitions grew in the final quarter of the century. By defeating China in the war of 1894–5, Japan gained control of Taiwan. It also curtailed China's long-standing influence in Korean politics. Likewise, its defeat of Russia in 1904–5 curtailed Tsarist imperial ambitions on the peninsula. The United States was by now the only major power capable of preventing a Japanese takeover of Korea. Given that the US was seeking to consolidate its gains from the Spanish–American war, it had no further territorial ambitions in Northeast Asia, it accepted Japan's ambitions in Korea on the proviso that Japan did not contest American rule of the Philippines (Oberdorfer 1997: 5; So and Chiu 1995: 91–2).

From the outset national security concerns motivated the founders of the colonial-era developmental state. Japanese leaders expressed their belief that security and prosperity were mutually reinforcing and complementary national objectives. Japan's self-strengthening movement, summarised in the term *fukoku kyohei* (rich nation, strong army), combined a state-sponsored strategy for 'late' development, the achievement of military parity with rival powers, and the foundation of a meritocratic civil bureaucracy capable of penetrating and mobilising the resources of society.

In this sense national security can be seen as a precondition for the developmental state – and for creating a developmental alliance. The existence of external threats provides a rallying point around which the state can galvanise national resources. Military threats also justify a 'big push' into heavy industries such as steel and chemicals, which serve both military and industrial ends. Park Chung Hee and his contemporaries were attracted to the notion of *fukoku kyohei*, especially its conception of 'national development as being based upon, and in turn strengthening social cohesion . . . both labour and business should accept state authority and function in the service of national development' (Moran 1998: 166–7).

In keeping with this logic, the developmental state in colonial Korea also sought to minimise the effects of globalisation by creating an autarkic colonial economy. Japan sought to inoculate this system from external economic forces, seeking self-sufficiency in the resources it would need to continue expanding the boundaries of the empire. Japan's rationale for attacking Pearl Harbor in late 1941 was that the United States and the other Western powers had hindered Japan's imperial ambitions in Southeast Asia by denying it resources – such as steel and oil – that were crucial to the empire's war-fighting capacities. The colonial-era state was thus designed to operate in an integrated, autarkic political–economic system.

In this way the industrialisation of Korea during the first half of the century served as a means to a wider Japanese end. Korea, as a colonial enclave, served as a 'semi-periphery' between Japan ('core') and the northern Chinese 'periphery' (Mason *et al.* 1980: 246).[5] After benefiting from the colonial state's investment in training and education during the first decades of colonialism, Korean technicians and bureaucrats were sent to Manchuria to oversee the expansion of the empire. Patterns of food production typified the commercial relations between the various components of the empire. Millet grown in the regions of northern China occupied by Japan found its way to Korean kitchens. Japan in turn imported rice from Korea. Similarly, Korean exports of cotton increased significantly after the invasion of Manchuria. Korea gradually moved closer to the core of the empire than the periphery (Cumings 1984: 13; Eckert 1996: 9).

The five-variable framework discussed in Chapter 2 allows us to analyse the state's exercise of infrastructural power via the bureaucracy, and its penetration of society in order to extract resources for the developmental

---

5 A contemporary Japanese analogy, popular especially after the beginning of the Sino–Japanese War in 1937, had Korea as an 'arm' joining the Japanese 'torso' to Manchuria's 'fist' (Eckert 1996: 12).

project (measured by the social pressures variable). Japan sought to eliminate opponents to its rule in Korea by co-opting Korean socio-political elites into the colonial state. In this way Japan sought to integrate Korean society into the broader empire. An initial means of strengthening control was thus to integrate the Korean economy, which was largely self-sufficient, into the imperial system. An additional motivation for Japan to build stronger institutional and commercial links with its newly acquired colony lay in breaking old loyalties (Jung 2000: 40–1; Yu 1972: 27–8). A major failing of the Korean state, and one that contributed to its loss of independence, was its inability to raise sufficient taxes to pay for national defence and other essential services. The land-holding gentry (*yangban*) dominated the civil service and treated their positions as sinecures and opportunities for petty graft. The chain of authority from the state was thus greatly weakened. This hindered even normally routine functions of the state such as tax collection (Eckert *et al.* 1990: 254–5; Woo–Cumings 1998b: 324). It was precisely these facets of the state apparatus that Japan sought to strengthen.

To remedy these dysfunctional aspects of the governance structure, the colonial state sought to establish a professional civil service in the years following the formal takeover of Korea in 1910. Bruce Cumings refers to the colonial state that launched the 'forced modernization' as being 'over-developed' insofar as its 'political, administrative, coercive and economic functions were extensive even by international comparisons' (quoted in Moran 1998: 163). The scale of the bureaucracy was immense compared to other colonial enterprises of that era: with about 100,000 civil servants, Japan mobilised almost thirty times as many bureaucrats as France did in Vietnam (Y.-G. Kim 1991b: 234).

A second element of Japan's reform of the Korean state involved the police force, which not only performed conventional tasks such as maintaining law and order but also complemented the new bureaucracy's efforts to collect taxes and carry out a detailed land survey in the colony. More generally, the police sought to bring landlords and village elders into the colonial power structure (Kohli 1999). Local political leaders were co-opted to dissuade the nationalist impulse in Korea, which manifested itself in peasant rebellion, guerrilla war and rural–urban drift. Opposition to Japanese rule was never eliminated, as the assassination of colonial leaders and collaborators testified. Nonetheless, a 'highly articulated, disciplined, penetrating colonial bureaucracy' would replace the old Korean state, and created the conditions for economic development (Cumings 1984: 11–12; see also Lie 1998: 164–5).

In this way imperial officials used the landlords to strengthen their grip on the colony. While landlords would be later vilified for their collaboration with the colonial power, they had little choice but to comply with the wishes of the colonial state or face the loss of their holdings (Cumings 1984: 11). A comprehensive land survey conducted soon after the Japanese takeover clarified property rights throughout the colony. Landowners were forced to prove that they held title to the properties they possessed. Those who could not prove clear title to their land risked having their holdings taken over by the colonial state. The livelihoods of the peasants, in turn, became extremely tenuous because they had no formal right to own and occupy the land they tilled. This had the pernicious effect of dissuading overt opposition to the colonial government and to the expropriation of agricultural surplus (Kohli 1999: 125).

The colonial police supplemented the landlords' role in social control by intervening, brutally when necessary, to suppress the sporadic peasant uprisings against Japanese rule. The demands of industrial workers for better wages and conditions met a harsh response. The colonial period witnessed the birth of the Korean working class, as land reform encouraged the rural population to seek employment in urban areas. Lest the working class meld into a force capable of challenging Japanese rule, the state restricted trade union activity and intervened forcefully on the side of capital during industrial disputes (Cumings 1984: 14; Kohli 1999: 126).

For Park and his cohorts, who were then serving in the colonial army, these forms of statecraft became an object lesson about the capacity of the state to mobilise societal resources for the developmental alliance. However, the colonial state exploited Korea in such a way that benefits to society were minimal. The co-option of socio-political elites largely insulated the state from social pressures. Resistance to Japanese rule was so strong that colonial authorities did not contemplate the engagement of civil society in economic development. State power in this period was *despotic* in nature rather than *infrastructural*. That is, it was predatory rather than productive.

Discussion of the colonial state's interaction with social forces brings us to the final variable, economic conditions, and the incorporation of business elites into a nascent developmental alliance. The restructuring of the old Korean state and the implementation of a system of social repression allowed the colonial authority to enter a 'production-oriented' alliance with landowners and business in order to achieve rapid growth. The state's control of financial institutions and the bureaucracy supplemented the developmental capacities of the colonial state (Burmeister 1986: 131; Schneider 1998: 111; Woo–Cumings 1999: 9).

The legacy of Japanese colonialism would be felt during Korea's industrialisation in the 1960s and beyond. The colonial period's political economy, which featured 'high growth and repression', was revived in later decades (Kohli 1999: 95; see also Eckert 1996). The colonial state fostered growth and repressed society through the integration of state, financial, corporate and security institutions. This 'predatory developmentalism' would be Korea's 'institutional template for later development' (Woo–Cumings 1999: 9). It would take the installation of the Park Chung Hee regime in 1961 to revive the institutional links with Japan. However, Korean bureaucrats, security officials, military officers and capitalists viewed Japan as a model for the development of their own country (Eckert 1991: 255; see also Onïs 1991).

In partnership with the colonial state, industrial capital and a tightly controlled banking sector formed a 'mighty trio' aimed at furthering Japan's imperial ambitions. The *zaibatsu*, the family-owned industrial conglomerates that dominated the Japanese economy in the early twentieth century, carried out the forced development programme. In particular, chemicals and other heavy industries were founded to serve the Japanese war effort in the 1940s (Cumings 1984: 10; Eckert 1996: 13).

Instead of partaking in commercial activity for their own gain either independently or as part of a broader developmental alliance, Korean capitalists during this period 'lacked the independence to decide policy that enhanced their own interests . . . Japan exercised complete control over labourers, the forces for capital accumulation, and policies of taxation and finance' (Jung 2000: 44–5). The colonial era can thus be distinguished from the post-war period insofar as the latter was far less coercive. That is, whereas Korean (and Japanese) capital partook in the colonial state's forced development project to further imperial ends, Park's regime would induce the *chaebols* to participate in the DA during the post-war period.

The paucity of indigenous capital's structural position in the colonial economy was stark. Korea's economic growth during that period is estimated to have been about 4 per cent per year, which was roughly the same as Japan. However, there was little direct Korean involvement in the most important sectors of the economy. Indeed, over 90 per cent of authorised capital was Japanese. Korean-owned establishments had little involvement in sectors such as metals, chemicals and power generation (Mason *et al.* 1980: 75–6).

To induce Japanese investment in these pillar industries, the colonial state was willing to 'socialise' the risk of investment through implicit guarantees and preferential access to finance. This strategy would be a common feature of industrial policy in both Korea and Japan in later decades (Woo–Cumings 1998b: 325). Indeed, the term *zaibatsu*, defined as 'a system of highly centralised family control through holding companies', itself hints clearly at the intimate links between Korea and Japan, and between each country's capitalist development throughout the last century more broadly. In the Korean language, *zaibatsu* is rendered as *chaebol*, the name given to the conglomerates that have played a driving role in Korea's industrialisation. Consequently the origins of the Korean DA can be found in the colonial era, both in terms of the material and institutional links between the two countries and also in terms of the mode of development that Japan bequeathed to Korea (Mason *et al.* 1980: 285–6; Woo 1991: 41–2). However upon assuming power in Korea, Park would not find the *chaebols* as compliant as the *zaibatsu* had been under the colonial state during the first half of the century.

These institutional ties, the precursor to what this book refers to as the developmental alliance, were a significant legacy of the period. Korean entrepreneurs had little leverage because they were confined to the lower levels of the economy while Japanese firms dominated the most developed sectors of industry. Korean landowners were complicit in the suppression of civil society rather than economic development. The incipient ties between the state and the corporate elite would be revived later in the course of Korea's development. The colonial experience was not the sole influence on the Korean model. Indeed, the links between former colonialists and suspected collaborators were broken, often violently, during the process of decolonisation. Thus those who had served in the colonial state, including both capitalists and landowners, were tainted by their associations with Japan (C. Song 2003: 58–9).

How and why, we must ask then, did Korea retain so many features of the developmental model from the Japanese era? And yet why did it take almost two decades for it to become operational once again? To answer these questions, we next examine the role of the power that occupied Korea following the end of Japanese rule – the US – and its priorities in the post-war era.

Geopolitics and the imperatives of the Cold War

To understand how Korea came under American military rule for three years following the Second World War, we must first briefly examine great-power politics in the final years of the war. In 1943, the allied powers agreed at the Cairo summit that those countries that were subjugated by the Axis powers would be granted independence at the end of the war. Fighting in the European theatre came to a close in late 1944 with the defeat of Germany. In a boon to the Western allies, the Yalta Summit in February delivered a commitment from the Soviet Union to join the fight against Japan in the Asian theatre. This would expedite the war that America and the Commonwealth countries were winning in Asia.

As the war against Japan continued in the first half of 1945, the cooperation evident at Cairo and Yalta dissipated. The reasons were numerous, including the fact that two of the three war leaders present at Yalta – Theodore Roosevelt and Winston Churchill – no longer held office. The Soviet Union's impending superpower rivalry with the US was consuming the attention of the third leader, Josef Stalin. Another summit was held at Potsdam in July. The US had by then successfully tested the atomic bomb, the use of which in Japan may have hastened the end of the war by several months. With the common enemy in Germany now defeated, consensus broke down among the Western allies and the Soviet Union. In the absence of 'hot' war, the Cold War began in earnest (Cumings 1990).

Distrust between the war victors had consequences for Korea upon its 'liberation' in August. The Soviet Union had invaded and occupied Japan's northern islands, while America and the Pacific allies attacked from the south. The Red Army next entered Korea from Siberia. Honouring an agreement with the US, it occupied only the northern half of the peninsula. The area north of the 38th parallel was designated the Soviet zone, while the US would later occupy the southern half. An American military government was installed as an interim measure while the future of the country was debated at the United Nations (Oberdorfer 1997: 5–6).

The onset of the Cold War in the late 1940s precluded a swift, amicable solution to the question of establishing a representative Korean government. Neither the Soviet Union nor the US was willing to see the Korean peninsula fall under the other's domination. Nor was neutrality an option, given Korea's chronic incapacity to defend itself from external attack. The US was determined to prevent the spread of communism in East Asia. It viewed the southern half of the peninsula as a component of a 'great crescent' stretching from Japan through Southeast Asia to India that restricted communism to the Asian mainland. If the peninsula fell under Soviet tutelage, America's main Asian ally, Japan, would also become vulnerable to attack (Cumings 1990: 49; Dodds 2003: 210–11; Woo 1991: 48).

Defending Korea was not as simple as it seemed. Isolationists in the US Congress sought to cut funds to the army, which was footing the bill for the occupation. The War Department in turn was not convinced that it was worth the sacrifice in terms of American money and lives to remain in the southern half of Korea. The 'military–strategic' value of the country was low, insofar as Korea would be difficult to defend in a conventional war. The War Department recommended a swift withdrawal. In contrast, the State Department believed that any move to abandon the anti-communist forces in Korea would signal that America lacked the will to resist the Soviet Union's expansion. Korea had high 'political–strategic' value, as its abandonment would encourage the Soviet Union to test American resolve elsewhere (Woo 1991: 46–8). Ultimately, strategic interests outweighed economic ones. The US succoured its ally with largesse in order to make Korea part of a broad anti-communist alliance. This took the form of 'patron–client' relations, whereby 'the client receives security assistance at the cost of political autonomy, and the patron supports the client's economy for military and ideological reasons' (Shin 1994: 122).

The US decided to hand the problem of Korea to the United Nations (UN). America used its control of the UN system to assemble a commission that would oversee elections throughout Korea. In the event, the United Nations Transitional Commission on Korea (UNTCOK) was not as malleable as expected. Its members clashed with the American military government due to the bias shown to right-wing forces, especially Syngman Rhee and his followers. After failing to gain access to the Soviet zone, UNTCOK suggested that elections be held in the south. It recommended that the police and right-wing youth groups be purged of corrupt elements, and that prosecution should commence against those individuals guilty of violent crimes against trade unionists and leftist politicians. The US studiously ignored this suggestion. In 1948 Rhee's party gained power by dubious means with American blessing (Cumings 1990: 74–7; Moran 1998: 163).

After the departure of American troops in 1949 the US sought to maintain the existence of an independent South Korea through military and economic aid. Despite this assistance, the South was vulnerable to attack from its northern counterpart once US troops were withdrawn. A series of provocations from both sides ensued, before the North launched an attack on the South on 25 June 1950. Northern troops swiftly poured into Seoul and surrounding regions. Within days of the attack, the UN Security Council voted to intervene on behalf of the South. A total of sixteen countries contributed troops to the venture, with the US supplying the vast majority.

Although UN forces helped to slow the advance, the North held the entire peninsula by September – except for the region surrounding the southern city of Busan. At this point, the US landed at Incheon, near Seoul. American troops soon disrupted the North's supply lines, liberated Seoul, and regained all territory south of the pre-war border. Not content with these gains, American and South Korean officials were determined to push further north (Downs 1999).

The People's Republic of China (China) warned that it would intervene if the American-led forces conquered the North. US president Harry Truman sought to bring the entire peninsula into the anti-communist camp. He reasoned that this would be a devastating, and perhaps fatal, blow to the Soviet bloc in the early stages of the Cold War (Matray 1979: 314–15). Pyongyang and other key cities in North Korea fell to the UN forces by October, and the northward push continued. China lived up to its promise. It sent almost one million troops to assist the North. UN forces were sent into retreat, and Seoul once again changed hands in the winter of 1950–1. American troops and their allies regrouped south of Seoul in 1951 and pushed north again, retaking the capital. They established a front line at roughly the same point as the 38th parallel, the pre-war boundary. At this point, the US spurned a proposal to seek a ceasefire (N.-G. Lee and K.-J. Cho 2003).

Two years of trench warfare ensued, with little or no change in territorial holdings. Meanwhile, American officials (representing the UN) continued to meet their North Korean and Chinese counterparts to negotiate a ceasefire or another means of ending the war. Eventually an armistice was declared on 27 July 1953, just over three years since the outbreak of the war and almost two years since the re-establishment of the original front line (Downs 1999: 25–7).

Troop strength of the American-dominated United Nations forces peaked at about 450,000 during the first year of the conflict. That number decreased by the end of the decade with the signing of the armistice and the reduction in hostilities. All Chinese troops and Soviet advisors departed from the North, and non-American forces from the UN side did likewise in accordance with the armistice agreement. However about 60,000 American troops were to stay on in the South (Zhai 1993: 163).

The exigencies of war reconfirmed America's commitment to Korea and to its leaders. Bruce Cumings describes America's tolerance of the question-able practices of its client states as the limitations to US preferences emanating from the demarcation of a 'grand area' of strategic interest. Allies such as

South Korea, Japan and Taiwan 'were enmeshed in a hierarchy of economic and political preferences whose ideal goal was free trade, open systems, and liberal democracy but which also encompassed neo-mercantile states and authoritarian politics' (Cumings 1990: 6).

The East Asian allies took some time to adopt this 'ideal' goal. To further the global struggle against the Soviet bloc, the US wanted to present its allies as paragons of non-communist growth and stability. This entailed the provision of generous aid packages to bolster the military capabilities of the front-line states. The US turned a blind eye to the unconventional growth strategies that its allies pursued, as well as the egregious practices of their security forces (Huff *et al.* 2001: 717; Stubbs 1999: 342; Wade 1990: 84). As Meredith Woo–Cumings notes, 'security concerns have been used to justify the logic of industrialization since the end of the Korean War' (1998a: 428).

National security concerns thus influenced the initial stages of Korean economic development and the formation of the developmental alliance. Given that security concerns were prevalent throughout the colonial era, the US military's rule of the late 1940s and on into the Rhee, Chang and Park eras, it is reasonable to claim that national security was the primary building block of the DA.

In terms of the model that would function as the bedrock of Korea's development for much of the second half of the century, the implications of the decision by the US to tolerate non-conventional growth strategies (mercantilist practices such as import-substitution industrialisation – ISI) were significant. As a result of America's toleration of such strategies, the patterns of political economy that emerged during the colonial period, and the institutions that supported them, could continue (Cumings 1998: 46–7; M.-G. Kang 2000: 344–5).

While anathema to the American ideal of development, the state-centred 'deviant form of capitalism' served as the basis for rapid development in the post-liberation period. Woo–Cumings argues: 'development in East Asia is a temporal phenomenon . . . It took place in the context of a kind of benign neglect by a hegemonic power' (1994: 415). The US also provided its allies with opportunities to benefit economically from wars in the region. Just as the Korean War was a 'gift from the gods' for Japan, Vietnam would bolster the Korean economy during the early phases of its industrialisation (Woo 1991: 55).

The impact of these opportunities was substantial. The threat of outbreak of war 'played a critical formative, reformative, and redistributive role' in East Asian development (Stubbs 1999: 344). It provided an incentive to improve infrastructure, such as roads, railways and ports, which would later contribute to the economic development of America's allies in the region.

As mentioned above, another component of America's support for its allies was the tolerance of, and abetment to, the suppression of leftist political forces and independent labour organisations. The Korean War was an opportunity for Rhee to influence state formation by suppressing social pressures.

Under the cover of hostilities with the North, the regime eliminated or neutered leftist opponents. This purge continued the American practice of scuttling attempts by even moderate leftists from partaking in legitimate political activity after 1945 (No *et al.* 2002: 77–81; T.-G. Park 1991; So and Chiu 1995: 187).

In contrast, the US did not purge Korea's security, commercial and bureaucratic institutions of collaborators from the colonial period. Likewise in Japan, campaigns to ban officials who served in the war era were half-hearted at best, and abandoned within a few years of the war's end. Thus the East Asian allies defeated the challenge of those who sought to dismantle the extant model of political economy (Cumings 1990: 235–6; Ikenberry 2001: 199–200). Reform was defeated when it was viewed as playing into the hands of the Soviet Union. A genuine revolution would have required the accession to power of figures untarnished by the imperial government. That would preclude all but the socialists, who the US would not tolerate. Thus the decision was made to stick with the war generation bureaucracy that staffed the incipient developmental state in Japan and colonial Korea (Cumings 1981: 175–8; 1984: 16–17).

In sum, by the early 1950s the US had forged a military alliance with an unstable client on the frontline of the Cold War. American military assistance in the Korean War was the first tangible instalment of what has to date been a decades-long commitment to Korean security. From the outset that commitment also involved an investment in Korean prosperity, and the ideal model for generating that prosperity would in time prove to be the very Japanese developmental state that was at odds with America's preferred model of capitalism. Korea, however, was to experience nearly two decades in which the state-led development model fell into disuse. It was only after the tumultuous Rhee period that Park Chung Hee would launch his bid for power.

The Rhee interregnum

Syngman Rhee ruled from the establishment of a Korean government in the southern half of the peninsula in 1948 until his resignation in the face of student-led demonstrations and subsequent exile in 1960. His time in power also encompassed the Korean War. Rhee returned to Korea in 1945 after spending the period of Japanese occupation (1910–45) living in the United States. There he garnered support for the liberation of Korea from Japanese rule. As such, his credentials as a nationalist could not be questioned. Indeed, Rhee opposed American plans to re-connect Korea's economy to that of Japan after the war. His lobbying did not deliver support for Korean independence prior to 1945. American policymakers showed little interest in opposing Japan's suzerainty over Korea until the bombing of Pearl Harbor in late 1941. As the previous section of the chapter noted, the US was more concerned about Japan's expansion into Southeast Asia. In any case, Rhee's uncompromising stance against communism made him America's favoured candidate to lead a government in the southern half of the Korean peninsula (Cumings 1997: 305–6; D. C. Kang 1995a: 583–4).

The political economy under Rhee differed in several ways from the colonial period and also from what would follow under Park Chung Hee. An aspect of Rhee's system of control that had roots in the colonial era was land reform. The main motivation of this reform was to strengthen socio-economic control. However instead of co-opting landlords into the system of social control, Rhee overturned the entire structure of landholding. The state acquired swathes of land that were devastated during the Korean War and offered them for sale to the peasants, who were able to own the land they tilled for the first time. Landowners typically had the highest levels of education in the country. The state encouraged them to turn their acumen and the money they received from land sales to commerce. Former landlords would also later transfer to mid- and high-level positions in the bureaucracy and the *chaebols* (Cumings 1989: 12; Lie 1998: 164–5; Woo–Cumings 1998b: 326).

Further, the state purchased agricultural output and compensated the peasants at prices that were below market rates. This resulted in a ready supply of cheap food. In later decades, this also allowed the proceeds from the surplus to be used for the fostering of the export-oriented industrialisation (EOI) drive that would occur under Park. Meanwhile, the low profitability of agriculture pushed surplus peasant labour into low-wage manufacturing. The rural sector in Korea thus subsidised the remainder of the country and the developmental project. It provided markets for industrial and service output as well as inputs of labour, food and other raw materials. The state controlled access to fertiliser, credit and irrigation, strengthening its grip on rural society (Kay 2002; Kuznets 1981; Wade 1990: 85).

While the state under Rhee was developmental insofar as land reform could be considered successful, it did not have a coherent strategy to promote economic development. Land reform was a means to reduce the appeal of socialism. There were sporadic peasant uprisings both during the colonial period and following liberation due to poor living standards and the insecurity associated with not holding title to one's fields. Giving title to the peasants reduced the incidence of anti-state activities. Rural voters were older and more conservative than their urban counterparts. Thus farmers invariably supported the government when given the chance to vote (Amsden 1990: 24; Kay 2002: 1079–80).

Like Japan, Korea witnessed a significant reconfiguration of class relations during the early stages of industrialisation. Without the removal of their feudal orders, it is doubtful whether either Japan or Korea could have launched successful developmental projects. While the Philippines had the most propitious conditions for development in East Asia at the end of the war by dint of its plentiful resources and education levels, its developmental record stands in contrast to Japan and Korea insofar as land reform failed. Filipino socio-economic elites retained substantial influence after the war, and a similar tendency for power to remain in the keeping of rural-based elites was evident also in Latin America (see Kay 2002).

The paucity of Rhee's developmentalism was more apparent in his relations with the business elite. In addition to extensive and ongoing political support from the US, Rhee's pre-eminent position in South Korea relied on donations to political campaigns from leading industrialists. Most of these had survived the transition from the colonial period with their entrepreneurial skills – if not their reputations – intact. Like the military and police, the business class was complicit in the colonial enterprise. They needed the political cover of post-war authorities to avoid retribution at the hands of those who had suffered during the colonial period and those who wished to see the collaborators brought to justice. Thus in the years following the end of the war, the main figures from the colonial era reconvened under American tutelage (Cumings 1990; Kay 2002).

The bureaucracy had little influence because Rhee and his regime dealt directly with the business elite. In the absence of a developmental alliance, the bureaucracy did not play the significant role as interface between the state and business. In the absence of policymaking autonomy, the bureaucracy was unable to play the role traditionally delegated to it. Unlike the 'production-oriented' nature of the colonial-era phase of industrialisation, in the 1950s Rhee aimed merely to provide opportunities for patronage. American officials and other observers at the time were wont to dismiss Rhee as a senile, rambling octogenarian whose predilection for anti-communism and corruption knew no bounds (Cumings 1990: 227–9). Woo instead argues that there was 'a method to his madness', as Rhee managed to extract maximal concessions from his American patron and business. The sources of patronage that Rhee traded were financial support, access to American aid projects and ownership of assets from the Japanese period (Woo 1991: 44; H.-S. Yoon *et al.* 2003: 352–3). Business had poor access to both resources and political legitimacy. Moreover, it was reviled for its collaboration with the Japanese colonial state. Hostility deepened when news of business leaders' corrupt dealings with Rhee and their rampant war-time profiteering came to light (Moran 1998: 164–5).

Rhee's corruption aside, America was also concerned that the regime's foreign policy was adversely impacting on US regional objectives. It was part of wider American geopolitical strategy to reintegrate the economies of Japan and Korea, so that each would assist the other's post-war reconstruction. Aid dollars could be 'recycled' by, for instance, Korean commodities serving as inputs to Japanese industry, whose produce could then be exported to Korea (M.-G. Kang 2000: 344–5). A State Department internal memo outlined four lines of argument for Korea to integrate its economy with that of Japan's:

> Rapid Korean economic development, crucially necessary for stability, would be materially accelerated by Japanese economic aid additive to continued US aid ... Korea would gain greater access to Japanese markets for her exports, thus providing further major stimulus to Korean

economic development ... A significant impediment to Free World unity and strength in Asia would be removed ... ROK prestige would be bolstered in the increasingly serious competition with the Communist North Korean regime.

(Quoted in Keefer *et al.* 1996: 567)

However, the nationalist Rhee government sought to stymie this strategy, which attempted to capitalise on Korea's alleged 'comparative advantage' in commodity production. Rhee, whose tenuous grip on power was built on the slogan of anti-communism and the stoking of anti-Japanese sentiment, feared that it would consign his country to a subordinate position vis-à-vis Japan. He argued that this would replicate the dependency of the colonial period, when Korea was but one component of Japan's imperial economy (M.-G. Kang 2000: 315).

In contrast, the ISI strategy contributed to the achievement of two of Rhee's goals: the continuation of external support from the US, and economic independence from Japan via the development of an autonomous industrial economy (Woo 1991: 52–4). Rhee's successors would continue this quest for autonomy. Even though Park, for instance, attempted to deflect the constraints of globalisation by insulating Korea from external economic forces, this bid – like that in the colonial period – was bound to fail.

Rhee offered business a number of ways to join the ruling alliance. For instance, financial capital was scarce following the war, so business repaid the ruling party through political donations. This gained business elites access to the most vital of resources – money. The state also offered tenders for business licences or import permits on a non-competitive basis. Only generous and well-connected supporters benefited from this arrangement. Of most value were the opportunities for entrepreneurs to acquire economic assets that the state inherited from the colonial period ('vested properties'), or to begin a new line of business, especially in light manufacturing. American aid projects delivered a plethora of opportunities for local firms to get a foothold in industry. The state controlled access to the tendering process for these projects too. The vested properties accounted for most of the colony's industrial output, and – as with other benefits that the Rhee government offered potential backers – provided an invaluable opportunity for small-time capitalists after liberation (K.-D. Kim 1976: 467–9; W. Lim 2000: 7–8; Mason *et al.* 1980: 249–50; Woo 1991: 67; C.-H. Yoon 1999: 2–3).

Nonetheless, while some collaborators became wealthy industrialists after the Japanese period, there was little Korean participation in the upper echelons of the colonial economy. Only a minority of *chaebol* owners in the early 1990s had accumulated wealth in the Japanese era. Moreover, the Korean War destroyed much of the extant capital in the country. Entrepreneurs were forced to rebuild their firms after the Armistice in 1953 (Y.-I. Chung 1985: 17; Kagan 1998: 40–1; E. M. Kim 1997: 92; Woo 1991: 65–6).

Rather than directly benefiting from the colonial period in terms of wealth, it was more typical for future Korean entrepreneurs to make their first significant forays into business through the acquisition of vested properties or contracts with the US military. These 'political capitalists' (Woo 1991: 66) learnt during the Japanese period that cooperation with the state was vital to their success. Timothy Lim thus uses the term 'petit capitalists' (1999: 618) to describe those entrepreneurs who had minor involvement in the colonial-era economy before rising to prominence after the war.

For instance, Lee Byung-chul, the founder of the Samsung conglomerate, dabbled in rice trading, trucking, real estate, noodles and brewing prior to liberation. Hyundai patriarch Chung Ju-yong's first lines of business included auto repairs and rice. Indeed, the owners of most of the biggest *chaebols* began their careers in such a fashion. This left them well placed to capitalise on the opportunities offered at the end of the colonial period (Eckert 1991: 254; T. C. Lim 2001: 113).

Even so, they did not have adequate autonomy from the state to wield structural power in a developmental alliance. That would await the coming to power of a regime that was committed to using its powers in a productive rather than predatory manner. The near-monopoly that this group of entrepreneurs held over access to economic resources generated a significant degree of structural power. Further, the state sought to pursue economic development in order to construct a society capable of warding off the communist threat. This would require substantial input from business and thus inducements from the state. The emerging capitalist class was well positioned to dominate the economy. The state would entrust economic development to these entrepreneurs because they were the only Koreans capable of running a business properly, skills they attained during the colonial era (T. C. Lim 2001: 623–5).

It was not only out of concern for national development that the state offered opportunities to the emerging capitalists. Far more was at stake. By extension, the viability of the state and the institutions inherited from the colonial era were also under threat from economic stagnation. As the next chapter will show, policymakers in the US and Korea recognised that a developmental alliance would contribute to the broader battle against communist expansion. Revolutions are born in stagnation and upheaval, not prosperity.

From the viewpoint of the remnants of the colonial period, a robust economy was required to maintain the system of payoffs that greased the wheels of the extant political economy. When the axles supporting those wheels threatened to break, all bets were off (No *et al.* 2002: 105–6).

Conclusions

The twin objectives in the Japanese empire's quest for modernisation were national security and the developmental project. The exigencies of the Cold War encouraged the continuation of the incipient developmental state arrangements despite their standing in sharp contrast to the preferences of

American policymakers. State–business relations in the colonial period served the needs of *imperial* expansion. It answered to Tokyo rather than Seoul. And the imperatives of the United States would determine the capacity of the state–business alliance to contribute to state building under Park, as it did under Syngman Rhee before him. Short of autarky, state–business inter-action in Korea would be subject to the effects of external economic, political and security factors. Invasions and wars involving neighbouring states abound in Korean history. The state has subsequently sought autonomy from external threats. Rhee, too, was imbibed with this desire, as witnessed by his intent to avoid subjugation at the hands of Japan.

The colonial state in Korea was an appendage to the Japanese empire that was on the losing side of the Second World War. The capacity of the empire to combat threats to its independence, rather than the specific form of statecraft practised by colonial authorities, determined the autonomy of the colonial state. This highlights the ongoing importance of *national security* concerns, and specifically the support of the US, to the developmental alliance in Korea. It also hints at the struggle that was to come as Park and his successors sought to combat what they considered to be political interference on the part of the US in domestic affairs and also the impact of external economic factors, or *globalisation*, on the Korean state.

If addressing national security concerns is a primary requirement of the developmental state (and thus a developmental alliance), then a competent and developmental *bureaucracy* is the second. As Chapter 2 noted, state infrastructural power must interact with the structural power of capital for state–business relations to constitute a DA. The Japanese empire employed despotic rather than infrastructural power. Its promotion of heavy industries in Korea was an exploitive activity aimed at furthering imperial expansion. It was a 'forced development' project, aimed at furthering Japanese imperial interests, rather than the national development that the Korean state pursued in the second half of the century. Similarly the colonial bureaucracy sought to extract resources such as foodstuffs and labour from Korea. This process of extraction may have contributed to the imperial economy, but business had limited capacity to combat the despotic powers of the state through structural power.

In effect the Japanese colonial state used a crude form of infrastructural power, one that heavily relied on the state's coercive powers to mobilise resources and cooperation from business. There was no real attempt to usefully incorporate societal groups into the capitalist economy except in the most exploitative manner, as *social pressures* were ruthlessly suppressed. In particular, the colonial state sought to keep its subjects on a war footing and prioritised the military in resource allocation. The sustainability of this mode of mobilisation is certainly open to question, raising the possibility that a modicum of democratic accountability in fact provides a creative tension for the DA.

The state bypassed the infrastructural tools of the bureaucracy in the Rhee period, instead establishing mutually beneficial yet unproductive relations with business leaders. State power was despotic insofar as Rhee's political economy focused on regime security rather than the promotion of economic development. The state sought to prevent challenges to its rule through an extensive security apparatus and a well-funded political machine. However, protecting the regime in this manner was expensive, necessitating generous support from the corporate elite. The state in turn handed lucrative business opportunities to a select number of entrepreneurs, reducing their material incentive to be developmental. This indicates that structural power only emanates when there are conditions for productive activity. Otherwise business is prone to corruption.

This chapter contrasted the actions of the state in the colonial period to deliver a mode of 'forced development' with the predatory actions of the Rhee period. That is, the legacy of the Rhee period was to be an absence of policy autonomy for the bureaucracy, a key component – along with a commitment to national security – of the developmental state. An activist state requires its pilot agency to be adequately insulated not only from interest groups but also from the debilitating effects that stem from the cronyistic relations that Rhee's regime shared with the business elite. The coming to power of Park brought an end to this mode of state–business relations, and so changed the course of Korean economic development by launching the developmental alliance with the *chaebols*.

4 Forming the developmental alliance

Introduction

The coup d'état of 1961 marked a turning point in the fortunes of modern Korea: with Park Chung Hee forcibly taking the reins of leadership, the key focus of the political elite shifted away from self-aggrandisement and towards national development. Although initially greeting the coup with some reservations, the United States offered a substantial degree of military, economic and political support to Park and his coterie. The US also encouraged Japan to foster and support Korean industrial development from the end of the decade. With the support of such powerful allies, the Korean state was well placed to take a lead role in developing the national economy. The Korean state under Park was also able to deploy a significant degree of coercive power, evident in the suppression of the labour movement and political dissent. This coercive power was harnessed in support of Park's developmental project, with a commonly cited manifestation of this being the disciplining of big business (*chaebols*). Alice Amsden (1992), for instance, argues that the state both supported and disciplined the *chaebols* through its control of credit. In this way the state was the 'senior partner' in the developmental alliance with business.

The state was also enmeshed in an expensive and risky partnership with big business. Park envisioned that the Korean state could oversee the developmental project in a similar manner to Japan during the colonial period. He considered state–business relations during the colonial era to be a positive illustration of the virtues of state-led development, while viewing the Syngman Rhee presidency as a period of developmental failure. The Park regime, however, faced considerably more constraints than the colonial state in constructing a state–business relationship in which it was the domineering partner. The structural power that capital had accrued in the post-war period dictated that the state adopt a more collaborative approach to development.

That relationship between state and business is best illustrated through the use of Michael Mann's (1984: 191–3) concept of 'infrastructural power', which explains the capacity of the state to extract resources from society and mobilise them for the developmental project. The state becomes dependent on society because it draws economic resources from society to enhance its own powers. However the state can use societal resources for ends such as the developmental project, which society cannot pursue autonomously. Thus the *political* dynamics of the nascent Korean developmental alliance were crucial to the shaping of policy itself as well as to its implementation and monitoring. While the state had the capacity to coerce the *chaebols* into productive behaviour, the imperative to retain 'business confidence' necessarily reduced its incentive to exercise disciplinary powers or to enact remedial measures. Given that the exercise of despotic power carries heavy risks to a regime with an imperative for sustained economic growth, a strong political imperative for the developmental project enhances the structural power of capital. The *chaebol* leaders, as the only individuals with the capacity to convert economic resources into viable enterprises, thus possessed a certain structural power that largely protected them from the exercise of state power. It was the interaction between the infrastructural power of the state and the structural power of capital that would set the parameters for the Korean developmental alliance.

This chapter examines the relationship between the state and capital in Korea by drawing on the five contextual variables discussed in Chapter 3. First, by referring to previous discussions of infrastructural power, it explains how the *bureaucracy* re-emerged as a tool of state power in the 1960s. Given that the focus of the state was on the accumulation of despotic rather than infrastructural power in the years after the Korean War, Syngman Rhee and Chang Myon were unable to satisfy the conditions for a developmental alliance.

The chapter next recounts Park's coup of 1961, the American reaction to it, the stabilisation of the regime in a civilian format, and the subsequent formation of a developmental alliance with business. This reminds us that *national security* is the cornerstone of the developmental state. With both the justification of security concerns, and a state apparatus capable of penetrating society in place, the Park regime created the conditions around which the state could amass infrastructural power and thus enter into a developmental alliance. The chapter then examines the *economic conditions* of the early phase of Korea's industrialisation, and argues that the imperative for rapid growth endowed the *chaebols* with structural power. This required the state to strike a political bargain with big business, whereby the two parties became mutually dependent upon each other for survival. Consequently, when the forces of *globalisation* adversely impacted on Korea in the late 1970s, the state was forced to intervene and support the indebted *chaebol* enterprises.

Park was to pay a high price for the developmental alliance, both personally and in terms of the constraints imposed on his regime. The chapter concludes by considering the eruption of *social pressures*, which had been heavily suppressed during the initial phase of industrialisation, and their manifestation in political turmoil at the end of the decade.

In quest of infrastructural power

In the case of East Asian societies such as Korea, the developmental state has proven to be the preferred mode of state elites because it aligns neatly with the self-propagated presumption that strong, centralised state leadership is not only necessary but also inherently valuable. As argued in previous chapters, this developmentalist orientation – evident in both political elites and policymakers who head the bureaucracy – sets East Asia apart from the West. For Michael Mann, despotic power refers to 'the range of actions which the elite is empowered to undertake without routine, institutionalised negotiation with civil society groups' (1984: 188). This form of power entails the enforcement of the state's will on society, by violent or predatory means if necessary. In contrast, infrastructural power is 'the capacity of the state to actually penetrate civil society and to implement logistically political decisions throughout the realm' (Mann 1984: 189).

Particularly in the early phases of an economy's development, Mann argues, a centralised and coordinated state apparatus is necessary to ensure that all sectors of society are incorporated into the emerging capitalist order. The state exercises infrastructural power when it meets socially useful ends that society cannot meet itself. These ends include the redistribution of economic resources, the organisation of military forces for the purposes of national security and the supervision of a 'late development' campaign to upgrade the domestic economic base (Mann 1984: 201–2). This final task equates to what this study refers to as the 'developmental project' in Korea.

Discussion of the developmental state's emergence in Korea requires us to review America's expectations of its putative allies in East Asia. The US enmeshed Korea into a broad anti-communist alliance, and acceded to mercantilist practices and authoritarian rule on the part of its allies despite espousing the ideals of free markets and democracy. For the US, 'economic growth, the expansion of regional and world markets, and the fighting of the Cold War went together' (Ikenberry 2001: 200). States such as Korea sacrificed military and security autonomy in return for internal autonomy and capacity in 'patron–client' relations with the hegemon (W. Shin 1992, 1994). Despite the power asymmetry between the US and its Korean ally, the client state benefited significantly from the relationship. Jung-en Woo describes this as a process of attempting 'to wrest autonomy through interdependence' (1991: 159). By becoming an indispensable part of the Cold War effort, Korea thus turned its weakness in the international setting into strength at home.

Yet the tolerance of the US for its allies' actions was finite. As part of its quest to resist communist expansion, the US expected its allies to develop liberal economies and polities. They would thus serve as models of capitalist rather than communist virtue. Initially, at least, the Korean and Taiwanese states accumulated the despotic type of power rather than the infrastructural type. This was in part due to the communist insurgency in each country. It was also due to the authoritarian nature of the regimes that assumed power in the late 1940s. Ming-Chang Tsai notes that the Taiwanese regime strengthened the army, police and bureaucracy 'to enforce political order, land redistribution and effective taxation', which in turn 'generated widespread resentment from the urban middle class and the rural peasantry, but coercive state forces repressed any opposition' (1999: 103).

Rhee's staunch anti-communism endeared him to the US but the hegemon had reservations about his predilection for corruption. As noted in Chapter 3, the domestic business elite made political donations in return for patronage, such as access to scarce financial resources, import permits, participation in aid projects and use of nationalised industrial assets. Rhee also constructed a formidable security apparatus, but his power was despotic in nature, focusing on the maintenance of regime security rather than broader socio-economic ends. Another cause of consternation was his refusal to reintegrate the Korean economy with that of Japan.

The US attempted to reform some of the more egregious features of Rhee's political economy in the second half of the 1950s, setting in train events that led to his downfall. The main change occurred in 1957, when the US altered its aid dispensation from grants-in-aid (mainly used for equipping the military) to development loans. Aid recipients were required to repay the loans and also to use the funds for projects with a clear economic rationale. The US had not hitherto enforced such conditions on its allies lest it destabilise their regimes (M.-G. Kang 2000: 324–5; Tsai 1999: 104–5).

Moreover, development was seen not as a virtue in itself but as a way to expedite the winning of the Cold War. Spurred on by Walt Rostow's 'new look' at foreign policy, America would attempt to 'win the hearts and minds' of the post-colonial world by showcasing the material benefits of participating in the capitalist system (T.-G. Park 1999: 102–5). It would be explained to a Korean delegation in 1961 that John F. Kennedy:

> felt that the American people had become weary of foreign aid and needed a new program they could support with good conscience and some degree of enthusiasm . . . it seemed some aid given on a short-term basis had not been used to best advantage in some countries, including Korea.
>
> (Quoted in Keefer *et al.* 1996: 532)

A halving of American aid between 1957 and 1961 curtailed Rhee's discretion over spending. Rhee had previously used American aid to finance a security apparatus and a collusive relationship with the business elite. However, the US insisted that Korea use aid for economic development, a task requiring infrastructural rather than despotic power. The economy stagnated once shorn of its artificial stimulus, increasing the national rates of bankruptcies and unemployment. The rate of economic growth dropped from 7.7 per cent in 1959 to less than 2 per cent two years later (Woo 1991: 71–2).

Dissatisfaction with the government manifested itself in social unrest. Discontent spilled into the streets after Rhee used particularly egregious means to win the 1960 presidential election. Thousands of protestors demanded that Rhee resign. The regime responded by ordering the presidential guard to fire on protestors (Oberdorfer 1997: 49). The US at this juncture withdrew support for Rhee. The moderate Prime Minister Chang Myon formed a new government from the political opposition. Yun Bo-seon assumed the presidency, an office whose powers were reduced through constitutional amendments. Korea entered a (short-lived) period of government by the cabinet system. As discussed in the next section, the military did not intervene on Rhee's behalf, in part because junior officers such as Park Chung Hee believed that the misrule and corruption of the Rhee regime had seriously damaged the fabric of Korean society (Moran 1998: 168).

It was easier for the US to abandon Rhee given his lack of support among the public and also sections of the military. The removal of Rhee facilitated the changes that America had sought in terms of integrating its allies' economies. Chang was less nationalistic than Rhee, opening the way to normalisation of ties with Japan.

Despite his having better democratic credentials than Rhee, Chang struggled to revive the economy and quell social unrest. Protestors favoured the wholesale replacement of the extant political elite, including Chang, who they viewed as no less tainted than Rhee. The US was disappointed that Chang failed to restore social stability. Fears grew that North Korea might seize upon the unrest in the South and launch another invasion (W. Shin 1994: 123). Secretary of State Dean Rusk expressed concern about the future of Korea in a telegram to the US embassy in Seoul just weeks before the Chang government fell. Rusk bemoaned the lack of 'forceful leadership' and the 'serious weakness in moral fiber', which threatened to drive the South Korean populace into the arms of communism (quoted in Keefer *et al.* 1996: 436). The US had sought in vain a suitable candidate to lead Korea. One was soon to emerge who would provide the impetus for the socio-economic development that the US sought among its allies.

The view from Washington

As the previous section noted, Walt Rostow influenced the direction of American foreign policy in the late 1950s. Rostow argued that developing countries would spurn capitalism, and by implication the US, unless the market economy could deliver tangible socio-economic benefits. Given that the North Korean economy was faring better than that of the South, the propaganda value of improved economic performance was strong (M.-G. Kang 2000: 349–50). Rostow presumed that people from outside existing economic structures – namely, those from rural areas, youth and the military – would be cast into leadership positions. Coupled with a competent public service, this new 'modernising elite' could serve as agents of change by giving their countries the opportunity to create wealth for themselves. They would no longer rely on American aid (Brazinsky 2005: 85–6; T.-G. Park 2001: 58–61).

It was in the interest of the US, Rostow argued, to encourage precisely such self-sufficiency on the part of its putative allies. Above all, the state would need to focus on the developmental project in order to retain American support. This in turn necessitated a departure from the despotic nature of the regimes in the immediate post-war era. Korea would need to develop infrastructural power, which entails negotiation with society for the state to perform tasks that benefited society. Ming-Chang Tsai notes the conditional nature of infrastructural power, arguing that 'constrained, rather than unlimited, state power converted Taiwan's government from a predatory state into a development regime' (1999: 102). This again highlights the difficulty involved in accomplishing a developmental project.

Coming from outside traditional power structures, the junta's leading officials had little compunction about overturning the established political order. They were largely a product of – and complicit to – the Japanese colonial empire. Kim Jong-rak, the elder brother of Park's confidante and nephew-in-law Kim Jong-pil, notes that many of these officers were originally from the north of Korea. They were thus considered to be potential enemies of the South Korean state after the establishment of rival regimes in the North and South (Heo 1999: 408–10).

Park Chung Hee and his coterie viewed senior military leaders with disdain for being part of the ruling elite during the presidency of Syngman Rhee. Rhee's fall, and the continuation of cronyism under Chang Myon, demonstrated to Park that Korea was undergoing a failed experiment with democracy. The junta considered national morale to be in terminal decline, manifesting itself in corruption, inefficiency, immorality and dependence on external aid. As Park wrote later, 'It was really sad for me to see our dignity, our worth and our self-respect being forcibly swept away by alien things' (C. H. Park 1970: 57)

Park and a small band of followers executed a military coup on 16 May 1961. The junta pledged to: maintain Korea's commitment to anti-communism; fulfil its obligations to its allies; carry out an anti-corruption drive; revive the economy; create the conditions for non-communist unification; and return power to a civilian government after completing its self-appointed tasks (S.-J. Kim 1971: 93–4; No *et al.* 2002: 155–7).

Diplomatic records suggest that the coup came as a surprise to the US. However, this surprise was not an altogether unwelcome one. If Park was committed to fighting communism and pursuing a developmental project, Korea could become the ally that the US had sought since the end of the war. The junta's pledges were a good starting point for Park in securing the support of the US. Nonetheless, the official position of the US was to reaffirm its support for the elected Korean government: 'The Department of State . . . emphasized the need of the ROK to return to civilian constitutional government as soon as possible and remove the Army from any political power struggle' (quoted in Keefer *et al.* 1996: 463–4).

This unease was in part due to concerns that the coup was a communist takeover by stealth. There were reports that the Korean military had arrested Park in 1948 for heading a communist cell. Once the US was convinced that Park was not a communist, it was more disposed to support the junta. Indeed, the American government would soon argue that Park was qualified for the vexing task of leading Korea's economic development. Under Park, Korea thus appeared to satisfy the American expectation of an 'orderly, efficiently operated and politically friendly regime' (W. Shin 1994: 125).

The stabilisation of the regime, first as a junta and later as a civilian entity, was crucial to the creation of a developmental state. Regardless of the despotic power that it could wield – and this power was indeed substantial – the Korean state under Park would ultimately need to attain and exercise infra-structural power in order to achieve its goals. The most notable of these was the developmental project. Park's regime thus negotiated, via the bureaucracy, with society to extract the resources it needed to oversee that project. In particular, it would grant senior public servants – such as Kim Chung-yum, Kim Yong Hwan and Kim Yong-tae – a leading role in formulating economic policy, winning the confidence of both the US and the business community in the process.

Sensing that they lacked American support, Chang Myon and Yun Bo-seon stepped down from their roles. While in principle the US did not want a military-led government, it was willing to accept one in the name of stability. Secretary of State Rusk indicated a willingness in mid-1962 to tolerate the transformation of the regime into a civilian form. It was not

> realistic for us to insist on full-blown democracy and complete disap-pearance of military leadership in 1963. Pak [sic] is the only figure now in sight who seems to possess sufficient intelligence, vision, breadth of contact, forcefulness, personal reputation, and access to power (especially over military) to fulfil present leadership requirements.
>
> (Quoted in Keefer *et al.* 1996: 591–2)

For the US, Park was distinct from Syngman Rhee and Chang Myon due to his apparent understanding of the link between the twin components of modernisation: security and development. David Kang (1995b) argues that the state demonstrated a 'credible commitment' to the developmental project by not expropriating domestic capital. The capacity it attained from the American alliance provided a means of being *productive* rather than *predatory*. Unlike military regimes in other countries, the support of the American hegemon contributed to the state's capacity to pursue the developmental project.

Thus the potential for a transition to democracy was tempered by the belief, on the part of both Park's group and its American ally, that the military was the only institution capable of overseeing the modernisation of Korea. A reversion to a fully civilian government was mooted for 1963. However, the junta was unwilling to return power to the political class. Park would later claim that the regime was 'betrayed' during discussions about a reversion to civilian rule. 'Our naïveté, trusting in their humanity, was cruelly stamped underfoot . . . when I hoped that their old evils might disappear, they became more ambitious, knowing that I would not take part in civilian government' (C. H. Park 1970: 103). Arguing that civilian politicians were incorrigible and thus unfit for office, Park portrayed his prolonged stint in power as a reluctant one: 'It was a means to supervise the incipient corruption of the Third Republic, to prevent degradation and stop the recurrence of the tragedy of revolution' (C. H. Park 1970: 105).

The US was more concerned with regime stability than a transition to democracy, for its principal concern remained the broader foreign policy goal of fighting communism. Korea would also eventually become less of a burden on American treasure and blood if it could oversee a successful developmental project. The National Security Council suggested to the president's special assistant for national security, that:

> All in all, instead of urging Park and his Rasputin, Kim Chong-pil to be more democratic, maybe we ought to tolerate a little more dictatorship in this messy fief. Korea is still a mess (one of our great failures despite billions in pump priming). So I'd settle for a bit more stability, which would permit us to cut our bill some more.
>
> (Quoted in Gatz and Patterson 1999: 20)

A staunch commitment to anti-communism, which Park, Kim and the other junta leaders were displaying, would ensure ongoing American support. The only caveat that the US was attaching to its support was some improvement in socio-economic development, a condition Park fulfilled by including senior public servants in the devising of economic policy. After Park offered his country's support for the evolving conflict in Vietnam, the US was convinced of Park's alignment with its regional objectives. With American support, Korean policymakers were heavily involved in Park's ambitious bid for rapid economic development. American and Korean worldviews had reached a satisfactory level of agreement, with the shared goals of anti-communism and development becoming the main themes in bilateral relations.

Park Chung Hee defended his government's concentration on the developmental project rather than political liberalisation, arguing that 'In developing countries, the focus point of politics is "economic construction"; and democracy can prosper only in the fertile soil of economic construction' (Park and Shin 1970: 139). The emphasis on development over democracy dovetailed neatly with the nationalist logic of the developmental state, whose time had come in Korea.

An unruly alliance

Despite attaining US support and granting input to senior public servants, Park still faced the gargantuan task of reviving the Korean economy. In addition to its precarious geo-strategic position, Korea – unlike Latin America or Southeast Asia – also lacked the advantage of substantial reserves of natural resources such as arable land and extractable mineral resources, and was ranked among the world's poorest countries in the early 1960s (Doner *et al.* 2005). Given that its economic conditions were generally unfavourable, there was a strong imperative for the state to intervene and – armed with political and economic support from the US and later Japan – promote socio-economic development. Launching a developmental project in such inauspicious conditions, however, would require close cooperation with big business.

As noted at the outset, Alice Amsden considers a defining feature of the developmental state to be its playing of the role of 'senior partner' ('elder brother') in an alliance with business (1992: 14–15). This characterisation connotes a dominant role for the state in the process of development. Jonathan Moran also emphasises the tradition of the 'strong state' in Korea thus:

> Political power resulted in patron–client links being organized in the service of national development. Businesses could not adversely affect the developmental priorities of the state whilst the state could decide which groups to grant resources to in return for favours.
>
> (1998: 169–70)

While these authors highlight the capacities of the state, they do not fully capture the limits that accompany those capacities. In particular, these depictions grant little role to the *chaebols* in the developmental alliance. In contrast, the understanding of the developmental alliance in this book is based on Michael Mann's conception of infrastructural power, which is state action that furthers the common weal. This form of power is used to induce the complete participation of business in the developmental project.

Nonetheless, there were instances of the state using despotic power against the *chaebols*. James Crotty and Kang-Kook Lee note the capacity of the state to discipline subsidy recipients: 'if export and productivity targets were not achieved, financial support was withdrawn from the offending firms and forced mergers or bankruptcies imposed upon them' (2002a: 328). The state also acted against *chaebols* that did not support its political goals. For instance, Peter Morriss recounts that the Samhak group 'was driven into bankruptcy after it financed Kim Dae-jung in his (failed) presidential challenge against President Park in 1971' (1997: 50–1).

The puzzle here is how state power interacted with the structural power of capital *without* destroying the will of business to contribute to the developmental project. A starting point is to acknowledge that Korean development has *not* proceeded in accordance with the dictates of the state (Lie 1998). As noted earlier, infrastructural power is a resource that the state draws from society. A core component of this process is the inducement of business into a cooperative framework for national development. This in turn limits the capacity, and incentive, of the state to exercise its despotic power against business. If infrastructural power is a resource that the state extracts from society, then the state must negotiate with society.

Ming-Chang Tsai similarly argues that the developmental alliance was based on the notion of 'embedded autonomy' that Peter Evans (1995) suggests. That is, a 'synergistic tie between the state and the private sector' was the basis of a developmental project in late industrialising countries such as Korea and Taiwan. While the state disciplined subsidy recipients for substandard business performances, it also 'effectively responded to business interests' (Tsai 1999: 103). These state 'responses' stand in contrast with the depiction of an all-powerful state brooking no dissent from society. If the state did play the role of elder brother, it was to an increasingly demanding sibling. According to a famous anecdote about the 1961 coup, the regime frog-marched business leaders through the streets of Seoul with placards hanging around their necks and dunce's caps on their heads. The rationale for this spectacle was that business leaders should be contrite for the corruption of the Syngman Rhee and Chang Myon eras (Woo 1991: 83–4). The regime announced that it would fine the leaders of Korea's biggest enterprises and exclude them from business activities. According to former economic advisor Kim Yong-tae, the junta's radical elements even discussed the possibility of executing these businessmen (Y.-G. Kim and S.-H. Lee 2002: 287).

A spectacle was all these measures would amount to as the 'dunces' soon returned to their posts, albeit somewhat chastened by their dressings down. The state asked the leaders of the *chaebols* to 'contribute' to the developmental project instead of jailing, fining or barring them from business activity. The regime thus chose the carrot over the stick in its dealings with business. It elicited a promise – if not a guarantee – that the entrepreneurs would devote themselves to the developmental project in return for a waiving of the most serious charges against them. This purification drive was also a means of differentiating the new regime from the corrupt Rhee era (T. C. Lim 1998: 468–9).

Senior policymakers such as Kim Yong Hwan and Kim Yong-tae, as will be explained below, highlighted to Park that regime security was dependent on the incentive structure offered to the *chaebols*. The legitimacy of the Park regime, and ongoing US support, required the state to showcase the virtues of capitalism to the Korean public and other developing countries. At the same time, with the corporate elite seen as complicit with corruption, its fortunes were similarly linked to the success of the developmental project.

For instance, Park's senior economic secretary of the 1970s, O Wonchol (1996), notes that the regime could not achieve the developmental project alone. Through its 'engineering approach' to the developmental project, the state identified industries in which firms had the potential to be internationally competitive. It then provided incentives for business to invest in those sectors. Park thus acknowledged the need to create the conditions for the developmental project.

The path of state intervention, and thus the evolution of the developmental alliance, was thus very much informed by senior figures in the Korean bureaucracy. Economic advisors urged the junta to pursue the developmental project through partnership with business. Kim Yong Hwan calls the junta's measures to stimulate business 'an inevitable choice, not a privilege . . . [the state] respected the principle that business was the engine of economic development' (2002: 273). The regime came to view inducements to business as a necessary element of the developmental project. The ends justified the means, because only the *chaebol* leaders could develop the economy's resources in a socially useful manner. The Korean state thus largely dispensed with its despotic power and used the infrastructural variety to induce the *chaebols* into a developmental alliance.

For instance, one of the main means by which the state contributed to economic development was via its control of the banking system. By assuming control of the major national banks, the government could direct 'policy loans' to those *chaebols* who were invited to participate in projects earmarked as being of national priority (Woo 1991). Nonetheless, the state would need to give business sufficient incentives to participate in the developmental project largely free of the threat of despotic power. Kim Yong-tae, an advisor to Park Chung Hee, describes how he enlightened the junta's leaders on the need to cooperate with the *chaebol* leaders:

> I said, 'These men of ability have taken from 30 or 40 years ago to create. We can't now create talented people and use them. We have to use the entrepreneurs.' We got the entrepreneurs together in one place and discussed building the national economy . . . *Getting our entrepreneurs to participate voluntarily* was the main foundation of the miracle on the Han River.
> (Quoted in Y.-G. Kim and S.-H. Lee 2002: 287, emphasis added)

Consequently, the Park regime developed a measured approach to its dealings with the *chaebols*, and sought to provide an incentive structure conducive to maximal private sector activity. Kim Yong Hwan writes that Park 'had a strong belief in private-sector-led economic construction. He was well aware that in the early stages of economic development, the intervention of the government is inevitable' (2002: 111–12). Given that the exercise of despotic power against the *chaebols* would be detrimental to the developmental project, the imperative for economic growth necessarily limited the regime's capacity to discipline business. It would be difficult to reverse the logic of the developmental project once it had begun. For the state to move against business *as a whole* would destroy the confidence of firms to invest.

Vivek Chibber argues that the Korean case offers evidence for 'the constrained position of state in capitalist economies' (2005: 124), insofar as the state clearly relayed its commitment to economic development. While possessing substantial capacities, the state under Park was cognisant of the need to maintain business confidence. The state recognised that the *chaebols* were endowed with a substantial degree of structural power because they alone could convert economic resources into viable enterprises (T. C. Lim 1998). For this reason, the regime sought to convince business leaders that their interests coincided with those of the developmental project.

The limits of state power

For the Park government, economic development – and the launching of the developmental alliance – was not merely an abstract or aspirational goal. Given the precarious state of South Korea's geopolitical position, and the inevitable comparisons with the North, the DA represented a risky and ambitious strategy to deliver society from poverty to prosperity. The strength of the economy was equated with overall national strength and virility, indicating the way in which the regime saw – and portrayed – the pursuit of development as literally a 'life or death' struggle. An important element of Park's development strategy was to maximise national autonomy by relying on loans from international financial markets rather than foreign investment in order to fund the 'big push' in heavy industries in the 1970s. Unable to recoup the costs of investment in its small domestic market, the Korean government backed the ability of the *chaebols* to enter export markets in sectors such as ships, steel and automobiles (Woo 1991).

In this way, the state sought to go beyond a simple import substitution programme and instead focus on export-orientated industrialisation. An EOI strategy, Korean officials reasoned, offered the chance for Korea to surpass not just the Pyongyang regime's level of industrial development but also those of competitor nations in the Third World. Only by expanding scale of production to surpass the capacity of its own small markets could Korea break out of the cycle of underdevelopment. While continuing to discourage unnecessary imports, the government bolstered funds for industries with ample potential for generating export income (Luedde–Neurath 1988). Korea was exposing itself to the benefits – and risks – of globalisation. The investment risks of the *chaebols* were socialised – that is, the state (and, indirectly, the public) ultimately bore the risk of investments in heavy industries.

The developmental alliance amounted to a Faustian bargain, whereby the survival of the regime was tied to the well-being of business. Despite the powers available to the state, Park was reduced to imploring the *chaebols* to 'discard their habit of relying on protection as if they were plants in a hothouse, and to make assiduous effort to explore new markets, improve the quality of their products, rationalise management, and effect technical renovation'. Park, in 1966, acknowledged the need to appease the *chaebols*: 'some businessmen have lost sight of the ethical as well as social nature of business' (Park and Shin 1970: 129, 153).

The reluctance of the *chaebols* to act in the interests of society appeared to exasperate Park at times. For instance in May 1966, he urged business to 'think of the society and the nation before temporary excessive profits or the profit of "my company" or "my factory"' (Park and Shin 1970: 154). However, this advice appeared to go unheeded. Former policymaker and diplomat Kim Chung-yum notes that Park 'stressed that entrepreneurs had to feel responsible for the state and the people who had given them a chance ... Despite their vows, they did not show much compliance' (1994: 122). The true cost of the *chaebol* model would soon become apparent.

The regime could not guarantee that its pro-business approach would further the developmental project. To exercise its disciplinary powers, such as the confiscation of economic assets or the exclusion of certain firms from spheres of business activity, would risk a 'capital strike' on the part of business (Block 1992). Without sufficient incentives to invest, the *chaebols* would not participate in the developmental project. For instance, Lee Kwon-Hyung (1998) argues that the state needed to assure Korean carmakers of a significant share of the domestic market in order to localise their operations in line with the developmental strategy for that sector.

Kim Chung-yum (1997), reflecting on his decade of service to Park Chung Hee as chief of staff, also notes the paucity of the state's disciplinary powers. The *chaebols* publicly admitted to culpability for a debt crisis in 1972. This necessitated state-led bailouts of the most poorly run enterprises. However, the *chaebols* did not take substantial measures to improve their finances. This suggests that the state's approach involved plenty of carrots but few sticks. Cho Yeong-cheol (2003) claims that the developmental project thus created a 'market tyranny', whereby attempts to rein in the *chaebols*' power were futile.

Park's relations with the US deteriorated during the presidency of Richard Nixon (1969–74). This was due to an apparent weakening of US power in the shape of troop withdrawals from the region, the symbolic abandonment of the link between the American dollar and bullion, and a resort to protectionism in the US. Park's sense of abandonment impelled him to bolster Korea's industrial and military autonomy in the 1970s through the Heavy and Chemical Industry (HCI) drive. Korea's relations with the US reached a nadir during the presidency of Jimmy Carter (1977–81), when calls for Korea to improve its human rights record brought into question American support for the regime. The involvement of the *chaebols* was crucial to the success of the HCI drive (and the developmental project more broadly). Thus once again the political imperative of the state strengthened the structural power of business. That is, its structural power made business somewhat immune from the most powerful forms of coercion that the state possessed.

The HCI drive saw the *chaebols* undertake billions of dollars of investment in new industries with the assistance of subsidised finance. The top-ten *chaebols* increased their share of value-added to GDP from 5.1 per cent in 1973, the year in which the HCI drive was launched, to 10.9 per cent five years later (J.-S. Shin and H.-J. Chang 2003: 28). In addition to recording high sales volumes, the *chaebols* also created substantial employment directly and also indirectly through their relationships with downstream subcontractors. The benefits of the HCI thus spread across the economy, bolstering aggregate economic growth and – more modestly – income levels in the process. Consequently, their importance to the developmental project necessarily reduced the capacity of the state to coerce the *chaebols*. The state's disciplinary powers extended only as far as encouraging the *chaebols* to undertake practices that would serve both their own narrow interests and those of the developmental project.

Another example of the state's provision of incentives to the *chaebols*, and the limits to its coercive powers, was evident in the presidential directives of 1974 regarding the improvement of corporate performance. The state proposed to offer incentives to firms with good debt-to-equity (D-E) ratios, such as permission to list publicly. This would offer material benefits to *chaebol* owner–managers through windfall profits. The state also provided *disincentives* to those with weak debt structures, such as denying them access to new loan repayment guarantees and credit injections. Firms that refused to list would sacrifice these benefits. The state intended these measures to improve debt structures by delivering new capital to the *chaebols* through public listing, with a commensurate improvement in corporate governance practices.

Yet the *chaebols* argued that public listing would reduce their control over their corporate empires. The *chaebols* accused the state of adopting 'anti-business' measures. The state relaxed its performance standards in order to dispel this perception. Business leaders were slow to conform to the directive to list publicly. Kim Yong Hwan, an advisor and minister to Park during the 1970s, argues that those firms that had listed included few of the largest *chaebols*, at whom the directives were originally aimed (2002: 126–8). That is, the structural power of the *chaebols* limited the state's capacity to enact reform, even when it furthered both corporate and national interests.

The intensive investment in heavy industries in the 1970s, which was financed through generous state support, resulted in an unsustainable accumulation of debt. It also produced excessive investment in some sectors and a concentration of credit in a small number of borrowers. A painful recession began late in the decade, with a loss of employment and production.

The contradictions of the privileges granted to business became evident in the 1970s. So did the limits of the state's capacity to ameliorate the deleterious effects of the developmental project. Sung Il Choi (1983) argues that a vicious circle evolved whereby the state gambled on offering the *chaebols* privileged access to capital through low-interest loans. It expected that the *chaebols* would use these funds to invest in new industries and thus generate the income to repay the mounting level of foreign debt. To suddenly withdraw privileges risked default on national debt. This would spark a collapse of the financial system. By the late 1970s the contradictions of the *chaebol*-centred developmental alliance were becoming clear: the need for capital infusions and sales in overseas markets necessitated ongoing support for the *chaebols*, who, by dint of their structural power, were largely impervious to efforts by the state to rein in their excessive borrowing. Indeed it was the state that had encouraged this borrowing in the first place, in the name of national development. The Park regime was facing the consequences of its own economic policies.

Containing the backlash

For Park, economic development was a major element of a broader nation-building project. In light of the instability that had plagued Korea during the war and the Rhee years, one of the government's priorities was to placate a restive populace, which had proven itself willing to support the overthrow of administrations deemed to be incompetent or corrupt. The regime was thus cognisant of social pressures, and sought to legitimate its rule through the developmental project. For this reason it encouraged the *chaebols* to lift productivity and compensate workers through wage increases (Doner *et al.* 2005: 344–5). In the interim Park began to tighten political control in the early 1970s. Opposition leaders such as future presidents Kim Dae-jung and Kim Young-sam had been denied power through the rigging of elections, and the Korean Central Intelligence Agency (KCIA) monitored the opposition closely through an extensive security apparatus. The Yusin Constitution of 1971 formalised Park's intention to deflect challenges to his presidency, removing the number of terms a president could serve and handing responsibility for electing the president to an electoral college. Park appeared to believe himself an indispensable element of Korea's modernisation, and so took all and any challenges to his government as a personal affront.

The regime's agricultural policy, as noted in the previous chapter, had by the late 1960s succeeded in raising production levels to the extent that food shortages were largely eliminated. The 'New Village Movement' was part of the government's policy of raising living standards in rural areas by, for instance, providing grants to those villages and towns that had made visible efforts to improve health and hygiene standards. At the same time nothing could disguise the fact that incomes in rural areas were stagnant, encouraging young people to take up factory jobs in the cities (Kay 2002; Koo 1990).

The rapid transformation of Korean society, exemplified by the rural–urban drift, also wrought great changes to the structure of the Korean economy. Park's pro-*chaebol* strategy, while delivering high growth rates, had an uneven and destabilising effect on the economic structure. For instance, the financial system was heavily skewed in favour of the *chaebols*. This worked to the detriment of small–medium enterprises, which could not access credit on the preferential basis that the *chaebols* did. Depositors were also penalised in the form of lower returns on their savings, which the banks lent to the *chaebols* at concessional interest rates. In addition, environmental standards were lax, and the state suppressed aggregate wages to maintain the competitiveness of export industries. The imperative to maintain competitiveness left Korea vulnerable to a downturn in the global economy or protectionism in markets such as the US (Yu 1980: 23–5).

There were also significant discrepancies in working conditions between *chaebol* and non-*chaebol* sectors. In the light manufacturing sector – the labour-intensive production in industries such as footwear, clothing and textiles – there was an increase in the number of both blue- and white-collar workers. There was also a substantial influx of women into the workforce, with women being particularly prominent in the light manufacturing sector that required close work (Koo 1990). The YH Trading Company manufactured wigs, and thus did not receive the benefits that firms in targeted industries such as steel and electronics received. Such labour-intensive sectors were not priorities for the developmental project, but they illustrated the negative aspects of the Korean model. YH was notorious for exploiting its predominantly female workforce, who went on strike to protect their livelihoods when the factory owners absconded with the firm's funds. One of the strike's leaders, Kim Gyeong-suk, took her life in November 1978, highlighting the sense of hopelessness on the part of the workers. The strike and Kim's suicide became a magnet for opposition forces. Ko Un, contemporary Korea's foremost poet, led a public campaign to support the strikers (D. M. Choi 2003: 141–3).

Increasingly concerned about challenges to his rule, and with support from the US appearing to weaken, Park ordered the military to violently suppress the strikes. However, some elements of the government were concerned about Park's centralisation of power and the paranoia that had developed in the 1970s. While his ever-diminishing circle of confidantes supported his forceful responses to the deteriorating political, economic and social conditions, some argued that a more nuanced and conciliatory response was required. Late in 1979, the director of the KCIA assassinated Park after a heated argument in the presidential residence (see Cumings 1997). In an unexpected and sudden manner, Park's eighteen years as leader had come to an end, drawing to a close the initial phase of the developmental alliance.

Conclusions

This chapter shed light on the politics behind Park Chung Hee's developmental state. It demonstrated the limits of the 'strong state' thesis by highlighting the state's incapacity to combat the structural power of the *chaebols*. The Korean state relied to a significant degree on the *chaebols* for its survival, despite the support of the US and despite a preponderance of socio-political power. The attainment of infrastructural power, the means by which the state oversaw the developmental project, required the state to extract resources from society. Notably, this extraction necessitated the consent of the *chaebols*.

The chapter noted that the *bureaucracy* acted as an interface between the state and the *chaebols* during the Park era. Civil servants, shielded by the political cover that Park provided through suppression of external account-ability, shaped the state's approach to the developmental alliance. Leading civil servants, especially those in executive organs such as the EPB, were charged with producing 'sound' policy in a rarefied atmosphere, with the bureaucracy serving as the state's source of infrastructural power. The exalted position granted to the bureaucracy reflected the traditional reverence given to civil servants in East Asia and, as such, represented a return to the pre-war norm. The relatively low status granted to civil servants during the Rhee era thus appears as an anomaly to the longer trend, whereby bureaucrats held prominent positions in the machinery of government. It took a change of thinking on the part of the US, coupled with the ascension to power of a regime intent on achieving the developmental project, for the state to again grant the bureaucracy such a position of prominence and, more importantly, to nurture the infrastructural variety of power in Korea.

The second contextual variable that the chapter considered was *social pressures*. Although civil society could not remove Park from power through physical force due to the regime's preponderance of despotic power, the state relied on infrastructural power to execute the developmental project. Consequently the state sought to increase its legitimacy since infrastructural power in turn required at least a modicum of public consent to the develop-mental project. For example, Park introduced a limited form of democracy from 1963, and attempted to civilianise the regime that assumed power via the coup. However, narrow escapes from assassination in 1968 and 1974 (the latter of which cost the life of his spouse), along with waning support from the US, saw Park introduce the authoritarian Yusin Constitution of 1971 and later declare himself president for life. The regime thus sought to suppress social pressures more tightly, bearing the brunt of social discontent and thus granting space to the *chaebols* to concentrate on wealth creation.

National security was central to the founding of the developmental alliance. The US supported its Korean ally in order to contain communism in East Asia. However, its treatment of the Rhee and Park regimes differed in several respects. Walt Rostow's 'new look' at foreign policy called for a more holistic approach to fighting the Cold War. The US expected its client states to pursue socio-economic development as well as the attainment of sufficient military capacities to oppose communist expansion. It thus encouraged the fostering of infrastructural power. Park, in turn, adjudged the support of the US as vital to the goals – and the very survival – of his government, and thus committed Korea to its ally's side in the Vietnam War. At the same time, changing US goals under the Nixon and Carter adminis-trations increased Park's sense of paranoia, encouraging the regime to tighten political control and exacerbating American concerns about human rights. In this sense, national security worked in favour of the *chaebols* in the developmental alliance due to the state's overriding goal of furthering the developmental project. The US was more tolerant of the statist model during this period than it would be in later decades.

The *economic conditions* of the Park era also increased the structural power of the *chaebols* within the developmental alliance. The chapter showed that the Korean state struck a Faustian bargain whereby it entered a risky developmental alliance with the *chaebols* in order to increase its legitimacy. The political imperative of the state to achieve the developmental project explains the privileges showered upon the *chaebols*, and the corruption that accompanied the collusive relations with business leaders. The state relied on the *chaebols* to convert economic resources into wealth-generating enterprises. This in turn necessitated pro-business policies at the expense of wider societal interests. It is possible that Park was aware of the shortcomings of pursuing the developmental project, and that he presumed that the future would present him with an opportunity to resolve them. The regime's reticence to exercise despotic power in response to *chaebol* malpractices highlights the contingent nature of state capacity within the developmental alliance. Given that state capacity offers 'windows of opportunity' within which action must be taken, this book views it as a 'wasting asset' that can only be deployed in specific circumstances. As the prevailing economic conditions compelled the state to use its capacities to promote rapid growth through the HCI with relatively light sanctions on the *chaebols*, the state of the economy favoured the *chaebols*. However, following the recession of 1979–80, as Chapter 5 will explain, a new opportunity arose for the state to deploy its powers against the *chaebols*.

The launch of the HCI drive highlights Park's quest for autonomy from external interference in the shape of both the political and economic aspects of American hegemony. The regime's limited capacity to achieve that quest was apparent. Korea was incapable of independently funding the HCI drive. It thus relied on international financial markets to make up the shortfall. This exposed the domestic economy to the international financial system, however. It was the state that would bear the burden of this exposure rather than the *chaebols* through state guarantees for the *chaebols*' loans. Thus, like economic conditions, *globalisation* worked to the advantage of the *chaebols* within the developmental alliance. The state was obliged to offer incentives to the *chaebols* but had little means of disciplining them for excessive borrowing, which imperilled the national economy.

The Park period illustrated how the interests of the state were closely tied to those of the *chaebols* via the developmental alliance, substantially enhancing the structural power of capital. While these ties would endure in subsequent decades, Park's successors were intent on breaking this tight nexus with the *chaebols*.

5 The developmental alliance in flux

Introduction

The 'growth-first' policy stance that was central to the developmental alliance neatly encapsulated the tumultuous Park era. Whereas Park initially considered rapid economic growth to be merely the means of Korea's modernisation, by the late 1970s it had become an end in itself. The state's extensive support for the *chaebols* had created serious imbalances between big business and other economic agents. In the wake of the financial crisis that accompanied Park's death, Korea's new leaders appeared resentful of the way in which the state was held responsible for the crisis when, they reasoned, it was the *chaebols'* investments that had contributed to a substantial accumulation of foreign debt and the recession of 1979–80.

At the same time state leaders were confronted with a realisation that Korea's modes of economic and political organisation were out of step with the dominant paradigms emanating from Washington. While willing to overlook these discrepancies in earlier decades, by the early 1980s the US government's rationale for supporting the authoritarian regime in Seoul and its top-down development model were coming under ever-greater scrutiny. In this sense, the *national security* variable, which tracks the willingness of the US to support Korea, came into focus. Challenged from both within and without, the new Korean government was faced with a difficult political manoeuvre: admitting that its chosen mode of development contained certain structural faults while defending the case for state leadership. The self-appointed right to rule of the state elite remained, even if the DA was required to undergo some alteration in terms of governance mechanisms.

Referring to this book's five contextual variables helps to explain changes in economic policy and also in the DA more broadly. With the ascension to power of Chun Doo-hwan in 1980, policymakers atop the *bureaucracy* increased their influence on the developmental alliance. Liberal bureaucrats, many of whom were educated in the United States and thus inspired by the 'small government' mantra of Reagan and Thatcher, advised Chun to liberalise the economy and dispense with policy tools such as preferential access to credit. The economic liberals argued that the bailing out of the *chaebols* placed the financial system under great strain during the 1970s, making the economy hostage to the *chaebols*. In response to deteriorating *economic conditions*, the emphasis of economic policy shifted from 'growth' to 'stabilisation'. The government directed a relatively greater share of economic resources to small–medium enterprises (SMEs) rather than the *chaebols*. Despite the prevalent shift to deregulation in the US and Europe in the 1980s, the Chun government's adherence to neoliberal reform was limited, as evidenced by the 'restructuring' of sectors with excess capacity through debt rescheduling.

Relations between the state and the *chaebols* became increasingly tense during the presidency of Roh Tae-woo, who succeeded Chun to the leadership in the election of 1987. This was in large part attributable to civil society's articulation of new demands on the developmental alliance. The government responded with the rhetoric, if not the substance, policies more accommodating of *social pressures*, by adopting either a neutral or anti-*chaebol* stance. Viewing this change of attitude as a betrayal of the ethos of the developmental alliance, the *chaebols* sought to put their own position across in the public domain. The greatest act of defiance on the part of the *chaebols* was the decision by Hyundai chairman Chung Ju-yong to directly challenge the state by running for the presidency in 1992.

The first leader in thirty years not to come from a military background, Kim Young-sam sought to put even more distance between the government and the *chaebols*. For Kim, the *chaebols* symbolised the developmental alliance of the Park era. His catchphrase was 'globalisation' (*segyehwa*), the intention of which was to expose Korean industry and finance to greater international competition. The adoption of *globalisation* as an official policy, in rhetoric if not substance, was a consequence of more than a decade of neoliberal influence on state policy. However, the tilt to neoliberalism was not accompanied by a coherent strategy for protecting the economy from external shocks, leaving Korea vulnerable to a more serious version of the economic crisis that struck at the end of the Park era.

Retrenching the state?

As mentioned in the previous chapter, Park Chung Hee's assassination resulted from disagreement within the regime about the appropriate response to deteriorating socio-economic and international conditions. A recession coincided with Park's relations with the US reaching a nadir in the late 1970s. For these reasons the conditions were not ripe for the emergence of a civilian regime. Park and his contemporaries abhorred what they considered to be the decadence of the political class. They considered civilian politicians, such as Kim Young-sam and Kim Dae-jung, to be unqualified to lead the country. A younger class of military leaders, centred on Chun Doo-hwan and Roh Tae-woo, seized power within the armed forces and in national politics. Chun and Roh assumed control of the military – and also the powerful

Korean Central Intelligence Agency – in December 1979, actions that would earn them jail terms in the 1990s. Choi Kyu-hah was to serve as caretaker head of state but Chun and Roh were the most powerful figures in the country (Cumings 1997).

Popular opposition to the continuation of military rule was strong, especially in the southwestern Jeolla province. This region had been neglected during the process of economic development. Most industrial complexes were built in the Gyeongsang province, Jeolla's rival. The Jeolla people considered themselves to be victims of discrimination within their own country, especially since the Park regime arrested and tried to assassinate the region's most revered statesman, Kim Dae-jung. With the end of the regime, the Jeolla people hoped that Kim would become president after narrowly losing in 1971 amid credible allegations of vote rigging. The regime had also imprisoned the other prominent opposition leader, Kim Young-sam. The harassment of these political leaders encouraged dissent among their supporters. Kim Young-sam's supporters rallied near his hometown in the southeastern cities of Busan and Masan. The most extensive display of opposition to the new regime was in Gwangju, the capital of Jeolla. Weeks of demonstrations culminated in a popular revolt and a subsequent violent repression by security forces. The death toll was later estimated to be in the hundreds (Presidential Truth Commission 2004).

Chun and Roh solidified their grip on power after crushing the Gwangju uprising in May 1980. Chun assumed power as acting president later that year. The election of Ronald Reagan at the end of 1980 strengthened the position of Chun, who was sworn in as Korean president in early 1981. The events of 1980 appeared to merely affirm to the US that it needed a 'stable' ally in Korea. Given the history of America's clientistic relations during the Cold War, it came as no surprise that 'stability' usually connoted support for military regimes. Chun had the honour of being the first foreign head of state to visit the Reagan White House (Cumings 1997).

The ascension of the Chun regime also signalled change to economic policy. Kim Jae-ik, who had served in the bureaucracy since his return from the US in the early 1970s, advocated 'stabilisation' and liberalisation to respond to the recession that followed the HCI drive in the 1970s. In the view of liberals such as Kim, the state's provision of capital to the *chaebols* on generous terms resulted in high inflation, excessive indebtedness, the concentration of economic power in the hands of a small number of firms, and thus an economy highly sensitive to changes in the fortunes of the *chaebols* (B.-K. Kim 2003: 53–6; Thurbon 2003: 348).

This stance did not meet with universal approval, and it was certainly not uncontested. The pro-growth elements of the bureaucracy called for the new government to adhere to the tenets of Park's approach to economic policy. In contrast to those who championed a leading role for the state in the develop-mental alliance, senior technocrats such as Kim believed that 'minimizing the state's role is the best way to promote development . . . promoting strategic reduction of the state's role as the best route to increasing the state's efficacy' (quoted in Evans 1995: 232). The influence of the liberals grew. In return for financial assistance from the IMF, the caretaker government of Choi Kyu-hah adopted Kim's policies of stabilisation (limited growth in prices, wages and public spending) and liberalisation (less government involvement in bank lending, more competition for finance) after Park's assassination (Aghevli and Marquez–Ruarte 1985).

Chun was to continue the policies that Kim Jae-ik recommended to the interim Choi administration. By re-appointing Kim as director of the EPB, Chun indicated that he would accede to the policies of stabilisation. Kim, until his untimely death in 1983, would wield tremendous influence over the new government's policies due to his unique access to the president. Kim acted as Chun's personal tutor in economics. He used these private contacts to advocate a break from Park's policies (Clifford 1998).

While accepting of Kim Jae-ik's advice, some elements of the Park era remained, resulting in a policy mix that contained both dirigisme and market–liberal traits. Unlike Park, neither Chun nor his successor Roh professed to be adept at economics. Nor did they inherit the belief that Japan was the optimal model for Korea's developmental alliance. Subsequently they were willing to heed the advice of the US-educated liberals, such as Kim Jae-ik. The liberals argued to Chun that the recession of 1979–80 was attributable to excessive intervention, especially in the form of policy loans for projects such as the HCI drive. They added that Korea would not attract foreign capital without an explicit commitment to stabilisation (S.-G. Kim 1989: 255–60; Woo 1991: 190–1). That is, they argued, the increasing economic weight of the *chaebols* (their structural power) had destabilised the national economy.

The state took measures to help the economy recover from the downturn. Initially, at least, these accorded with the advice of the liberal bureaucrats in the EPB. The conditions of the IMF bailout loan required Korea to reduce its budget deficit and the rate of growth in the money supply. This necessitated the curtailment of 'policy loans' at low interest rates, tax breaks and research subsidies. The Chun government largely phased out these policy instruments during its early years. It also curbed wage rises in order to restore the competitiveness of the *chaebols*. The currency was devalued by 17 per cent, the effect of which was a rise in prices of imported oil. The economy returned to growth in 1981 due to the combined effects of the currency devaluation, wage stability and an increase in agricultural output (S.-H. Lee 1999: 23–30).

Despite the reformist zeal of the liberals, the political imperative to pursue economic development blunted the state's capacity to reform the *chaebols*. The stabilisation measures impacted on production costs in the form of higher costs of borrowing and inputs. Of far greater concern to the *chaebols* were proposals for sectoral reorganisation and corporate restructuring. The liberals suggested that the *chaebols* could improve their corporate structures by disposing of unprofitable affiliates and excessive real estate holdings. The opposition of the *chaebols* to these measures explained the generous terms of the restructuring in the early 1980s. The government's proclaimed goal of fewer producers in particular sectors would be met, but typically this came at a price. The state funded the rolling over or cancellation of bad debts for firms in sectors that it earmarked for rationalisation (B.-K. Kim 2003: 55–6).

Critics questioned the efficacy of sectoral rationalisation, given that it produced a consolidation of monopolistic and oligopolistic market structures. Invariably it was the largest *chaebols* that benefited. This again highlights the sensitivity of the state to the interests of the *chaebols*, dovetailing with this book's argument that the structural power of capital is positively correlated with the political imperative to further economic development. For instance, in 1985 the state provided low-interest loans to banks that carried massive non-performing loan (NPL) burdens. It halved interest rates for policy loans to 3 per cent in order to prevent a systemic collapse. In all, the state funnelled $2.1 billion into the financial system from 1985 to 1987. The loans favoured big business. This reinforced the reliance of the financial system on injections of public funds. The state sponsored further assistance to the financial system later in the decade, with $8.5 billion for the restructuring of insolvent firms, $5.25 billion for interest payment deferrals, and $1.2 billion for writing off bad loans (Clifford 1990: 226–8).

These injections were at odds with the liberals' exhortations that the state not support the *chaebols* with public funds. With few exceptions, the state failed to punish the *chaebols* for accumulating high levels of debt or for over-expanding productive capacity. This illustrates what Tat Yan Kong refers to as '*chaebol* non-reform' (2000: 84). Kong argues that the will of the state to forcibly restructure the *chaebols* tends to weaken once the urgency of a crisis has passed, and once the degree of short-term economic pain that would result from structural reform becomes palpable. This was certainly the case after the initial years of the Chun regime. Another reason for the weakening of reform was the death of twelve of Chun's ministers and advisers, including Kim Jae-ik, in the Rangoon bombing of 1983. Other liberals remained in the state apparatus, but none had Kim's degree of personal input into Chun's thinking (Clifford 1990).

The regime needed to cultivate closer ties with big business for its political survival due to a series of financial scandals in 1982 and 1983. This further reduced the state's will to enact reforms that the *chaebols* opposed. The *chaebols* provided Chun with increasingly generous political donations in return for a softer line on reform (Thurbon 2003: 348–9).

As mentioned earlier in this section, liberals such as Kim Jae-ik had urged Chun to abandon the traditional policy tools of the developmental state. They opposed the type of sectoral reorganisations that the Ministry of Finance (MOF) and Ministry of Commerce and Industry (MCI) oversaw intermittently during the Park era. The EPB proposed that the private sector initiate the rationalisation of insolvent firms. However, the MCI and MOF opposed this suggestion in both style and substance. These ministries, which championed a significant role for the state in economic development, argued that the state needed to call the *chaebols* to account. The EPB liberals urged greater respect for the sanctity of the divide between the state and the private sector.

Restructuring was more than a mere difference of opinion: it represented a significant schism in the bureaucracy and thus in the way in which the state participated in the DA. The dirigiste ministries were concerned that the EPB was usurping their authority. The MOF and MCI argued that issues such as sectoral rationalisation were their remit rather than that of the EPB. They restructured six industrial sectors between 1982 and 1985 through M&As, publicly funded bailouts and tax breaks (M.-H. Lee 1993: 307–10). The reformist EPB subsequently acted as a counterweight to the conservative ministries in terms of overall policy. However, its influence on micro-level issues such as restructuring was limited.

The EPB was more influential on the macro-level issue of stabilisation and the liberalisation of the financial system. It was the measures that the state took to liberalise finance that would have greater consequences for the developmental alliance. The measures in the financial sector to reduce the concentration of economic power benefited the *chaebols* rather than reducing their influence. Especially during the capital-intensive HCI drive, the state encouraged the concentration of economic power in the biggest *chaebol* groups. It rewarded successful groups with more opportunities to expand their empires (Leung 2003: 49–50).

Without a radical reorganisation of corporate ownership, the liberalisation of financial markets would ensure that the biggest and most indebted borrowers continued to dominate access to capital. Although the government retained indirect influence of the banks, their gradual privatisation during the Chun era signalled a loosening of the state's disciplinary power over the *chaebols*. The expansion of secondary financial institutions (non-bank financial institutions, NBFIs) allowed the *chaebols* to access funds free of state control, further weakening the banks–business–state nexus that had evolved after the government's takeover of the banks in the 1960s. NBFIs took an ever-larger share of bank deposits from the mid-1970s. From less than one-fifth in 1975, their share rose to 30 per cent in 1980, 45 per cent in 1984 and just over half of all deposits in 1987 (Hahm 2003: 81–3; Woo 1991: 197).

The state remained responsible for ensuring the liquidity of the financial system despite these changes to the source of finance. The state's *explicit* guarantee to support the *chaebols* through policy loans transformed into an *implicit* guarantee to rescue the financial sector in the event of a systemic collapse. Such a transformation eroded state autonomy, because the state had at least earmarked policy loans for specific aspects of economic development (Y.-C. Cho 2003: 158). The state continued to guarantee the stability of the financial system. However, it lost the means of disciplining the *chaebols'* use of loans. The balance of power in the developmental alliance moved in favour of the *chaebols* as they attained a greater degree of autonomy from the state.

This is not to say that the state did not attempt to re-impose its will upon poorly performed *chaebols* or those that did not comply with its political agenda. Indeed, the most notable case of the state's using despotic power against the *chaebols* occurred in 1985, when it forced the mid-sized *chaebol* Kukje into bankruptcy. While it is true that the Kukje Group's debts were high compared to other *chaebols*, indebtedness had long been a feature of the *chaebols*. Kukje's more serious failing was that it declined to contribute to a political fund the president had established. However, this alone was probably not enough to ensure that the Chun government would force it into bankruptcy – three factors coincided at that time: a highly indebted *chaebol*, the perceived political snub, and the desire of the government to prove to the biggest *chaebols* that its guarantee for their debts was not inviolable (Clifford 1998: 219–20). The Kukje incident was an attempt to discipline the *chaebols*, insofar as the state dismembered the group and stripped its owners of their assets. Such a display of despotic power was anathema to the other *chaebols*, whose own vulnerability was made all the more stark.

The state's use of despotic power in this way was a calculated risk. It was possible because the economy had recovered to such a degree that the political imperative was relatively low. It was also the case that other *chaebols*, while chastened perhaps by this display of state power, did not suffer any damage from the Kukje incident. Indeed, several benefited when the state disbursed Kukje's assets to other groups (Schopf 2001: 702–5; Underhill and Zhang 2005: 17–18).

The democratic interlude

Relations between the state and business became increasingly tense during the presidency of Roh Tae-woo, who succeeded his military colleague Chun Doo-hwan to the leadership in the 1987 election. The significance of the Roh period lies in the degree to which the expectations of Korean society impacted on the developmental alliance. Scholars such as Alice Amsden (1992) have praised the capacity of the state to inoculate economic development from the vicissitudes of politics. Despite the best efforts of the Chun regime to crush opposition to its rule, workers, students, church groups and the *minjung* (people's) movement all challenged the legitimacy of the government. These disparate sources of opposition found common cause, culminating in massive strikes and protests during the spring of 1987 (Koo 1999; Wells 1995).

David Martin Jones argues that the developmental state holds the middle classes 'effectively in its thrall' (1998: 156). The state pre-empts political change and thus constrains its deleterious effects. Roh used the protests as an opportunity to further his own political ambitions, announcing a transition to democracy. Roh's strategy in 1987 was to harness the power of civil society towards a less authoritarian version of the developmental alliance. He nominated himself as the government's candidate and adopted populist policies to improve his chances of winning the poll. Roh won a three-way contest against Kim Dae-jung and Kim Young-sam.

The policy changes were to sour relations with the *chaebols*, whose leaders resented the insinuation that they benefited improperly from economic development. With the democratisation of Korean society, the *minjung* movement articulated a deep-seated popular resentment that big business had collaborated with, and benefited from, both the colonial Japanese state and the post-liberation authoritarian governments of Rhee, Park and Chun (C. Song 2003: 58–9).

Roh made significant political mileage from adopting even a moderately anti-*chaebol* stance. One example was the government's directive in May 1990 that the *chaebols* should sell some of their real estate holdings in order to reduce pressure on the property market. This was an issue of concern for an emerging middle class with aspirations of buying homes or starting businesses (Clifford 1991: 60). Yet even these measures were more about style than substance, and did not significantly impact on the *chaebols*' financial interests. The biggest *chaebols* promised to sell 15 per cent of their holdings immediately. However, most sales occurred in rural areas and thus did not ease the demand for urban housing (Friedland 1990: 62).

One of Roh's most notable changes was his approach to industrial disputes. The Park and Chun governments forcefully intervened on the side of business to end strikes, minimise wage claims and restrict union organisation. However, Roh took a more hands-off approach. This forced the *chaebols* to negotiate directly with trade unions, which had become well entrenched in the massive industrial estates that formed the basis of heavy industries such as shipbuilding and automobiles. The unions used their relatively high densities to campaign for wage increases (Bellin 2000: 200–1). The outcome was an upsurge in strikes, hefty pay increases and improved working conditions. Roh's stance had an immediate effect on wage levels. After rising by 9 per cent in 1987, wage increases averaged 16 per cent from 1988 until 1992. This represented a cumulative increase of 115 per cent throughout the life of the Roh government (Y.-S. Kim 1999: 425).

Other examples of policy changes that the *chaebols* opposed included the scrapping of export credits and further reductions in low-interest policy loans. The state also strengthened the Fair Trade Law to reduce the prevalence of oligopolistic and monopolistic market structures (Clifford 1990: 47). Yet these measures were, at best, watered-down versions of the original bills. They had little effect other than to infuriate *chaebol* leaders, who accused the state of making political capital out of anti-business measures.

The state also sought to reduce the *chaebols*' concentration of economic power and to restrict the *chaebols* to a total of three 'core industries' of activity. The *chaebols* had long cross-subsidised their business activities. The 'convoy' (*seondansik*) system involved a *chaebol* group using profits from one sector to invest in an entirely different one. Critics argued that this wasteful and indulgent process did not follow economic logic. As will be seen in the next section of the chapter, Kim Young-sam also adopted these policies with similarly disappointing results (Y.-S. Kim 1999). The *chaebols* perceived this policy as a threat to their unique system of resource allocation and innovation. They viewed the core industries policy as an effort to dismantle their business empires. Nonetheless, the balance of power within the developmental alliance at the time was such that the state's capacity to enforce the policy was limited. Roh could only exhort the *chaebols* to comply voluntarily, and justified his approach several years later: 'So the direction of economic policy at that time was to tell the *chaebols* that they had to restructure for their own sakes and for the sake of the country' (quoted in Y.-S. Kim 1999: 437; see also H. Lee 1991).

The measures were provocative to the *chaebols*. They were reminiscent of the *chaebol* owners' experiences of 1961, when the state castigated them for their 'crimes' in the Rhee era. While the state had only infrequently exercised despotic power in the intervening years, possibility remained that the government would take arbitrary measures, such as tax audits, against the *chaebols*. The state could target the *chaebols* for 'punishment' at will (Bellin 2000: 200–1; B.-M. Lee 1993: 332). While the shift towards a 'core industries' policy had little impact on the capacity of the *chaebols* to expand their business empires, the *chaebols* viewed the government's stance as a betrayal of the ethos of the developmental alliance. This in turn encouraged the *chaebols* to defend their interests more strongly. Business leaders portrayed themselves as nationalists. They adopted slogans such as 'building the nation through industrial development' (*saneop ipguk*) and 'serving the country through entrepreneurial activities' (*saeop poguk*) to emphasise their contribution to economic development and Korean society more broadly (C. Song 2003: 60). Instead of being perceived as 'junior partners' who merely did the government's bidding, business tried to present a positive image of itself through its words and actions. The Federation of Korean Industries (FKI) exhorted public companies to be 'loved and trusted' by the people, and for 'autonomy and democracy' in both the economic and political realms (quoted in K.-M. Kim 1988: 385).

The state's inability to rein in the excessive investment and speculation of the *chaebols* after the boom of the late 1980s illustrated their growing power and willingness to oppose the government. After a surge in investment and expansion during the boom years, the Roh government sought to bring corporate investment back to more stable levels. The favourable conditions that had made the boom possible were dissipating. First, labour-intensive exports faced increasing competition from low-wage producers such as China. Those in capital- and technology-intensive sectors competed with Japanese producers, whose quality surpassed that of their Korean counterparts. The US and the European Community were taking measures to end what they considered to be mercantilist practices on the part of countries such as Korea. Multilateral negotiations resulted in harsher measures against dumping. Meanwhile, the trend towards regional trade agreements restricted access to Korean exports in key markets (C. S. Kang 2000: 81–5; B.-K. Kim 2003: 62–3).

Further, energy prices rose from their lows in the mid-1980s after Iraq's invasion of Kuwait. International oil prices doubled during 1991, reducing the competitiveness of the export-driven Korean economy. Finally, the currency appreciated as a result of the trade surpluses that Korea had accumulated. The yen rose from 120 to the American dollar in 1985 to 140 in early 1990. This further cut the competitiveness of exports vis-à-vis Japan. The trade surplus thus dropped sharply in 1989 and returned to deficit in 1991. The favourable external conditions disappeared along with Korea's trade surpluses (Y.-S. Kim 1999: 429).

Despite this deterioration in external conditions, the *chaebols* considered any attempt by the state to control investment decisions as an infringement of their managerial autonomy. The *chaebols* became bolder in voicing their opposition to state policies under Roh. As noted above, the FKI's 'declaration of independence' announced the autonomy of business from the state. The *chaebols* and their lobbyists began to publicise the contributions which business had made to Korean society through their role in economic development. This propaganda sought to counteract the criticism emanating from the *minjung* movement and some quarters of government and the media. The election to the National Assembly of several former businessmen – whose ranks from 1996 would include future president Lee Myung-bak – provided another venue in which business could defend its interests (K.-M. Kim 1988: 377).

The 'counterattack of the *chaebols*' began in May 1991. The chairman of the Hyundai Group, Chung Ju-yong, criticised government policy. Chung said, 'The sense of crisis in Korean politics and economy is because there are no firm leaders in whom the people can trust' (quoted in H. Lee 1991: 240). The FKI became a conduit for enunciating the position of the *chaebols*. It funded the publication of pro-business tracts, calling for a smaller role for the state. Apart from attempts to influence politicians and policymaking through informal networks, the FKI championed a private-sector economy in which state intervention would be minimised (Y.-B. Kim 1996: 149–50). The *chaebol* leaders, who comprised the FKI, also began to publish the content of their meetings. Their minutes revealed sharp criticism of the government for its expansionary policies in the face of rising inflation, calls for the privatisation of state-owned enterprises (SOEs), and recommendations that the state overhaul the tax system to induce corporate investment. An FKI representative argued, 'We must say what needs to be said' (H. Lee 1991: 241).

These actions brought the views of business to the public domain. They revealed that the direction of economic development reflected more than just the preferences of the state. The public domain became a venue for both parties to the developmental alliance to defend their interests and espouse their understanding of the most appropriate direction for economic development. The most significant act of defiance on the part of the *chaebols* was the decision by Chung Ju-yong to stand against the government's candidate in the 1992 election. Chung adopted the provocative slogan of 'get government out of business' (quoted in Evans 1995: 229). His actions heightened tensions between the state and *chaebols*.

The party of opposition leader Kim Young-sam and another small opposition party joined Roh in an expanded ruling party in 1990. The new ruling party, which espoused a return to a more conservative, pro-business approach to economic development, was called the Democratic Liberal Party (DLP). The name connoted the party with the most electoral success in Japan since the war, the Liberal Democratic Party. Indeed, there were fears that the three-party merger would transform the Korean developmental alliance into a facsimile of the 'Japan Inc' relationship between the Liberal Democratic Party and big business (G.-H. Kim 1990: 224).

With Kim as its candidate in the 1992 election, the ruling party developed a softer line on *chaebol* reform. For instance the DLP announced that it would defer the implementation of the 'real-name financial transaction system' (*silmyeongje*). This measure aimed to end the practice of political donations being made from bank accounts held under false names. The *chaebols* opposed it because such a system would limit their capacity to make campaign donations and to transfer funds within and between affiliates through false bank accounts. The government also announced an easing of restrictions on real estate holdings. Overall it would revert to a traditional growth-oriented approach rather than populist, redistributive policies (Y.-B. Kim 1996: 153). Despite these policy changes, the *chaebols* – especially the Hyundai Group – patently did not trust the government to defend their interests adequately. As the next section will show, Hyundai would pay a price for this defiance after the election.

Kim Young-sam and globalisation

Kim Young-sam won the presidential election in late 1992, with his long-standing opposition colleague-cum-rival Kim Dae-jung running second. Chung Ju-yong, the chairman of Hyundai, finished a distant third. The first leader without a military background in thirty years, Kim Young-sam sought to further distance the state from the *chaebols*. Some of his motivations were personal and some represented a deeper philosophical commitment to changing the developmental alliance. Kim launched a campaign of revenge against Hyundai only weeks after assuming office. The state indicted senior Hyundai officials for providing illegal funds to Chung Ju-yong's party during the election. It also pressured Park Tae-jun, Chung's confidante and running mate, to step down as chairman of state-owned steel maker POSCO (Paisley 1993: 16). Hyundai itself was later the target of intrusive tax audits. These actions were not aimed at destroying the group. They merely displayed once more the capacity of the state to hurt the *chaebols* if need be.

The Kim Young-sam government did not suffer in the eye of the public by humiliating such well-known public figures. Indeed, the hounding of Chung Ju-yong appeared to be part of a broader attempt by the new government to attract popular support. The president also purged 'political' elements of the military and forced corrupt politicians to resign during his first year in office. He thus removed a host of potential rivals, especially those with ties to Park Chung Hee.

Despite Chung's conviction for electoral and other financial malpractices in 1993, the new president agreed to pardon the Hyundai leader if he agreed to retire from political activity. The Hyundai chairman did not serve a day in prison (Morriss 1997: 40, 49). In public at least, the president was critical of the influence that the *chaebols* had on the national economy. Once again, a sharp divide was apparent between the substance and rhetoric of reform. As one insider commented:

> President Kim personally felt that if the *chaebols* performed poorly, they could cause fatal damage to the national economy . . . He directly witnessed the arrogance of the *chaebol* owners resulting from the concentration of economic power in the *chaebols* and the concentration of ownership . . . And before the Hyundai incident, President Kim's view of the *chaebols* seemed naïve. After it, his understanding of the *chaebol* problem became clearer.
>
> (Quoted in B.-M. Lee 1993: 330)

Despite arriving at such a negative prognosis of the *chaebols*, the state remained cognisant of the limits of its disciplinary capacity. Wholesale reform of the *chaebols* was impossible given their sheer scale. The state thus tended to enact piecemeal and half-hearted reforms (Kong 2000). The state had to trust the *chaebols* to reform themselves or instead delegate this task to 'the market', as liberals advised. The Kim government's capacity to discipline the *chaebols* was even more limited than that of its predecessors. Kim abdicated responsibility for reforming the *chaebols* by adopting the slogan of 'globalisation' (*segyehwa*). The prime intention of globalisation was to turn Korea into a market economy by opening domestic industry and finance to international competition (C. S. Kang 2000: 86–7). Misguided though it would later appear, the government's intention was for globalisation to force the *chaebols* to lessen their domination of the economy.

The main problem with relying on the passive forces of globalisation to enact *chaebol* reform was a weakness that lay at the heart of the developmental alliance. With few resources of its own, Korea relied on the international economy as both a market and also as a source of finance. The state thus imperilled the economy by opening hitherto protected domestic markets to competition, for it simultaneously reduced its capacity to prudently oversee capital inflows. A generous reading of the Kim period would be that the president was merely naïve about *chaebol* reform. It would perhaps be more accurate to say that it was negligent of Kim to propose his globalisation policy as a solution to the very real problems that the *chaebols* posed for the Korean economy.

Unlike his predecessors Park, Chun and Roh, Kim Young-sam lacked experience in running large organisations such as the military or bureaucracy. His years in opposition denied him the knowledge of components managing the economy on a day-to-day basis. Kim thus relied on his policymakers, especially the liberals, to shape his globalisation policy. The key bodies of the Korean economic bureaucracy, the MOF and the EPB, had complemented each other under previous governments. The EPB was responsible for long-term planning and the MOF managed economic development on an ongoing basis. These competing sources of advice had provided Park, in particular, with a balanced view of both long-term and immediate concerns about economic development (Thurbon 2003: 351–2). Proponents of a more activist state complained that some of the EPB's advice was needlessly theoretical. EPB director Lee Ki-ho defended his agency against charges that it was too abstract in its advice about the economy:

> The EPB plays the future-oriented role of investigating all problems that can occur. Sometimes the EPB can make abstract and nonsensical statements but I think that this is a phenomenon that occurs early in the process and that will be reduced in the process of public consultation ... Differences of opinion and clashes between ministries will intensify. We must have a moderator in order for economic development to be possible.
>
> (Quoted in Y.-G. Kim 1991a: 307)

The two bodies merged in 1994 despite the objections of the EPB. The merger undid the balance in policy advice that the liberal EPB and the more conservative MOF and the MCI provided. The new entity could not prevent, predict or manage a financial crisis because the state's infrastructural power, which it needed to oversee the liberalisation of the economy, was impaired. In particular, the merger dulled the capacity of the new Ministry of Finance and Economy (MOFE) to oversee the liberalisation programme (Thurbon 2003: 353–4).

Globalisation, both as a policy and as a phenomenon in international political economy, thus adversely affected the state's capacity to combat the power of the *chaebols* in the developmental alliance. For their own narrow interests, the *chaebols* certainly did not oppose measures to further liberalise the financial system. Kim's '100-day plan for the new economy' ostensibly aimed to strengthen the national economy and prepare the *chaebols* for globalisation. The *chaebols* also approved of proposals to privatise state-owned enterprises and restrain wages.

The most significant easing of restrictions occurred in the financial sector. The *chaebols* favoured the curtailment of policy loans because their high borrowing from domestic banks encouraged the banks to continue lending to them. They were also the best-placed entities to benefit from new sources of capital, such as the stock market and the secondary financial market. The availability of these funds ended the *chaebols'* dependence on the state (Evans 1995: 231). The 'easing of restrictions' on the financial sector was thus a euphemism for letting the *chaebols* act free of all restrictions (Y. B. Kim 1996: 154).

Foreign borrowing was even more perilous for the national economy. The liberalisation programme gave the *chaebols* perverse incentives to borrow funds from overseas, especially through short-term loans. The *chaebols* were concerned that financial liberalisation would raise domestic interest rates and thus raise costs. It would also increase competition in the banking sector and imperil their position of relative strength that emanated from their size (Underhill and Zhang 2005: 14). The *chaebols* found a new source of funds, one that would remove these pressures. International capital markets provided a way for the *chaebols* to continue expanding free of the oversight of domestic supervisory agencies. The financial sector reforms of the 1980s permitted the launch of NBFIs, which were capable of providing funds from foreign institutions at cheaper rates than the domestic banks. Borrowing from the unregulated NBFIs soon outstripped that from the official sector (Y. J. Cho 1999: 9–14).

Although the state's regulatory capacity was declining, the markets still expected it to act as the 'lender of last resort' to the Korean financial system in the case of a liquidity crisis. The state was no longer obliged to provide capital directly, but the liberalisation of the capital account only made the *chaebols* less accountable to the discipline that had accompanied policy loans. Now free of state control, the banks should have acted as the primary source of discipline over the *chaebols*, but they failed to do so (Y.-C. Cho 2003: 157). By the mid-1990s the liquidity of the Korean financial system relied on inflows of short-term loans from NBFIs to finance the *chaebols'* long-term investments and speculative activity. The economy was thus vulnerable to crisis because the state no longer provided coordination and discipline. Problems emerged when the *chaebols'* capacity to repay their loans fell sharply. It was here that the true legacy of the implicit government guarantee for the *chaebols* became apparent: international banks allowed the *chaebols* to continue lending on the assumption that the state would bail them out (Hahm 2003: 94–5).

The fate of the semiconductor and automobile industries illustrates this problem. Korean firms were world leaders in semiconductors but the industry suffered a glut due to an increase in new production facilities in the middle of the decade. Sales of dynamic random access memory (DRAM) fell from $42 billion in 1995 to $25 billion in 1996. This severely impacted on the profitability of Korean chipmakers, despite an increase in the volume of DRAM sales. This hinted that the core problem lay in over-investment and excess capacity (C. S. Kang 2000: 95).

Similarly, the automobile industry suffered from over-capacity. There were already four carmakers in the relatively small Korean market when the state gave Samsung permission to enter the industry in 1994. Samsung did not begin production until 1998, but its imminent entry to the industry put pressure on existing carmakers to increase market share. The impending entry of a new producer spurred a massive expansion in capacity, which doubled between 1990 and 1996 before peaking at 4 million units in 1998. Most expansion was funded through loans. This raised D-E ratios to well over 400 per cent on average in 1995 and 1996. Exports were vital to the survival of Korea's carmakers given their low profits in the domestic market. However, there was already a worldwide glut in the industry (B.-H. Lee 2002: 61–2).[6]

The Kim government was aware of the issue surrounding the *chaebols'* profitability – or lack thereof. One of Kim's first 'reforms' after assuming the presidency in early 1993 was to revive the core industries policy, with the intention of reducing the non-profitable business interests of the *chaebols*. At the behest of his liberal advisors, Kim's approach did not include compulsory asset swaps and sectoral reorganisations – needless to say, the *chaebols* also opposed such disciplinary measures. Not only was the attempt to restrict *chaebol* activities to a narrow range of industries a failure but the shift towards financial liberalisation encouraged expansion into even more sectors. Roh's former finance minister thus claimed that the Kim government had encouraged an investment binge by the *chaebols*: 'there was talk of "new Korea" and "new economy", and the previously restricted investment desires of the *chaebols* were relieved' (Y.-S. Kim 1999: 439).

The state's decision to allow Samsung to enter the automobile industry illustrated the laxity of economic policy. Kim argued that the decision furthered the policy of globalisation. Even if the automobile industry was overcrowded, it was not for the state to tell market participants to enter or leave the industry. Participants should make those decisions on the basis of market conditions. Despite the government's exhortations for voluntary compliance, the *chaebols* resented the pressure that was brought to bear on them. As the president of one powerful company said, 'The business world has worried a lot since the inauguration of the new government that *chaebol* groups would be thought of as an object for "control". This has made them stand firm' (quoted in W. Park 1993: 44).

The intent and capacity of the *chaebols* to oppose the state's objectives were now apparent. There was little that the state could do to ensure that the *chaebols* acted in a way that furthered economic development. However, as an FKI official commented in 1993, there was no guarantee that the state's exhortations for the *chaebols* to act in a socially responsible manner would have the desired effect. 'Basically it's like preparing a feast (measures

---

6   A representative of Hyundai Motor informed this author in 1994 that Hyundai's profit margin for 1993, the year prior to the state permitting Samsung to enter the industry, was about 1 per cent. Chapter 6 discusses Samsung's entry to – and exit from – the automobile industry in further detail.

to stimulate the economy) for someone (big business) who doesn't have an appetite (investment sentiment) . . . You can lead a horse to water but you can't make it drink' (quoted in B.-M. Lee 1993: 330–1).

Another significant aspect of the decision to allow Samsung to make automobiles was that the plant would be located in a depressed part of Kim's home province of Gyeongsang. The region had suffered for several years from the offshore migration of labour-intensive industries such as footwear. There were concerns from many quarters that Samsung's entry into the car industry would exacerbate the problems of over-capacity and excess competition. It would also set the stage for a costly exit from the industry on the part of at least one existing producer (Ravenhill 2001: 9). Kim was adamant that Samsung would enter the industry and build its plant in Gyeongsang. The economic logic against the decision was irrefutable but the political logic in its favour was equally strong. The building of Samsung's automobile plant had the predictable effect of solidifying Kim's support in his home region.

Such blatant politicisation of industrial policy was a departure from the ethos of the developmental alliance. Although economic development had long been a political objective of the state, earlier regimes had at least cloaked political favours in the garb of 'national interest'. Samsung's entry into the automobile industry also allowed the president to take further revenge on Hyundai for opposing Kim at the election. Kim could continue his revenge on Chung Ju-yong for his temerity to run against the government's candidate by assisting Hyundai's rival, Samsung (Baek 1995: 387–90; H.-J. Chang 1998: 437–8). The Samsung venture again highlighted the ineffectual core industries policy. Like other *chaebol* groups, Samsung was entering a new field on the basis of profits gleaned from existing business lines, perpetuating the trend for the biggest *chaebols* to seek a stake in all major industrial sectors (Joh and Kim 2003: 108–10).

The *chaebols* had secured a powerful position in the developmental alliance by the second half of the 1990s. They could access almost all the resources they needed at low cost and with minimal state oversight. Further, the industrial conglomerates dominated domestic markets and enjoyed significant success in exports. Their sheer economic weight and contribution to economic development also put the *chaebols* largely beyond the reach of the state's despotic power. The corruption scandal that erupted in late 1995 illustrated the importance of the *chaebols* to economic development. The state prosecuted a number of businessmen for making political donations to former presidents Chun and Roh. However, subsequently, 'the very people who drew up the indictments . . . stated that some business leaders who gave money to Roh were not prosecuted because of "possible adverse effects on the national economy" if they were' (quoted in Morriss 1997: 45).

Yet at their most powerful, the vulnerability of the *chaebol* leaders was also apparent. Despite the unique influence that structural power imparts, the *chaebols* and the national economy were vulnerable to a slump in liquidity in the financial system. Given the low profitability of the *chaebols* in the early 1990s, the stage was set for a credit crunch. This is precisely what occurred when the willingness of foreign financial institutions to continue lending to the highly indebted *chaebols* suddenly ended. The Asian financial crisis began with a wave of capital outflows from Thailand in July 1997. This shook investor confidence about the capacity of the 'miracle' economies of East Asia to continue their growth trajectories. Capital had flowed into the region since the early 1990s despite warnings about corrupt banking practices and over-investment in some sectors. Investor panic spread across Southeast Asia. Within a few months lenders became concerned about the debt levels, investment patterns and corporate governance practices of even Korea's *chaebols*. Skittish foreign lenders detected some of the problems apparent in South East Asia in Korea too. Lenders were thus reticent to extend new loans to Korean borrowers.

These external shocks coincided with deterioration in the profitability of the *chaebols* due to a slowdown in exports and the emergence of more financial scandals. Of particular concern was the collapse in early 1997 of a mid-sized *chaebol*, the Hanbo Group. Following the group's collapse, auditors discovered that the *chaebol* had proffered large-scale bribes to government officials in order to secure loans. Hanbo's loans came at low interest rates and allowed the group to record an extraordinary D-E ratio of almost 2,000 per cent in 1996. This was three to four times higher than most *chaebol* groups (Schopf 2001: 709–10). These revelations made international investors question the capacity of the state to steer the course of national economic development.

The government also blundered when it passed a raft of anti-labour bills in a secret pre-dawn session of the National Assembly on Boxing Day, 1996. This resulted in a 'winter of discontent' during which massive strikes disrupted economic activity. The government caved into demands to repeal the most egregious sections of the new labour legislation (Koo 2001). Financial markets reacted negatively to this display of indecision. The mood in the markets became even more pessimistic when Korean banks signed an 'anti-bankruptcy pact' in the spring of 1997. This pact prevented the banks from demanding that insolvent firms repay their loans. Banks instead made additional payments to insolvent firms by recalling loans from healthier firms, driving even well-managed firms into bankruptcy (S.-J. Chang 2003: 4).

The net effect of these developments was that new loans dried up by the final quarter of 1997. This exposed the mismatch between the *chaebols'* pattern of short-term lending and long-term investments. The state could not provide repayment guarantees for the *chaebols'* and domestic banks' loans. The country had no choice but to apply to the IMF for an emergency loan to repay the outstanding loans to foreign lenders.

No way out?

This chapter examined the power relations between the state and the *chaebols* from 1980 to 1997. The *bureaucracy* was both a constraining and enabling feature of the state apparatus. As the previous chapter showed, the bureaucracy provided the means during the Park Chung Hee era by which the state could cultivate a developmental alliance with business through infrastructural power. Bureaucrats informed Park of the potential of these capacities to contribute to economic development. In contrast, the bureaucracy in the 1980s and 1990s informed the state about the liberal policy that it espoused with increasing intensity. Conflict and rivalry within the bureaucracy also degraded the infrastructural capacity of the state. In the words of Byung-Kook Kim, the government suffered from a 'cognitive failure' (2003: 74) when it came to *chaebol* reform: Kim Young-sam failed to appreciate what reform really meant and how to execute it. With conflicting advice being offered by various arms of the bureaucracy, the state's infrastructural power capacities were seriously impaired.

Social pressures were also significant to the power dynamics of the developmental alliance. However, the effect of this variable was mixed. On the one hand, the state was forced to consider the interests of civil society due to electoral imperatives. This entailed at least a rhetorical loosening of ties with the *chaebols*. In turn, this elicited accusations from the *chaebols* that the state had adopted an anti-business stance. The garnering of popular support helped Roh Tae-woo and later Kim Young-sam to attain power. On the other hand, the state had few means of disciplining the *chaebols* due to the ongoing retrenchment of the developmental state. Social pressures thus did not greatly improve the standing of the state in its relations with the *chaebols*.

National security concerns did not loom as a large influence on the developmental alliance due to the waning of the Cold War during the period under review. The loss of subsidies from the Soviet Union contributed to the steady decline in the North Korean economy and its military capabilities. The attainment of a reasonable degree of affluence in the South also reduced the political imperative for rapid growth. Nonetheless the US continued to influence the developmental alliance. This occurred through the ideational power of liberalism, which seeped into the state through reformers such as Kim Jae-ik. The ubiquity of the neoliberal paradigm will be discussed further in Chapter 6.

Economic conditions were generally sound during the presidencies of Chun, Roh and Kim. However, financial crises marred the beginning and the end of the period under review. The relatively buoyant economic conditions thus did not strengthen the structural power of the *chaebols*. However, their influential position within the economy and the retrenchment of the state's policy tools gave the *chaebols* greater independence from the disciplinary powers of the state.

Globalisation, as a feature of international political economy and as a policy that the Kim Young-sam government consciously pursued, also benefited the *chaebols* during the 1980s and 1990s. The state's liberalisation policies took the form of market opening. However, inadequate supervisory measures accompanied the *chaebols'* access to new financial resources. In the absence of such compensatory measures, the increasing integration of the Korean economy into the international economic system significantly damaged the state's capacity to discipline the *chaebols* and thus oversee the developmental alliance. Perhaps the only surprising aspect of this loss of state capacity was that it was such a self-conscious development. As Chapter 6 will show, liberalisation – and the rhetoric surrounding it – could prove to be a powerful tool in the hands of the state. The post-crisis period would witness another reformulation of the Korean developmental alliance.

6 Realigning the alliance

Introduction

This chapter investigates the evolution of Korea's developmental alliance in the wake of the financial crisis, a period in which the state enacted the reforms in return for bailout loans from the IMF. The process of reform contributed heavily to a realignment of the power relativities within the DA. Contrary to some expectations, neoliberal reform did not necessarily weaken the influence of state elites. Indeed, some state elites (particularly President Kim Dae-jung and his senior ministers) were able to utilise the reform process to increase their influence within the developmental alliance.

The variables highlighted at the outset of the book provide a schema for explaining the seemingly anomalous strengthening of the state amid conditions of financial crisis. First, the sharp deterioration in *economic conditions* provided a rationale for state intervention. A significant part of the impetus for reform came from Korean political and policymaking elites rather than the IMF, and the crisis provided an opportunity for the state to complete earlier reforms, rather than conceiving them *sui generis* in the wake of the crisis. This is not to underplay the significant pressure brought to bear on Korea, but we need to distinguish between: a) the external pressure from the IMF and the United States to reform what they viewed as an outdated mercantilist economy (*globalisation* and *national security* variables); and b) the influence of liberal reformers resident in the Korean state apparatus for at least two decades prior to the crisis (*bureaucracy*). Previous chapters have illustrated that liberal influence was evident in the policy approach of successive governments, but especially in the Kim Young-sam period that preceded the financial crisis. The crisis represented an opportunity for liberal elements to refashion the Korean state in a way that would be less deleterious to what they perceived to be the goal of national economic development. Rather than wielding the despotic variety of power, liberals sought to use infrastructural power to elicit market-converging behaviour from the *chaebols*.

The final contextual variable – *social pressures* – also contributes to our explanation of state–business relations in the wake of the financial crisis. The state's success in 'refashioning' itself was, in part, due to the support of the public, who were vehemently opposed to the *chaebols'* continued dominance of the economy. The strong anti-*chaebol* sentiment that the Kim Dae-jung government and the public shared resulted in attempts to rein in, rather than nurture, the *chaebols*. Thus the post-crisis period would witness a realignment of state–business relations and the subsequent transition from a traditional state-centric mode of discipline to a market-centric one. As part of this transition much of the reform agenda would focus on reforming financial institutions in such a way that they would apply sanctions to business groups that behaved in a manner that did not concur with the development of the national economy. In this way the Korean state continued to exhibit developmentalist tendencies while at the same time strengthening market principles in the national economy.

The paradox of neoliberal reform

Previous chapters of this book illustrated how the United States supported – albeit reluctantly – the emergence of an activist Korean state in the early stages of industrialisation. The US also accepted mercantilist practices such as the fostering of national champions in protected domestic markets. However, American tolerance for mercantilism in East Asia had waned considerably by the 1980s, and US relations with the region increasingly revolved around efforts to open the product and financial markets of Korea and Japan. With the easing of Cold War tensions, the US thus treated these strategic allies as economic rivals (Cumings 1998), and national security concerns no longer favoured the *chaebols* in the developmental alliance. That is, US pressure on Korea to ensure pro-business policies was replaced, in the post-Cold War period, with criticism of the Korean model of development. The role of the *chaebols* was a particular concern for the US.

American power thus weighed in on the side of the reformist elements within the Korean bureaucracy. Reformers advocated changes to the economic policy mix that would significantly alter the types of support that the state had provided to the *chaebols* since the presidency of Park Chung Hee. Chapter 5 noted that in 1994 the liberal EPB merged with the MOF, a stronghold of bureaucrats who advocated a greater role for the state. A fierce battle began within the newly created body (the Ministry of Finance and Economy) over the most appropriate policy stance in the mid-1990s. Elizabeth Thurbon argues (2003) that instead of offering competing views to government on the most appropriate policy stance, the merger resulted in a dangerously inconsistent and incautious policy mix. One significant outcome was that the government, influenced by the liberals' urging for openness, and wishing to distance itself from past regimes, largely abandoned the most powerful policy instruments of the Park era. In particular, the removals of restrictions upon international finance and the licensing of NBFIs meant that the *chaebols* were able to access capital free of the strictures that had previously accompanied policy loans.

The financial crisis presented an opportunity for reformist elements to press for further changes to the state's approach to economic management. While it is possible to argue that the *raison d'être* of the Korean state has changed markedly in the wake of the liberal reforms, this chapter contends that the crisis and accompanying reforms only expedited changes that were already underway. Both the US-trained technocrats and the political elites of the Kim Young-sam government had sought to change the statist paradigm. This trend became even more apparent after the inauguration of Kim Dae-jung. The ideological and institutional bases of state participation in the national economy were gradually eroded. This resulted in a form of liberalisation that ostensibly sought to weaken the developmental capacity of the state (Weiss and Hobson 2000: 62).

While some commentators catalogue this shift as a lineal departure from the pragmatic intervention of the Park era to a blind acceptance of the logic of neoliberalism (for instance, H.-C. Lim and J.-H. Jang 2006: 447), this study argues that the governance style that emerged after the crisis was more nuanced. In particular, it is noteworthy that the Kim government sought to consolidate state leadership within the context of the DA while envisaging the market as a mechanism of *chaebol* discipline. Even Korea's reformist elements did not envisage the wholesale retrenchment of the state. In place of the state's traditional policy instruments, the Kim Dae-jung government would introduce market-based disciplinary mechanisms to ensure that the *chaebols* contributed to economic development.

Learning to love the IMF

Some commentators referred to the International Monetary Fund reforms as a 'mistake' imposed on an unwilling country under crisis conditions. For instance, Martin Feldstein (1998) chided the IMF for overstepping the mark during the crisis by insisting that loan recipients undergo major structural and institutional change. Steven Radelet and Jeffrey Sachs (1998: 18–20) meanwhile claimed that Korea's macroeconomic policies were generally sound and that the crisis was attributable to the destabilisation of international financial markets and investor panic. They argued that the response to the crisis should have been more moderate. Instead of over-reacting and requesting wide-ranging institutional reform, the IMF should have calmed markets and allowed the crisis countries to resume growth while implementing regulatory reforms that would have helped their financial systems resist sudden shifts in capital flows.

There have been many attempts to assess the appropriateness of the IMF package for Korea, but to concentrate too much on the content of the reforms deflects attention from the way in which Korean officials were complicit in the implementation of the reforms. In particular, Korean state elites welcomed the opportunity to reshape the power dynamics of the developmental alliance in a way that would rein in the power of the *chaebols*. Kim Dae-jung and his senior ministers had called for *chaebol* reform well before the financial crisis provided the opportunity for such reform to proceed. Kim himself authored several volumes from the 1980s that championed root-and-branch reform of the authoritarian developmental model typified by the developmental alliance. Kim's economic advisor and later finance minister Kang Bong-gyun summarised the government's approach to the economy as 'getting rid of the factors that have prevented the market mechanism from working over the past few decades' (quoted in Kwon 2000: 76). That is, the government identified the *chaebols* as the chief impediment to a stronger national economy. In turn, the state presented itself as the legitimate body to discipline the *chaebols* in accordance with the requirements of the market economy.

The new president's view of the most appropriate form of state–business interaction thus differed significantly from those of his predecessors. Kim confirmed this at a press conference on the day after his election in December 1997, when he enunciated his view of the market economy. He claimed that his government would 'totally rescue firms from the chains of power *and from the protection of power* . . . only firms that adapt to the market economy and are victorious in global competition will survive' (D.-J. Kim 1997, emphasis added). Upon assuming power two months later, it soon became apparent that Kim Dae-jung's ideal-type developmental alliance would not involve the mutual support and reliance that characterised the Park Chung Hee era, when the state and the *chaebols* were allied against the remainder of society.

According to one insider, Kim would have pursued the sort of reforms that the IMF had demanded even if the financial crisis had not occurred. 'When President Kim was running for office, he once said in private "It's worked out for the best" after the IMF demanded that the *chaebols* be reformed' (quoted in Y.-H. Yoon 1999: 272). The president-elect believed reckless investment had imperilled not only the *chaebols* but also the national economy. Kim Dae-jung thus saw the financial crisis as an opportunity to carry out much-needed but long-delayed reform of the *chaebols*. 'Cosmetic reform', Kim said in response to the initial restructuring plans of the *chaebols* in January 1998, 'will not be permitted this time' (quoted in C. S. Lee 1998: 61; see also J.-S. Shin and H.-J. Chang 2003: 2–4).

The new president's call for tangible signs of change highlighted how the Kim government consciously repositioned the state as the solution to the *chaebol* problem. The government wholeheartedly committed itself to the reforms encapsulated in the IMF rescue package. Kim's comments in June 1998 revealed the government's will to produce signs of tangible progress. He called on the FKI, the main business lobby group, to promptly display its commitment to reform:

> Big business has contributed to our economic development but what caused the IMF crisis was also big business . . . Since external conditions have improved to such a degree, the FKI must take the lead. It's been

half a year since the IMF system [reforms]. From the viewpoint of the public, the FKI must show some kind of tangible, clear resolution.

(Quoted in Ahn 2002: 141)

The *chaebols* reacted by trying to seize the initiative from the government, arguing that they were best qualified to implement changes. Daewoo Chairman Kim Woo Choong said 'We're all trying hard. But restructuring is complicated so it'll take some time for big business to produce clear results. If it doesn't work out, I'll accept responsibility . . . Clear results will emerge' (quoted in Ahn 2002: 141–2). However, the government was to show little faith in the capacity of the *chaebols* to initiate reform. The government's appointment of itself as the agent for change was consistent with its diagnosis of the *chaebol*-centred economy. While the government placed the onus for reform on the *chaebols*, senior officials also implied that previous regimes had erred in their stewardship of the DA. This suggests that, under Kim Dae-jung, the Korean state was laying the ground for a new developmental alliance rather than its replacement. In the new alliance, the state would play a markedly different role to what Kim and his ministers viewed as the problematic Park-era manifestation.

Kim's initial finance minister, Lee Kyu-seong, claimed that previous governments and the *chaebols* were jointly responsible for the crisis. Lee argued that the crisis was attributable to three sets of factors: a) the accumulated ills of an 'authoritarian political–bureaucratic economy' (*gwanchi gyeongje*) that delayed the development of democracy and a functioning market economy; b) a faulty 'globalisation' policy that opened financial markets without introducing the market principles of responsibility and punishment; and c) the failure of the *chaebols* to restructure in response to the changing conditions of the global economy (K.-H. Kim 1998: 169–70). The latter two of these ills would – as the next section illustrates – be approached in the formal reform process. The broader question of reforming state–business relations would, however, prove to be a bigger task again.

Repositioning the state

The Korean government – first under Kim Young-sam and then under the new Kim Dae-jung administration – negotiated a reform package with the IMF after the *chaebols* encountered difficulties in repaying loans to international banks in the second half of 1997. As noted, the government did not wholly oppose these reforms because they largely coincided with the policies that Kim had long championed. The government thus became more than just a willing accomplice to the IMF during the crisis. It attempted to reconfigure the developmental alliance with the *chaebols* by leading the reform agenda. By siding with the IMF, the state was able to reposition itself as an agent for change, and by default, it was the *chaebols* that were in need of reform (see Hundt 2005).

The repositioning of the state was evident in the reform package itself. Of the five main areas of reform, two involved direct changes to the configuration of the state apparatus. First, the government tightened fiscal and monetary policies in order to reduce inflation and the budget deficit. It also raised taxes and diverted funds from defence to welfare in preparation for the anticipated increase in unemployment. The budget would later resort to a significant deficit position due to the burden of industrial and financial restructuring (H. J. Park 2002).

Second, the government reorganised the functions of the state. Launched with the goal of creating a 'smaller but more efficient' government, the reorganisation transferred the functions of some ministries to local governments and lower-level civil servants. Other aims of public sector reform were a reduction in the size of the public sector workforce, the privatisation of state-owned enterprises, and the introduction of 'performance-based' remuneration and employment in the public service. The state also delegated more control over economic policymaking to the office of the prime minister (E. M. Kim 1999: 43–6; No et al. 2002: 380–1).

Neither of these broad reforms greatly impinged on the capacity of the state to formulate and implement policy. Likewise these reforms did not detract from the capacity of state elites to informally influence the developmental alliance. In short, although the configuration of the state changed, there was little that emanated from the reforms that directly impacted on the functioning of the state. In contrast, the third plank of the agenda – labour market reform – was to have a far greater impact on the economy. During the Korean financial crisis the IMF argued that some jobs would be lost during the restructuring of the *chaebols*. Formed in January 1998 with the goal of improving flexibility, the Tripartite Commission on Industrial Relations elicited agreement from trade unions to layoffs in 'unavoidable' circumstances. The unions in return received permission to form political parties and to extend their coverage to hitherto non-unionised fields, such as the public service and education (S.-J. Kim 1998: 135).

The labour movement had demonstrated its organisational capacity during the general strike of 1996–7. This proved to be a high watermark for the movement given that the state's revision of the Labour Relations Law in March 1997 resulted in trade unions acceding to the notion of limited job security in return for greater freedoms for union activity. The IMF reforms thus largely removed the expectation of job security. Management was required to re-hire dismissed workers only if economic conditions improved. The government established a multi-billion dollar fund to compensate workers for job losses resulting from restructuring (No et al. 2002: 376–7).

In terms of the politics of the developmental alliance, the significance of labour market reform was that the state could claim to be promoting a market economy. Labour market 'flexibility' is a key component of the neoliberal agenda, insofar as it shifts the balance of power from labour to capital. The *chaebols* had long complained that rising wages and the high incidence of labour disputes had crippled their competitiveness from the late 1980s. The post-crisis reforms thus represented a credible response on the part of the state. With workers suffering acute cuts in living standards, the onus was back on the *chaebols* to bear their share of the reform burden. As will be discussed later in the chapter, the state sought to neutralise union militancy via the Tripartite Talks.

The fourth component of the reform agenda, that relating to the financial sector, likewise placed the onus on the *chaebols* to alter their practices. The IMF claimed that introducing greater competition to the financial sector would improve the performance of the sector and encourage the closure of insolvent institutions. The overall performance of many institutions was poor because NPLs impaired their financial condition. Foreign investors purchased some institutions while others merged with better-run domestic rivals. The government re-capitalised the surviving institutions after initiating the process of rationalisation. The IMF argued that the net effect of these changes would be a more competitive, better capitalised and more market-oriented financial sector (Choong 2001: 461; Haggard 2000: 149).

The IMF also advised Korea to enhance the independence of financial supervisory agencies and the Bank of Korea (BOK). A new supervisory agency, the Financial Securities Commission (FSC), would complement the newly independent central bank. The FSC was an amalgam of four separate agencies that had supervised different aspects of the financial system prior to the 1997 crisis: commercial banking, securities, insurance and merchant banks (S.-J. Kim 1998: 131; Pirie 2005b: 26–7).

Financial sector reform would be crucial to attempts by reformers to institute a new disciplinary regime. Whereas the dismantling of the state-centric disciplines in the 1980s had allowed the *chaebols* to indulge in the risky investments that imperilled the national economy, the post-crisis reforms sought to create a stricter disciplinary regime than either the Park era or the liberalisation of the 1980s. In effect, the state would delegate some of the responsibility for disciplining the *chaebols* to the market. Important safeguards, in the form of the new supervisory agencies and more stringent borrowing requirements on financial institutions, would reduce the proclivity of the *chaebols* to partake in excessively risky behaviour. In unison with new civil society actors such as Chamyeo Yeondae (People's Solidarity for Participatory Democracy – PSPD), the government introduced new internal governance reforms that would affect the way in which the *chaebols* managed their enterprises. For instance, the PSPD gave particular weight to the liberal agenda by pushing for greater shareholder rights and the appointment of outsider directors to *chaebol* boards (H.-C. Lim and J.-H. Jang 2006: 449–51).

The final set of reforms targeted the *chaebols'* style of management (governance) and production processes (restructuring). Improvements to corporate governance would involve the 'five-plus-three' principles. The initial five principles were: greater transparency; better accounting and reporting; greater accountability by owner–managers; abolition of mutual guarantees among *chaebol* affiliates; and a streamlining of the *chaebols'* operations. The government later announced additional measures to improve corporate governance. Supervisory agencies were to oversee more rigorously inter-subsidiary investments and the *chaebols'* control of NBFIs, a source of much of their credit. The state would also dissuade illicit collaboration among *chaebol* owners by banning 'irregular inheritances' and gift giving (Mo and Moon 2003: 128–32).

To emphasise the need for industrial restructuring, the IMF argued that one of the main causes of the crisis was low profitability. This in turn was the result of over-capacity and excessive investment in industries such as shipbuilding, automobiles, electronics and semiconductors. In the words of Lee Kyu-seong, 'In the past, companies had a finger in every pie and concentrated on expanding their power quantitatively, but now that kind of indiscriminate expansion is instead acting as a burden' (quoted in Y.-M. Song 1999: 97). The proposed remedies were: the elimination of surplus capacity in the form of the outright shutdown of plant and equipment; asset swaps between *chaebols* in similar industries ('Big Deals'); and 'workouts,' whereby the state re-capitalised big business in return for the elimination of mutual debt guarantees between *chaebol* affiliates (Cumings 1998: 63–4; D. Shin 2000: 191–4).

While relying on the IMF to provide political cover, the reform package offered the Korean government an opening to enact long-awaited reforms to the *chaebol* model. For Kim Dae-jung, the political outcomes of the reform project were just as important as the economic ones.

The taming of the two

The mode of state–business interaction of the Park era would change significantly if the incoming government altered the developmental alliance in this way. No longer would heavily indebted firms grow on the basis of government favours and maintain close ties with political leaders (H.-S. Yoon *et al.* 2003: 358–9). These illicit relations (*jeonggyeong yuchak*) were precisely the set of arrangements that Kim Dae-jung's government sought to reform after the crisis. As FSC chairman and later finance minister Lee Hun-jai would say in 1999:

> Since this government has a degree of distance from business unlike those in the past, it's got wide scope for policy choice and it can form a basis on principles, and it can also be relatively free in its actions. In the past, a positive interpretation would be to say that the government, business and banks delivered economic development by cooperating but a negative reading would be that it took the form of an illicit union.
>
> (Quoted in Yoo 1999a: 229)

The distinction between the old and new versions of the developmental alliance was also evident when Lee Kyu-seong discussed how the financial sector could help discipline the *chaebols*. He emphasised that the *chaebols* would have to be 'institutionalised' to the market economy. In particular, the government was intent on reducing the propensity of the *chaebols* to accumulate high debts. Lee explained:

> Through the logic of the market economy, through institutionalisation, sanctions come into force . . . When a company with a debt ratio of over 200 per cent to a bank takes out a loan, it must arrange collateral of 5 per cent against bad loans. If [its debt ratio] exceeds 400 per cent, it must arrange around 20 per cent, someone's got to be looking out for it. That's precisely what we mean by a market-based approach and institutional-isation . . . The basic difference between the *chaebol* policy of past governments and that of the current government is that we're trying to make the *chaebols* healthier through institutionalisation.
>
> (Quoted in Yoo 1999a: 234–5)

In short, the reform agenda allowed the state to position itself as the main agent for change in the post-crisis period. Much like a doctor armed with a new set of instruments, the Kim Dae-jung government approached the reform agenda with relish. However, the *chaebols*, the putative patients in this venture, were less than enthusiastic about the surgery that the state was planning.

This hinted at the incoming government's intention to introduce a new disciplinary regime and an amended rendition of the developmental alliance. The government could claim that the reform package would stimulate the market economy and thus reduce the authoritarian nature of Korea's political economy; reform would also continue to open the economy, but adequate safeguards would be put in place to ameliorate the adverse effects of globalisa-tion. However, it would be the third problem that Lee identified – *chaebol* reform – that would prove to be the centrepiece of the Kim government's agenda following the financial crisis. The onus to change was squarely placed on the *chaebols*. The examples of the Daewoo and Samsung Groups illustrate two ways in which the government used infrastructural power in the developmental alliance in order to rein in the power of the *chaebols*.

Given the significant economic concentration of the *chaebols*, successive governments had been reluctant to allow groups such as Daewoo to collapse due to fears that their failure would impact on the economy as a whole. However the Daewoo Group represented a particularly egregious case of corporate profligacy even by the standards of the *chaebols*. These malpractices only strengthened the belief of government leaders that the business practices of the *chaebols* needed to change.

The Kim government's willingness to publicly criticise the group's slow progress in restructuring exacerbated Daewoo's predicament. The state expected each group to proffer a blueprint for its own restructuring. Daewoo's plan clearly failed to impress the Kim government. Foreign investors seeking Korean joint venture partners interpreted the government's negative prognosis of Daewoo's proposals for restructuring as meaning that the state was unlikely to give the group new capital injections on favourable terms or that it might even allow it to collapse (C.-H. Lee 1999: 262).

Daewoo came to serve as the litmus test for the reform agenda. Whereas most *chaebols* proffered restructuring plans that at least paid lip service to the state's goal of reducing D-E ratios to 200 per cent, Daewoo actually increased its levels of debt by about 30 per cent during 1998. Auditors later estimated that the group's debts were twice their reported level, and the Financial Supervisory Commission uncovered 23 trillion won ($18 billion) in accounting errors (Ravenhill 2001: 3; Y.-H. Yoon 1999: 268–72).

It would take a Herculean effort to save Daewoo this time. A government official said: 'Of the big-five groups, the one that needs the most restructuring is Daewoo, and it needs to sell off its prize assets' (quoted in Ahn 2002: 144). Presidential economic advisor Lee Ki-ho, another EPB alumnus in the Kim government, commented that Daewoo 'hasn't kept its promises properly . . . If it doesn't carry out [restructuring], it will be entrusted to the creditors' delegation, so Chairman Kim will be removed from the management of the company after he has been dealt with' (quoted in Ahn 2002: 144). It was apparent by the second half of 1999 that Daewoo's belated efforts to restructure would not meet the expectations of the government. President Kim said only weeks prior to the announcement that the state would not prevent the Daewoo Group from going bankrupt:

> the restructuring plans suggested on several occasions by Daewoo haven't attracted the trust of either the domestic or international markets. I hope that Chairman Kim . . . takes full social responsibility as a genuine entrepreneur who the public expects to carry out restructuring properly.
> (Quoted in Ahn 2002: 144–5)

The government appeared to fully understand the salutary effect that Daewoo's bankruptcy would have on similarly recalcitrant *chaebols*. That is, the government was both unlikely and unwilling to bear the consequences of a series of collapses on the same scale as Daewoo. However, it might have allowed a handful of other *chaebols* to go bankrupt. Other *chaebol* owners, not wanting to imperil the survival of their groups, heeded the lessons of Daewoo and made more substantive efforts to restructure their operations. Within two years of the financial crisis over half of the biggest *chaebols* had entered receivership or undergone restructuring processes such as workouts.

Daewoo seemed to badly misread the government's determination to proceed with restructuring, presuming that the state would again bail the group out. This presumptuousness alone appeared to pique the government. As Kang Bong-gyun said, 'Chairman Kim ultimately didn't carry out restructuring. Of the various *chaebols*, Daewoo's speed of change was the slowest. There weren't any clear results' (quoted in Ahn 2002: 142).

The Daewoo case illustrated the Kim government's pursuit of an initial goal of reform, the lowering of debt levels. This had great symbolic value given the *chaebols'* notoriously high levels of borrowing. The state's handling of Daewoo thus represented a re-assertion of state power within the developmental alliance – the exercise of state power in a manner that differed from previous decades. By allowing Daewoo to collapse, the state could claim to be enforcing market principles on the *chaebols*.

While Daewoo was a *cause célèbre* for the state's campaign to introduce a market-based governance structure for the economy as a whole, Samsung Motor's exit from the automobile industry illustrates the state's success in changing the internal governance structures of the *chaebols*. The state sought to end the practice of cross-subsidisation, whereby the *chaebols* used funds from one business unit to subsidise another (G.-J. Lim 1999: 224). The FKI defended this practice, arguing that the national economy benefited from *chaebols* using profitable business units to subsidise the development of newer and less profitable ones.

The *chaebols'* understanding of the system of cross-subsidisation sharply contrasted with that of Kim Dae-jung and his senior advisors. The government argued that the practice resulted in unprofitable business units dragging down entire *chaebols* and ultimately imperilling the national economy (H.-K. Kim 1998: 174). Samsung's controversial venture into the automobile industry proved to be the crucible for the battle of wills over the *chaebol* model. The electronics division was the Samsung Group's main profit centre from the 1980s. It provided the funds for the group to enter the automobile industry, but a collapse in the price of semiconductors and electrical goods in 1995 and 1996 adversely affected the financial structure of the entire group. The curtailment of international lending during the financial crisis only exacerbated this problem. To the government, the Samsung case was a typical example of a profitable activity (electronics) subsidising an unprofitable one (automobiles).

Even worse in the eyes of the government, Samsung indicated an interest in taking over the embattled Kia Motors. Kia, then the country's fourth-biggest carmaker, had collapsed during 1997 with debts of over $13 billion. The Kim Young-sam government nationalised the carmaker later that year. Kim Dae-jung sought to sell Kia to foreign interests because his government believed that allowing one of the established carmakers (Hyundai, Daewoo or Ssangyong) to acquire Kia would only perpetuate the overcapacity problem. The government was opposed to Samsung solidifying its position in an already overcrowded industry by acquiring Kia. The industry's capacity fell marginally when Daewoo took over Ssangyong in January 1998. This reduced the number of carmakers to four, and it worsened Daewoo's own financial position, of course. Nonetheless, Samsung Motor, which only began production in 1998 after spending billions of dollars building its automobile plant, applied to acquire Kia. The perpetuation of the 'too big to fail' (*daema-bulsa*) logic was precisely what the government sought to eliminate. Kim Dae-jung's economic team instead courted foreign interests during 1998 to acquire Kia.

The government did not meet with success. Hyundai eventually acquired Kia, returning it to profitability in 1999 (B.-H. Lee 2002: 66).

The government suggested that Samsung, as the newest and least profitable producer, should merge with Daewoo. This proposal came to naught, as Samsung and Daewoo failed to agree on the terms of a merger (Yoo 1999b: 256–7). Samsung was forced to withdraw despite its intention to remain in the industry when it was unable to secure funds to either acquire Daewoo or survive independently. As noted above, Daewoo's well-publicised debt binge in the post-crisis period did not endear it to the government. In late 1998, less than a year after producing its first automobile, Samsung Motor ceased to exist as an independent entity. The group declared its motor division bankrupt in June of the following year (H.-S. Kim 1999: 296–7). It would resume production later in 1999 after selling 70 per cent of the division to Renault for $100 million plus a share of future profits. This represented a massive discount on Samsung's cumulative investment in production and research. Renault also assumed responsibility for some of Samsung's debts. Daewoo's takeover of Ssangyong and Hyundai's acquisition of Kia resulted in an industry structure of two large producers and the smaller Samsung–Renault venture. The Hyundai–Kia grouping controlled nearly three-quarters of the domestic market (Ravenhill 2001: 5–11).

Daewoo collapsed in the second half of 1999, and General Motors subsequently acquired the *chaebol* group's automobile unit (Y.-M. Song 1999: 96). The automobile industry thus illustrated the intent of the Kim government to rationalise sectors that it perceived to be uncompetitive, and this serves as one of the most vivid examples of the new market-based disciplinary regime. While in some respects standing in contrast to the forcible dismantling of the Kukje Group some fourteen years earlier, the decision to allow Daewoo to collapse was arguably a more momentous decision in terms of the Korean state's relations with the *chaebols* in the context of the developmental alliance.

The rationalisation of the industry raised numerous questions about the Big Deals. At least in the case of the automobile industry, the state-led process of industrial restructuring had resulted in an oligopoly market, albeit one with greater foreign involvement. This hints at the inherently *political* nature of the reform project. The Kim government seemed less interested in the economic outcomes of reform and instead focused on the political consequences. That is, the reforms reduced the power of the *chaebols* and thus represented a reassertion of state power within the developmental alliance. The long-term impact on the growth capacity of the Korean economy was less clear, as will be discussed later in the chapter.

The politics of *chaebol* discipline

The Daewoo and Samsung restructurings were the first attempts by the Kim government to apply the new market-based disciplinary regime to the *chaebols*. In spite of Samsung Group chairman and chief shareholder Lee Kun-hee's personal and longstanding passion for the automobile industry, Samsung was forced to cede this prized asset to foreign interests following the financial crisis. Yet the state did not dismember Samsung. Indeed, the group received a handsome reward for ceasing independent production in the automobile industry. The state permitted Samsung to publicly list its life insurance unit at a price that delivered massive windfall gains to Lee and other key shareholders (Yoo 1999b: 258–9).

The exit of Samsung nonetheless represented a shift in the power dynamics of the developmental alliance. The state illustrated that it could play a role in enhancing the national economy by both spurring on the *chaebols* through the substantial resources that remained in its keeping and also enabling financial institutions to punish particularly egregious behaviour. However, the developmental alliance lost some of the intimacy and exclusivity that characterised its early phases. While the *chaebols* would continue to be important components of the growth strategy, their relative importance had declined. At the same time, the state could not justify such an exclusionary developmental alliance in light of the political changes that had occurred in Korea since the 1980s.

Subsequently, the state adopted a populist stance. This involved casting the *chaebols* as the villain in the piece. The state also cast itself as a neutral, responsible, necessary and thus legitimate contributor to the national economy. While his critics expected Kim Dae-jung to find common cause with trade unions, Kim's natural constituency was the middle class. The president's political strategy was to reach over the heads of the unions and directly to the public. In one of his first public statements after winning the 1997 election, Kim stated that job losses were unavoidable. As Lee Kyu-seong would later comment, 'I think that the public must understand that reducing employment by 10 to 20 per cent through restructuring is a way to prevent a situation where 100 per cent of jobs are lost to unemployment in the future' (quoted in Y.-M. Song 1999: 91).

The middle classes, who were less likely to be affected by layoffs, traditionally distrusted trade unions and felt that militancy was inappropriate during a national crisis. Moreover, this section of the public was wary of any group that appeared to share the *chaebols*' opposition to reform. The government capitalised on the anti-*chaebol* sentiment to paint strikers as anti-reform and, by implication, as working in the interests of the *chaebols* and against those of the country as a whole. For instance, Roh Moo-hyun, then a parliamentarian from the ruling party, commented on the strike by the Hyundai Motor Workers Union (HMWU): 'All of the people of Korea, even the workers, thought that redundancy was inevitable . . . all the people denounced HMWU . . . The workers had no choice but to accept it' (quoted in Neary 2000: 3).

The *chaebols* responded to the charge that they, and by implication the *chaebol* system, were responsible for the crisis with a propaganda offensive of their own. Implicit here was a defence of the *modus operandi* of the *chaebols* in the developmental alliance. For example, Daewoo chairman Kim Woo Choong claimed – in what proved to be a futile attempt to stave off the collapse of his enterprise – that there was nothing wrong with the *chaebol* system. He said in response to criticism from the government that the *chaebols* were not properly complying with the process of restructuring, 'What on earth have the *chaebols* done wrong? . . . It's not right to enforce the Big Deals, which are not suitable to the current conditions' (quoted in Ahn 2002: 140).

Former FKI chairman Sohn Byung-doo reinforced the message that the *chaebols* were not solely responsible for the crisis. 'Wasn't the main cause sheeted home to just the excessive investments of the *chaebols*? . . . There's a clear responsibility on the *chaebols* but they weren't the culprits' (quoted in N. Lee 2003: 223). He claimed that the *chaebols* had contributed significantly to Korean society through the developmental alliance. 'Aren't firms the driving force behind the creation of national wealth? . . . Our society has accepted the free market economy system and enjoyed its benefits but we don't seem to really understand its strengths and blessings' (quoted in N. Lee 2003: 223).

The FKI would later warn that the strength of anti-business sentiment, which has long permeated Korean society due to the Confucian disdain for entrepreneurship, was detrimental to the normal operations of business. The anti-*chaebol* feeling is in part a product of culture and history. The traditional East Asian social order of *sanonggongsang* divides society into four classes, whose prestige is ranked in the order of scholars, farmers, artisans and tradesmen. One social scientist was quoted as saying that since Korea's 'traditional culture, which venerates scholars, is extremely anti-capitalist, it is hard to imagine a social environment that grants a positive meaning to the accumulation of wealth and rich people' (S.-K. Lee and I.-H. Woo 2004; see also Seo 2004). This confirms the restraint that social pressures has placed on the power of business in the developmental alliance. Social pressures thus acted in favour of the state in its attempts to reassert itself as a legitimate contributor to the national economy. This form of pressure reinforced the market-based disciplinary regime, which sought to make the *chaebols* act in a manner that would comply with the goals of economic development.

The mutual antagonism between the state and business in the Daewoo and Samsung cases resulted in less cooperation in the post-crisis period. This was significant given that close collaboration between these parties is a hallmark of the developmental alliance. The government's reassertion of influence over the alliance particularly disturbed the *chaebols*. Whereas in previous decades the *chaebols* had substantial input into the policymaking process, their leaders began to complain that they could not respond to the reform agenda. They were unsure of its aim and extent, and they could not communicate directly with the government. The *chaebols* argued that there was no sense of mutual trust because 'talks' merely meant a rubber stamp to the government's policy (Y.-G. Kim 1999: 4).

The *chaebols* also claimed that the government was interfering in matters that should be left to the private sector to decide, most notably decisions about restructuring. Indeed, the government's senior economic officials claimed the right to intervene selectively. It was the duty of the government to provide leadership if, in the words of Kang Bong-gyun, 'autonomously managed systems and traditions are not in place' (quoted in Y. Kwon 2000: 77). Kang cited the example of the selection of a new FKI chairman to replace Kim Woo Choong, who resigned following Daewoo's collapse. Similarly, Lee Hun-jai stated his belief that in principle market forces should operate, but only if the market operates smoothly. The government appropriated the right to decide when this was the case (H.-K. Kim 1998: 176). Lee Kyu-seong, meanwhile, claimed that it was appropriate for the state to intervene in the restructuring process and to force banks to raise interest rates. Lee added that 'we're in a crisis situation where the autonomous market mechanism is broken, so it's impossible to fly with instruments and we've no choice but to rely on sight' (quoted in K.-H. Kim 1998: 172).

These comments indicate that some elements of the developmental state had survived the reform agenda. This was an unsettling combination for the *chaebols*. The realignment of the developmental alliance thus entailed the introduction of a market-based governance structure, in which the state used infrastructural power to compel the *chaebols* to behave in accordance with market principles. The concept of the state 'controlling' or 'regulating' the *chaebols* was quite a sensitive one in the post-crisis era, in which the tenets of liberalism supposedly dictated the direction of economic policy. As one official commented on the body charged with guiding the process of financial and industrial restructuring:

> It's not the main goal of the Financial Supervisory Commission to regulate the *chaebols*; rather, it aims to oversee a sound financial system. The FSC regulates the use of industrial capital to some degree, but that's really the duty of financial markets. *You really can't say that the chaebols are regulated in Korea.*
>
> (Author interview, June 2004, emphasis added)

The *chaebols*' distrust of the government was becoming patently obvious, as witnessed by claims that Kim Dae-jung and his advisors were determined to destroy the *chaebol* system that had served Korea well. An advisor to the FKI said that despite the myriad rationales provided for *chaebol* reform, they amounted to a project that would end the *chaebol* system:

> The government claims to be in favour of *chaebol* reform, not the break up of the *chaebols*. However the *chaebols* will be broken up if all the policies that the government has suggested are implemented ... the government is just using the expression of reform.
>
> (Quoted in C.-H. Lee 1999: 254)

Trust was also eroded due to broken promises. Sohn Byung-doo complained that the government's approach to the Big Deal process was seriously flawed because it kept few of the promises it initially made. The FKI requested that the government and banks provide large-scale financial assistance to expedite restructuring. It argued that the *chaebols* would have no incentive to carry out the Big Deals without D-E swaps, low-interest loans and tax breaks. However, Sohn claimed that 'the government abrogated responsibility for the model of assistance . . . they kept on dragging their feet' (quoted in N. Lee 2003: 226).

The *chaebols* resented the Kim government's use of coercive measures, such as the setting of timetables for compliance with restructuring. The government threatened to investigate non-compliers on the grounds of criminal activities such as selling shares illegally and fixing share prices (G.-J. Lim 1999: 225). The FKI criticised officials such as Kang Bong-gyun for underhand tactics: 'although the government talks about negotiations, it interferes through telephone messages and directives. Since there's potential for problems to develop in the future, they don't want to document anything' (quoted in C.-H. Lee 1999: 255–6). The government stood accused of intimidating business leaders:

> Is it negotiating to haul business leaders in front of the president and tell them to sign an agreement . . . The leaders of the top-five *chaebols* aren't saying anything and trembling in front of the president; would they even dream of resisting? This is close to a reign of terror.
>
> (Quoted in C.-H. Lee 1999: 255–6)

Widening the alliance?

In keeping with its efforts to maximise pressure on the *chaebols*, the Kim government sought to lend the weight of organised labour to the reform agenda. Consequently the state was also aiming to recruit labour as an ally in its political rivalry with the *chaebols* by instituting a limited form of corporatism after the crisis. While re-regulating the labour market in the wake of the financial crisis, the state also offered political concessions to peak union bodies as a means of compensation. Labour market reform is one of the most symbolic parts of the neoliberal agenda, and featured prominently in the reforms that the IMF negotiated with Korea in the wake of the financial crisis. Agreeing to measures that would make it easier to dismiss workers was an attempt by the state to win favour with not only the IMF but also international investors, whose input would be needed to revive the Korean economy.

As noted earlier in the chapter, the Tripartite Commission brought big business and the trade union federations into a social pact to facilitate 'burden sharing' in the post-crisis period. In January 1998, the three parties negotiated the Tripartite Agreement for Fair Burden Sharing. In order to save jobs, the previously militant unions accepted wage freezes. This was a form of 'business-first unionism', whereby unions sought to save Korean companies for the sake of jobs and the national economy (Kong 2004: 26, 2006: 118). Union leaders reluctantly accepted the state's argument that economic recovery would only be possible if labour bore a share of the pain involved in restructuring. Thus they agreed to layoffs in 'unavoidable' circumstances. Another outcome of the tripartite talks was the legalisation of 'dispatch centres', which employed workers on short-term contracts for less than regular wages. The unions also received permission to form political parties and to extend their coverage to hitherto non-unionised sectors such as the public service and education. The state also established a fund to compensate workers for job losses resulting from restructuring.

The trade union movement emphasised the symbolism of the talks. For instance, Yoon Young-Mo of the Korean Council of Trade Unions (KCTU) argued that the tripartite talks represented an opportunity to offer input to the developmental alliance for the first time: 'Labour could now be included and recognised as a pillar of the society, as a value in itself as an organised progressive force. In this way you could philosophically change the way in which labour was perceived in society' (quoted in Neary 2000: 4). While this process of incorporation provided labour with some social protections and legal rights in return for the acceptance of the flexibility provisions, the talks did not signal a commitment from the state to genuine corporatism. The state was more concerned with asserting leadership over the *chaebols* than with the intrinsic value of corporatism. Especially under the Kim government, the tripartite talks thus served as a way to suppress labour militancy. *Chaebol* restructuring was considered a far more important goal than corporatism (Y. Lee 2005: 289–90; Y. Lee and Y.-J. Lim 2006: 317).

Problems arose almost immediately when the union federations returned to their members with the details of the agreement. Delegates of the KCTU voted to reject the agreement struck in the commission, and the federation subsequently called a general strike in protest against the agreement, which placed the brunt of the burden for reform squarely on the shoulders of workers. It argued that the new legal protections did not prevent job losses resulting from the equally new 'flexible' dismissal mechanisms. Also, the promised buttressing of the social safety net would only apply to workers in big companies, which accounted for a minority of the workforce (D.-O. Chang and J.-H. Chae 2004: 432–4; Kong 2004: 34).

The limited corporatism was to have substantially negative effects on the quality of employment in the post-crisis period. For instance, a lower proportion of Korean workers found themselves in 'regular employment' in 2003 as compared to 1995. The 8 per cent reduction in the proportion of workers in this category – from 58 per cent to 50 per cent – precisely matches the increase in 'temporary employment' in the same period. Further, the Gini coefficient – a measure of the gap between rich and poor – widened from 0.302 in 1996 to 0.374 in 2000, marking a shift from the longer-term trend of growing egalitarianism during the period of rapid growth (H.-C. Lim and J.-H. Jang 2006: 454–5).

The experiment with tripartism proved to be short lived, in part because of the divergent motivations of each party for the tripartite talks and their respective interest in pursuing corporatism. The talks represented a way for the state to pursue its reform objectives. The *chaebols* opposed the mooted restructuring model and failed to arrive at meaningful solutions of their own. Only the trade unions showed an ongoing commitment to the corporatist project. The breakdown of the talks did not end the state's dialogue with its putative corporatist partners. Indeed, the state appeared almost to play one peak body off against the other in order to further the post-crisis agenda of reasserting state leadership in the DA.

From crisis to recovery

As noted throughout the book, a key source of the *chaebols'* structural power has been their capacity to play a unique role as economic manager, especially in respect to large-scale investment. The leverage of the *chaebols* increased due to the Korean state's preference to minimise the role of foreign capital in national economic development. The state sought to restrict the involvement of foreign enterprises to sectors where indigenous capital did not possess comparative advantage, and also provided substantial inducements for the *chaebols* to invest in priority sectors such as heavy industries. In this way the *chaebols* solidified their pre-eminent status in the Korean political economy. The industrial structure became divided into a relatively small group of large *chaebols*, who participated in projects that were the targets of industrial policy, and SMEs, which tended to act as subcontractors to the *chaebols*.

A key condition of the IMF rescue was that Korea would greatly liberalise restrictions on foreign investment. For instance, the proportion of foreign ownership in Korean enterprises would rise significantly, and it would also become far simpler for a foreign enterprise to launch a hostile takeover of a Korean firm. In addition, the restrictions on foreign involvement in 'sensitive' sectors would be dramatically reduced.

The state viewed the greater involvement of foreign investment in the economy as a means of complementing the Big Deal process mentioned earlier in the chapter. That is, the state identified the corporate structures of the *chaebols* as a key source of instability in the financial system and also as a factor encouraging irresponsible behaviour on the part of *chaebol* leaders. Impelling the *chaebols* to concentrate on their 'core competencies' would result in more rational business practices and also reduce the capacity of the *chaebols* to use their leverage against the state.

The Big Deals, as noted previously, did not go as initially planned in that they did not result in large-scale asset swaps *between* the *chaebols*. In the wake of the financial crisis the *chaebols* had limited capacity to buy new industrial assets, and instead were forced to cede business units in order to meet the new, lower debt-equity requirements. The *chaebols* were thus forced to sell a number of prized assets to foreign buyers. The change in ownership structures was dramatic. For instance, by early 2002, foreign investors owned more than one-third of listed stock in Korea. A majority of shares in firms such as Samsung Electronics, POSCO and Hyundai Motor had passed to non-Korean hands (Crotty and Lee 2002b: 673–6; J.-S. Shin and H.-J. Chang 2003: 112).

It is thus not surprising to learn that some *chaebols* – such as Hyundai – can no longer be considered 'groups' in the sense that they were prior to the crisis. In the case of Hyundai, once the biggest of the *chaebols*, the dissolution of the central holding company has seen various arms of the once multifaceted group – such as construction and shipbuilding – spun off as independent enterprises. While these business units are powerful and market leaders in their own right, the reform agenda has to some degree succeeded in breaking the nexus between ownership and management of *chaebol* enterprises (see Jwa and Lee 2004).

While foreign investment acted as a disciplinary force on the *chaebols* insofar as they were forced to reduce their debt levels, the state has less influence over the owners of Korea's main industrial assets, because ownership of those assets was dispersed between the *chaebols* and foreign investors. Even prior to the crisis the state could not compel the *chaebols* to invest. Its substantial capacities were better geared towards providing incentives for investment rather than penalising non-compliers. The exercise of sanctions against the *chaebols* risked a 'capital strike,' and this risk continued even after the financial crisis (J.-C. Kim 2004).

The post-crisis period has witnessed significantly lower levels of new investment. For instance, it is notable that facilities investment increased at an annual average of 8.5 per cent from 1980 to 1997, and almost 10 per cent for the seven years prior to the financial crisis. By contrast, this form of investment increased by less than 1 per cent in the seven years following the financial crisis. The pace was even slower during the period from 2001 until 2004, suggesting that investment increased immediately after the financial crisis and then slumped (H. Kwon 2006: 263–4).

The change in ownership composition helps explain this trend. While foreign capital has entered Korea in substantial quantities, this has been largely in the form of portfolio investment. That is, it funded the purchase of industrial assets from the *chaebols* rather than investments in new productive capacity. This explains the apparent jump in investment in the years immediately following the financial crisis. Those foreign enterprises that have operated in Korea since the financial crisis have thus not provided much new stimulus to the national economy. In the case of Lone Star, an American private equity fund that was one of the most prominent purchasers of Korean industrial assets in the years following the financial crisis, public sentiment has been particularly aroused. After initially welcoming foreign involvement in the local market, the Korean government, especially under Roh Moo-hyun, sought to address concerns that foreign capital – as exemplified by Lone Star – was acting in ways detrimental to Korean interests (Fifield 2007: 21).

A second way in which the state sought to reduce the leverage of the *chaebols* over the national economy (and within the developmental alliance) was to encourage the growth of the SME sector. As part of the reforms to the financial sector, the state restricted the amount of finance that the *chaebols* could access from a given bank. Not only was each enterprise required to reduce its D-E ratio, specific shares of bank credit were reserved for the non-*chaebol* sector. The result has been that SMEs have relatively better access to resources. One measure that has benefited both SMEs and the *chaebols* – and that indicates continuity with previous forms of industrial policy – is the 'SME Coexistence Scheme'. This measure has involved government support for joint research ventures between upstream and downstream producers in the shipbuilding industry, a high value-added sector with substantial potential for localised production and employment (S. Kim 2006: 21–4). In the face of growing competition from China and other low-cost producers, the government has sought to protect this valuable industry.

While the greater involvement of foreign capital and SMEs has somewhat reduced the economic concentration of the *chaebols*, neither of these sets of actors can play the role of the *chaebols* over the past four decades. They are simply too well entrenched and too great in scale to be readily replaced. The state appeared to recognise this in 2004, when President Roh Moo-hyun, newly returned to office after escaping impeachment charges, called for a summit with the *chaebol* leaders (J.-C. Kim 2004). After veiled and sometimes overt warnings that Korean business would invest overseas rather than in the domestic economy, the top-five *chaebols* announced a string of massive new investments. These multi-stage and multi-year plans envisaged thousands of new jobs in the domestic economy, at a time of increasing uncertainty about the capacity of the Korean economy to reach the growth rates of the pre-crisis period.

However the quid pro quo for these investments was a relaxation of regulations on *chaebol* control over their financial affiliates. The Roh government had proposed reducing the capacity of *chaebols* to exercise their voting rights in financial affiliates, which represented a potential conflict of interest in the eyes of reformers. Once again, the state was forced to offer an incentive to the *chaebols* to invest without any commensurate power to discipline the *chaebols* for non-compliance. In this sense the *chaebols'* structural power, emanating from their role as key investors and thus agents of economic change, remained evident even after the financial crisis. While the state remains authoritative and seeks to exercise strategic intent, the effectiveness of its authority remains limited in terms of investment coordination.

Conclusions

The IMF reforms were an opportunity for the Kim Dae-jung government to strengthen the state's position in the developmental alliance. The state facilitated the process of industrial and financial restructuring that was required as a condition for the emergency loans. It thus operated in accordance with a markedly different template than the early stages of economic development.

The *bureaucracy* gained influence during the post-crisis period, strengthening the state within the developmental alliance. The process of *chaebol* restructuring illustrated that the state retained some dirigiste elements, especially in its sponsorship of Big Deals. While this represented a strengthening of the state's standing vis-à-vis the *chaebols*, the long-term impact of the reforms appeared to weaken the state's developmental capacity.

Social pressures were increasingly influential to the power dynamics of the developmental alliance during the post-crisis period. The Korean public provided a crucial pillar of support for the state during its enactment of the reform programme. The *chaebols* were the target of popular resentment about the hardships that Korea experienced after 1997. Yet the high cost of corporate and financial restructuring limited the state's capacity to offer tangible benefits to the public in the form of an expanded welfare system. This in turn limited the public's support for the Kim government. Conservative elements of society would claim that the government's approach to the *chaebols* was endangering the growth capacity of the Korean economy. Nonetheless, social pressures favoured the state during this period, regardless of the unsatisfactory results of the Tripartite Talks.

The reduction in the economic concentration of the *chaebols* reduced their importance to the national economy. Thus *economic conditions* did not further the interests of the *chaebols*. The Korean state still relied to some degree on the *chaebols* and foreign-invested enterprises to act as the engine of the national economy.

National security concerns impacted to a far smaller degree on the developmental alliance under Kim Dae-jung. The US was unlikely to allow a close ally such as Korea to collapse under the weight of its debts in 1997–8. However, this was also the case for other countries within the sphere of American interests. The US contributed directly to the bailouts of most Asian crisis countries. It also exercised influence at the board level of the IMF, where it holds veto powers, to ensure that these countries did not default on their loans. It could be said that the US was protecting its global interests in the maintenance of the international financial system rather than a specific interest in Korea. The conditions attached to the IMF bailout package, which the US was closely involved in negotiating, suggest that the US saw the crisis as a long overdue opportunity to reform the *chaebols*. National security concerns thus acted in favour of the Korean state rather than the *chaebols* in the context of the developmental alliance. However, the exertion of American power also contributed to debasement of the state's developmental capacities.

Globalisation should serve the interests of the *chaebols* in the developmental alliance because its logic is to subsume national economies into transnational structures. This manifested itself in the gradual retrenchment of the developmental state's most potent policy tools prior to the 1997 financial crisis. Yet in the post-crisis period the effect of globalisation was mixed, given that liberals castigated the *chaebols* for their reckless behaviour. Critics claimed that the *chaebols* represented the worst form of national capitalism rather than the globalised variety. The reform package increased the degree of competition in the Korean economy and also the level of foreign ownership. The reforms further downgraded the capacity of the state to act against the *chaebols* in a despotic manner. However, the increasing globalisation of the Korean economy did not work in the favour of the *chaebols* within the developmental alliance. Instead globalisation favoured the state's promotion of market-centric governance structures.

The state sought a renewed mandate in the post-crisis period. It did so by playing a vital role in Korea's economic recovery. Yet it may have dealt a fatal blow to business confidence in the process, with implications for the *chaebol*-centred developmental model. These will be discussed in the concluding chapter of the book.

7 The alliance in retrospect

Introduction

This chapter reassesses the empirical and conceptual issues raised throughout the book. The study investigated the interaction between the infrastructural power of the state and the structural power of capital during the industrialisation of Korea. The structural power of capital has been a key element of the developmental alliance, which shaped the formulation and implementation of policies that were conducive both to capitalist development and to the growth of the *chaebols*. This chapter draws on the findings of the historical narrative presented in the study in order to identify the specific patterns of power relations in the developmental alliance. It also highlights the dynamic nature of those relations.

The chapter first revisits each of the contextual variables that the study investigated in order to trace the variation in power relativities between the two parties in the developmental alliance. These variables were bureaucracy, social pressures, national security, economic conditions and globalisation. The chapter looks for variation in the respective influence of each variable on the alliance throughout the four periods into which the study divided Korean economic development. The chapter then searches for patterns and correlations between the variables. It investigates the impact of the variables on each period of the study, and seeks to explain how and why the variables changed in each period.

Three main issues arise from the analysis. First, the study seeks to explain the significance of the correlation between the economic conditions, globalisation and national security variables. These variables all worked in favour of capital during the Park and the 1980s–90s periods but then favoured the state in the post-crisis period. Why did the value of other variables change during the course of Korean development, favouring first one party to the developmental alliance and then the other? Why did the social pressures and bureaucracy variables show such a high degree of variation? Finally, this section extrapolates from the overall trends apparent in the analysis to predict future trends in the DA. Do the variables operate in cycles, favouring first one party to the alliance and then another? The chapter concludes with an overall summary and exploration of the implications of the analysis. Is it still relevant to speak of a 'developmental alliance' in Korea given the significant changes wrought upon state–business interaction in the past four decades? Given the indelible changes in relations between the state and capital that the financial crisis has produced, how should we assess the impact of these changes?

Bureaucracy

The Korean bureaucracy has strongly influenced the shaping of the developmental alliance, most notably by defining the goals of economic development. The book sought to identify the developmental ideology that guided each stage of the process, starting with the nationalist and state-led model of the 1960s and then the gradual rise of neoliberal thought from the 1980s. The bureaucracy has acted as a conduit between the state and *chaebols*, both informing the political elite of business concerns and suggesting appropriate responses to those concerns.

Chapter 3 argued that the bureaucracy was central to the pursuit of the colonial state during Japan's imperial expansion during the first half of the twentieth century. Japan fostered a penetrating bureaucracy that administered all aspects of Korean society. Its degree of control was rare among colonial powers. From the perspective of this study, the significance of this period was that Park Chung Hee witnessed, first hand, the colonial state's pursuit of economic development while serving in the imperial army. He also noted that the Korean state in the post-war period lacked the sense of developmental purpose of its predecessor. For this reason he sought to overturn the Syngman Rhee and Chang Myon governments and replace them with a state that was oriented towards the goal of Korea's own modernisation. This would entail the founding of a developmental alliance between the state and the *chaebols*.

Chapter 4 noted that the bureaucracy acted as an interface between the state and the *chaebols* during the Park era. Senior civil servants shaped the state's approach to economic modernisation, the result of which was the developmental alliance. The influence of the bureaucracy enabled the state to employ infrastructural power. The bureaucracy acts as the main point of contact when the state seeks to engage society or extract resources. Senior policymakers such as Kim Chung-yum and Kim Yong Hwan, along with the US, encouraged the Park government to adopt a developmental ideology and overcome the temptation to punish business leaders. Overall the effect was to strengthen the state's willingness to enter an alliance with capital. Thus while the bureaucracy worked *in favour of the state* during this period, its advice discouraged the state from exercising the despotic form of its powers against the *chaebols*.

Chapter 5 noted that the bureaucracy was both a constraining and enabling feature of the state apparatus. During the Park era the bureaucracy provided the means by which the state could cultivate a developmental alliance with business through infrastructural power. Bureaucrats informed Park of the potential of these capacities to contribute to economic development. In contrast, the bureaucracy in the 1980s and 1990s informed the state about the liberal policies that it espoused with increasing intensity. The overall effect was to encourage greater emphasis on market principles on the part of the state. This would later manifest itself in the transformation from a state-centric governance structure to a market-centric one.

The bureaucracy discouraged despotic action against the *chaebols*, such as the dismantlement of the Kukje Group. The state's action against Kukje was very much the exception to the rule. Conflict and rivalry within the bureaucracy also downgraded the infrastructural capacity of the state. This hindered its capacity to perform tasks such as overseeing the financial system. The bureaucracy contributed to a shift in the balance of power within the developmental alliance *in favour of capital*. Instead of operating in accordance with a market-centric governance structure, the economy was still vulnerable to the unregulated behaviour of the *chaebols*.

Chapter 6 argued that the bureaucracy attained new levels of influence during the post-crisis period. The IMF reforms allowed the state to regain influence because of the rhetorical power of neoliberalism that the Korean economic bureaucracy had advocated for two decades. The bureaucracy strengthened the state in its power relations with the *chaebols*. Analysis of the Kim government's approach to *chaebol* restructuring indicated that some statist elements remained. These elements were most evident in the Big Deal and 'Workout' programmes launched after the financial crisis. The *chaebols* found it difficult to combat this combination of: a) reforms intended to compel them to comply with market principles; as well as b) measures such as the state's directing the process of industrial and financial restructuring. The state was also less nationalistic in its definition of the interests of 'capital', embracing foreign interests to a greater degree than previous governments. During the post-crisis period market principles became a weapon in the hands of the state in its relations with the *chaebols*. This worked *in favour of the state*. However, the long-term impact of the reforms that the Kim Dae-jung government enacted may yet weaken state developmental capacity.

Social pressures

The study also considered the effect of social pressures on the developmental alliance. The partners to the alliance initially shared an interest in inoculating the policymaking process from social scrutiny. If the corporatist arrangements remained in place, social pressures would matter only to the extent that economic development required a degree of assent and thus cooperation from society. This book expected social pressures to work in favour of capital and capitalist development. However, if the state adopted a populist stance and drew on public support to attack business, social pressures could serve the state rather than capital.

Chapter 4 noted that society could not remove Park Chung Hee from power through physical force due to the regime's preponderance of despotic power. However, the state relied on infrastructural power to pursue economic development. This required at least a modicum of consent on the part of the public about that project. Park actively sought public support for his regime during the initial phase of his rule, as witnessed by attempts to convert the junta into a civilian format, the public dressing down of 'illicit profiteers' in 1961 and measures to improve the living standards of rural voters.

The regime gathered insufficient public support to rule without resorting to illicit means, such as the harassment of political opponents, use of illegal campaign funds (supplied by the *chaebols*) and the blatant rigging of elections. After a series of close election results, Park defied public sentiment by announcing the Yusin Constitution and further tightening political repression during the 1970s. These events hastened the end of his regime as both its domestic and its American support weakened. The public rejected the state's ongoing political rule despite material improvements in socio-economic conditions. Social pressures thus worked *in favour of capital* in the developmental alliance because the state shielded the *chaebols* from public criticism about political and economic issues without attaining legitimacy for its own rule.

Chapter 5 noted that social pressures were also significant to the power dynamics during the 1980s and 1990s, although their effect was mixed. On the one hand the state was increasingly forced to consider the interests of civil society due to electoral imperatives. This entailed at least a rhetorical loosening of ties with the *chaebols*, eliciting accusations that the state had adopted an anti-business stance. The garnering of popular support helped Roh Tae-woo and later Kim Young-sam to attain political power. However, the state had few means of disciplining the *chaebols* due to the ongoing retrenchment of the developmental state's policy tools. Responding to the demands of society reduced the state's autonomy both in terms of its policy preferences and also in terms of its relations with the *chaebols* within the developmental alliance. The state's change of stance encouraged the *chaebols* to openly oppose the state for the first time. Given the loss of its disciplinary powers, this adversely affected the state's standing within the developmental alliance and thus somewhat negated the benefit of social pressures to the state. The pressures of Korean society thus worked *in favour of the state* in its power relations with the *chaebols*, albeit to a low degree.

Chapter 6 argued that social pressures were increasingly influential on the power dynamics of the developmental alliance during the post-crisis period. The Korean public provided a crucial pillar of support for the state in its enactment of the reform programme during that period. The *chaebols* were the target of popular resentment for the hardships that Korea experienced after 1997. Yet the high cost of corporate and financial restructuring limited the state's capacity to offer tangible benefits to the public in the form of an expanded welfare system. This in turn limited the public's support for the

Kim Dae-jung government. Conservatives would later claim that the government's approach to the *chaebols* was endangering the growth capacity of the Korean economy. The state presented itself as a defender of wider social interests than just the traditional developmental alliance during this period. In contrast to the previous period, this acted *in favour of the state* to a moderate degree.

National security

The US provided ample military and economic aid to Korea due to its prominent position in the frontline of the Cold War, drawing attention to the importance of national security to the formation of state capacity during the initial phase of Korean development. However, this support was not unconditional. The US pressured Korea to pursue policies conducive to economic development. So this study expected national security to act in favour of capitalist development but not necessarily in favour of the *chaebols*.

Chapter 3 argued that national security concerns were vital to the survival of the Korean state and the revival of the colonial era mode of state–business relations. This was because the US viewed Korea as a cornerstone of its regional containment strategy. Support for the littoral states in East Asia, including Japan, Korea, Taiwan, Vietnam, the Philippines and Indonesia, furthered America's overall Cold War goal of preventing the expansion of communism beyond continental Asia. The US envisioned that Japan, like Germany, would become a regional economic stabiliser and mainstay of the alliance. So an anti-communist regime in the southern half of the Korean peninsula was central to the defence of Japan and other regional objectives. American interest in Korea per se was not particularly high given that its potential for development appeared to be low. However, its strategic value was deemed to be high due to the evolution of the Cold War. This was especially the case after the outbreak of the Korean conflict in 1950.

Chapter 4 viewed state capacity as a 'wasting asset' with a limited lifespan, given that the Park regime could not retain the capacity it accrued as a key ally of the US in the 1960s. National security concerns were central to the founding of the developmental alliance. The US supported its Korean ally in order to further the containment of communism in East Asia. However its treatment of the Park Chung Hee and Syngman Rhee regimes differed in several aspects. Most notably, Walt Rostow's 'new look' at foreign policy called for a more holistic approach to fighting the Cold War. Client states would be expected to pursue socio-economic development as well as the attainment of sufficient military capacities to oppose communist expansion. So the US provided the Korean state with the capacity to pursue economic development. American policies thus encouraged the fostering of infrastructural power.

The US was more tolerant of the statist model during this period than it would be in later decades. However, it expected client states such as Korea to pursue goals that were not inimical with overall American strategy. This would entail institutional reform along liberal–democratic lines. National security concerns provided the *raison d'état* for Park, but they also limited the regime's choices. This explains the state's attempts to attain greater autonomy through the HCI project. National security concerns thus worked *in favour of capital* in the developmental alliance. This was because the overriding goal of encouraging capitalist development was part of America's regional strategy.

Chapter 5 noted that national security did not loom as a large influence on the developmental alliance during the 1980s and 1990s due to the waning of the Cold War. Korea had attained a significant degree of socio-economic stability by the end of the 1980s, dissolving much of the rationale for US support for the authoritarian Syngman Rhee, Park Chung Hee, Chun Doo-hwan and Roh Tae-woo regimes. Thanks to three decades of rapid industrial-isation, South Korea first closed the gap in military capabilities between itself and the North, and then pulled ahead significantly (Bleiker 2005: 20–1).

The North was declining in terms of both military preparedness and socio-economic development. This was to intensify from the early 1990s when the collapse of the Soviet Union denied the North economic and military aid. East Asia was by this time the only region in the world where the Cold War continued. However, the intensity of the conflict was far lower due to the dissolution of the Soviet Union, China's prioritisation of its own economic development, and the economic travails of North Korea – which included a series of natural disasters and famine. Humanitarian organisations, which were permitted to operate in the country from the mid-1990s, estimate that up to 2 million North Koreans may have died as a result of famine and poverty during that decade (Seliger 2004: 3).

All these changes strengthened the national security of South Korea. This reduced America's incentive to overlook the elements of the dirigiste paradigm of which it disapproved. The US thus continued to influence the shaping of Korean development in terms of the power of liberal ideas, which seeped into the state through reformers such as Kim Jae-ik. The US also pressured Korea to liberalise its economy. National security concerns during this period thus worked *in favour of capital* to some degree.

Chapter 6 argued that the national security impacted to an even smaller degree on the developmental alliance under Kim Dae-jung. Given the gradual normalisation of Japan's military capacities and the growth of anti-American sentiment in South Korea during the late 1990s, the strategic value of Korea for the US fell commensurately. America's global priorities had changed markedly by the early twenty-first century. Terrorism had replaced commu-nism as the greatest threat to US interests. However, North Korea's member-ship of the 'axis of evil' ensured that it was still central to America's strategic thinking. As part of the global redeployment of American military forces to combat the perceived threat of terrorism, the US announced a timetable to reduce its troop strength in Korea by about one-third – to 26,000

– by 2008 (Department of Defense 2004). Its residual forces would be redeployed to positions south of Seoul. Instead of US troops being based on the border with North Korea and acting as a 'tripwire', ensuring full-scale American involvement in the instance of an attack from the North, they would be positioned to intervene in a renewed conflict or other regional contingencies.

This represents the largest reduction of American forces in Korea since the 'Nixon shock' of the 1970s. US forces based in Korea have thus taken on the status of a flexible entity that can be deployed in a range of contingencies rather than one purely ranged against North Korea (Scanlon 2004). Nonetheless the US was unlikely to allow a close ally such as Korea to collapse under the weight of its debts in 1997. The nature of the conditions attached to the bailout package, which the US were closely involved in negotiating, suggest that the US saw the crisis as a long overdue opportunity to reform the *chaebols*. Its tolerance for the statist paradigm appeared to be over. The US thus encouraged the neoliberal reforms that the IMF bailout entailed. National security, while less salient than in previous decades, thus acted in *the favour of the state* in the context of the developmental alliance because the reforms so squarely targeted the *chaebols*. The election to the presidency of Lee Myung-bak, who placed a higher priority on the US alliance than the Roh government had, would suggest a reinforcement of this trend (see, for instance, Onishi 2008).

Economic conditions

Chapter 3 posited that business could most effectively wield structural power when the national economy is in poor condition. This is because the state has a strong political imperative for an economic recovery, which in turn must be engineered through private sector investment. The political imperative for economic growth is lower when the economy is strong. This reduces the influence of structural power.

Chapter 4 noted that the state–business alliance in the colonial period served the needs of Japan's imperial expansion. Korean entrepreneurs were largely excluded from key industrial sectors such as chemicals and power generation. The alienation of Korean entrepreneurs from the key sectors of the industrial economy prevented state–business relations during the colonial period from constituting a developmental alliance. There was no indigenous developmental project in this era, and instead Korean capital served the interests of the Japanese empire.

Neither did state–business relations in the subsequent Syngman Rhee and Chang Myon eras constitute a developmental alliance. Upon assuming power after the war Rhee failed to replicate the 'production-oriented' political economy of the colonial state. Rhee bypassed the infrastructural powers of the state apparatus, such as the bureaucracy. The economic performance of the Rhee period was relatively unimpressive compared to the colonial period. State–business relations were not geared towards economic development.

In contrast, the salience of economic conditions increased the structural power of the *chaebols* within the developmental alliance during the Park Chung Hee era. Chapter 4 showed that the Korean state entered a risky developmental alliance with the *chaebols* in order to increase its legitimacy. The state relied on the *chaebols* to convert economic resources into viable enterprises and thus pursue economic development. This in turn necessitated pro-business policies at the expense of wider societal interests. The regime's reticence to exercise despotic power in response to *chaebol* malpractices highlights the contingent nature of state capacity within the developmental alliance. The state was incapable of acting with the same degree of impunity as the colonial state. Instead, the Park regime had to balance the urge to punish the *chaebols* with the imperative to encourage business leaders to focus on economic development. In keeping with the predictions of the study, the regime had a strong imperative for economic growth during its initial years in power. This manifested itself in a generally permissive attitude to the excesses of the *chaebols*. The study thus judges the impact of economic conditions during this phase to be *in favour of capital*.

While economic conditions were generally sound during the presidencies of Chun Doo-hwan, Roh Tae-woo and Kim Young-sam, financial crises marred the beginning and the end of this period. Chapter 5 argued that the relatively buoyant condition of the economy did not greatly strengthen the structural power of the *chaebols*. The study predicted that a strong economy reduces the state's political imperative for economic growth. This in turn reduces the salience of structural power within the developmental alliance. However, the *chaebols* attained a relatively high degree of independence from the disciplinary powers of the state during the 1980s and 1990s due to their structural position in the economy and the retrenchment of the state's policy tools (see the section on bureaucracy above). Thus economic conditions per se did not lend a great degree of leverage to the *chaebols*. However, the related phenomenon of their position within the economy *was* influential. In particular, the state was concerned about the potential for the *chaebols'* massive debts to destabilise the financial system. The state had little capacity to discipline the *chaebols* in this period. Financial markets nonetheless expected the state to guarantee the *chaebols'* loans from international lenders. The study judges the impact of economic conditions during this period to be *in favour of capital*.

Chapter 6 argued that the reduction in the economic concentration of the *chaebols* reduced their importance to economic development in the post-crisis period. The study predicted that the state has a strong political imperative for an economic recovery and that this would increase the structural power of business within the developmental alliance. However, Chapter 2 noted that adverse economic conditions could work *against* the interests of capital if the state espouses pro-market policies and if business appears to have performed poorly. This was indeed the case in the post-crisis period. The Kim Dae-jung government embraced neoliberal reform and vowed to restructure the debt-ridden *chaebols*. Thus economic conditions did not further the interests of the *chaebols* in this period. The Korean state also had less incentive to cater to the interests of business because the *chaebols'* economic concentration fell. This reduced their importance to economic development. Since levels of foreign ownership increased as a result of neoliberal reform, the *chaebols* shared the task of fuelling the Korean economy with foreign-invested firms and also the rejuvenated small–medium enterprise sector. Thus economic conditions worked *in favour of the state* during the post-crisis period.

Globalisation

The study expected to find that a higher degree of integration with the international economic system would work in the interests of capital within the context of the developmental alliance because the state tends to focus on *national* concerns. This is because integration with global markets reduces the dependence of domestic capital on the state. However, not all sectors of capital benefit equally, and the disciplinary powers of global markets penalises under-performers. In this sense globalisation can assist the state in a developmental alliance, especially if the state promotes policies of which markets approve.

Chapter 3 noted that Syngman Rhee, president of South Korea from 1948 to 1960, shared with his predecessors a fear of external domination. Korea has endured numerous invasions and wars involving neighbouring states. Subsequently the Korean state's struggle for autonomy from external threats has been more vigorous than that of other countries. However, this struggle has not necessarily been more successful. Rhee, too, was imbibed with this desire for autonomy, as witnessed by his intent to avoid subjugation at the hands of Japan. While the national security section of the chapter considered the military aspect of autonomy, this section focuses on the efforts of Rhee and his successors to avoid the *economic* aspect of external domination.

Chapter 4 noted that the HCI drive illustrated Park Chung Hee's quest for autonomy from external interference in the shape of both the political and economic aspects of American hegemony. The state guaranteed loans to the *chaebols* so that they could develop the heavy industries that Korea needed to attain a degree of industrial and military independence. The state thus assumed the risks of the HCI. These were substantial given the scale of foreign capital inflows needed for the project. While the state offered incentives to the *chaebols* to participate in the HCI project, it had insufficient means of disciplining them. It was the state that would eventually bear the costs of external instability, such as the oil shocks of the 1970s and the resultant downturn in the world economy. Like economic conditions, globalisation thus worked *in favour of capital* within the developmental alliance for the period as a whole.

The end of the Park regime resulted in a shift in economic policy. Chapter 5 noted that the liberalisation policies of presidents Chun Doo-hwan, Roh Tae-woo and Kim Young-sam took the form of market opening. However, these administrations did not ensure that adequate supervisory measures accompanied the *chaebols'* access to new financial resources. In the absence of such compensatory measures, the integration of Korea into the international economic system was detrimental to the state's capacity to oversee economic development. Globalisation, as a feature of international political economy and as a policy that the Kim Young-sam government in particular consciously pursued, thus worked *in favour of capital* during the 1980s and 1990s.

Chapter 6 argued that globalisation should serve the interests of the *chaebols* in the developmental alliance, because the logic of globalisation is to subsume national economies – and thus the state's regulatory capacity – into trans-national structures. Indeed, this tended to manifest itself in the gradual retrenchment of the developmental state's most potent policy tools prior to the 1997 financial crisis. Yet in the post-crisis period the effects of globalisation was decidedly mixed given that liberals castigated the *chaebols* for their reckless behaviour. Critics claimed that the *chaebols* represented the worst form of *national* capital rather than the globalised variety. The IMF's reform package increased the degree of competition in the Korean economy and also its level of foreign ownership. The reforms further downgraded the capacity of the state to act against the *chaebols* in a *despotic* manner. However, the increasing degree of globalisation in the Korean economy did not work in the favour of the *chaebols* within the developmental alliance. This study argued that it instead worked *in favour of the state*.

Patterns of change

This section collates the results of the analysis in the previous section and seeks to discover trends and patterns in the findings. It analyses the trends in terms of their impact on the developmental alliance. The study assessed each contextual variable's impact on the alliance, and the results appear in Table 7.1.

Immediately apparent is the fact that the variables generally changed from working in favour of capital (the *chaebols*) to working in favour of the state over the time covered in the study. That is, four out of five variables in the

Table 7.1 Impact of variables on the DA

	Bureaucracy	*Social pressures*	*National security*	*Economic conditions*	*Globalisation*
Park	State	Capital	Capital	Capital	Capital
1980–97	Capital	State	Capital	Capital	Capital
1998–	State	State	State	State	State

Park Chung Hee period and during the presidencies of Chun Doo-hwan, Roh Tae-woo and Kim Young-sam favoured capital. However all five variables worked in favour of the state during the post-crisis period. This appears to contradict the conventional wisdom that the decline in state capacity is inevitable, irreversible and terminal in the course of economic development. Thus business can accumulate a significant degree of structural power, but the state also retains and gains powers of its own. What this study seeks to discover is the conditions in which each actor is able to exercise its powers. In this respect the study's examination of the contextual variables that condition state–business interaction is significant.

The study found that four of the five contextual variables worked in favour of capital during the Park period. Only bureaucracy worked in the interests of the state. As Chapter 4 and a previous section of this chapter mentioned, this appears to coalesce with the arguments of this study about the imperative for the state to create conditions that are conducive to capitalist development in the early phases of the process of development. While the regime achieved its broad agenda of modernising Korean society, it is worth considering the price it had to pay. As Chapter 4 notes, the Korean state lacked the capacity to launch the process of economic development by itself, and the economy lacked the autonomy to deflect external political and economic pressures. Korea relied on foreign capital to pursue economic development, and it also relied on overseas markets to absorb its products on a scale that would allow local firms to establish themselves in industries such as steel, chemicals and automobiles. A previous section of the chapter mentioned that bureaucracy worked in favour of the state. However, this occurred in a way that encouraged the state to be developmental. In this sense the Park period witnessed the operation of a classical developmental state. The interests of the state in that era and, indeed, its very survival were intimately linked to economic development – and thus the *chaebols*.

While economic conditions, globalisation and national security all worked in favour of capital during the Park era and also from the 1980s until the 1990s, the effects of the social pressures and bureaucracy variables changed. Social pressures furthered the interests of capital in the Park period, but favoured the state under Chun Doo-hwan, Roh Tae-woo and Kim Young-sam. The opening of the polity strengthened the standing of the state within the DA during the transition from authoritarian rule to democracy. The state's legitimacy was closely linked to its capacity to oversee rapid economic development in the Park era.

Insofar as the state largely achieved that goal, social pressures worked in favour of capital because the state's engagement with society furthered capitalist development. However, this did not guarantee popular support for the regime, because the benefits of rapid economic development were not shared equally among all sections of Korean society. Thus in the wake of democratisation, the state sought to respond to public dissatisfaction through such measures as a more equitable distribution of wealth and a calling to account of those perceived to have benefited from the corruption of the authoritarian period. The state's adoption of populist measures, including policies that the *chaebols* perceived to be targeted at their interests, thus worked in favour of the state within the DA.

There was a contrary trend for bureaucracy. This variable worked in favour of the state under Park and then reversed to favour capital in the latter period. As the study noted earlier, liberals such as Kim Jae-ik used their influence within the bureaucracy in the early 1980s to argue for greater economic and political liberalisation. The *chaebols'* capacity to independently access resources increased at the same time as the state's capacity to discipline capital decreased. The *chaebols* entered new industries free of the constraints of state planning guidelines following the discontinuation of industrial policy in the 1980s. Further, the state's capacity to supervise the financial system diminished when the *chaebols* began to access funds through new sources, such as non-bank financial institutions. These sources replaced state-directed lending through the official banking sector. Thus economic and financial liberalisation worked in favour of capital within the developmental alliance during the 1980s and 1990s.

The transition from the Chun, Roh and Kim presidencies to the post-crisis period displayed an even greater change in the value of the contextual variables. Whereas only social pressures worked in the favour of the state during the 1980s and early to mid-1990s, this study found that all variables served the interests of the state in the wake of the 1997 Korean financial crisis.

This represented an almost complete reversal of fortunes from the Park period (1961–79). Social pressures continued to work in favour of the state in the post-crisis period, but the influence of this variable became even stronger. This was because the state used the authority it regained from overseeing the IMF reforms to compel the *chaebols* to behave more in a manner that conformed to a market economy.

Economic conditions, globalisation and national security also benefited the state in its relations with business in the post-crisis period. This was because the policies espoused by the state in this period were quite different from earlier decades, being strongly aligned with the recommendations of the liberal reformers within the bureaucracy and also the US and the international financial institutions.

This hints at the other variable whose direction changed during the post-crisis period: bureaucracy. As the previous section mentioned, the rhetoric of neoliberal reform became a powerful tool in the hands of the state after the crisis. The reform mantra had in previous decades served to reduce the influence of the state in economic development, with even the *chaebols* arguing for a more market-based approach. However the state turned neoliberal reform against the *chaebols* during the post-crisis period. While retaining some of the statist instincts of previous governments, Kim Dae-jung's economic team carried out the most extensive reform of the *chaebols* that Korea had ever seen, introducing for the first time a market-centric governance structure.

Understanding change

The study found that economic conditions, globalisation and national security are positively correlated. These three variables worked in favour of capital during the first and second periods of the study, but they worked in favour of the state in the post-crisis period. As the previous section of the chapter mentioned, the social pressures and bureaucracy variables worked in opposite directions during both the Park era and the 1980s–90s. Social pressures favoured capital and the bureaucracy worked in favour of the state during the rule of Park Chung Hee.

The opposite was the case in the two decades that followed. Economic conditions, globalisation and national security served the interests of capital within the developmental alliance in both periods. The combination of these three factors propelled the logic of economic development in the early stages of Korea's industrialisation. It also counteracted the impetus to state power provided by the bureaucracy during the Park era and social pressures during the 1980s and the 1990s.

It appears somewhat anomalous that these three factors worked in favour of the *state* in the post-crisis period. This study argued that this was because the state won the rhetorical battle within the DA in that period by attaining the support of the US and the international financial institutions (IFIs) through its adoption of the reform agenda. In previous decades the state's position was more precarious because it had overseen a heterodox development strategy that did not comply with liberal tenets. It relied on the acquiescence of the US to pursue economic development.

The state's degree of latitude narrowed in the 1980s when the trend towards neoliberalism strengthened both domestically and overseas. It was forced to retrench the most potent elements of the statist paradigm, such as control over the distribution of credit. The *chaebols* appeared to be passive victims of a misdirected state-led development strategy. However, they were the chief beneficiaries of economic development. The rhetoric of neoliberalism forced the hand of state, which ceded its only restraints on the anti-social activities of the *chaebols*. The 1990s thus witnessed almost unrestricted *chaebol* activity.

The result was an increase in borrowing and expansion into already over-crowded industries. The unrestrained profligacy of the *chaebols* became apparent when liquidity tightened in the latter half of the decade. However the financial crisis also exposed the degree to which the state had lost control of the economy, insofar as it could not play the role of lender of last resort in the domestic setting. It had no coherent strategy to pursue economic development.

Economic conditions, globalisation and national security all worked in favour of the state in the post-crisis period because the state could rectify the liquidity crisis. It could do so only by actively embracing reform and instilling a new element to its approach to economic development. The cornerstone of the state's *political* strategy was to target the *chaebols* for reform in order to improve the state's standing within the developmental alliance. Their high debts and expansion into new fields through cross-subsidisation came in for particular criticism and became the target of reform.

The state's position improved immeasurably because the reform drive had the full support of the US and the IFIs. These parties endowed the Korean state with the imprimatur of neoliberal reform. That is, they provided the political cover for the state to carry out economic reform that directly affected the *chaebols'* interests. Ordinarily this would be anathema in a market economy system, which liberals aim to universalise. However, liberals deemed that drastic measures would be required to compel the *chaebols* to change because their behaviour was so egregious. Critics of the reforms subsequently argued that some of the forced restructuring only solidified oligopolistic market structures in some sectors. There appears to be some evidence of this in the automobile industry, for instance, which has reverted to an oligopolistic market structure.

The analysis also revealed that there was only a single occurrence of a variable shifting from being in favour of the state to favouring capital. This was when *bureaucracy* changed from being in favour of the state in the Park period to being in favour of capital during the 1980s and 1990s. This variable would change yet again to favour the state in the post-crisis period. Each of the other variables, when it exhibited a change in effect, shifted from favouring capital to favouring the state.

This trend contradicts neoliberal expectations that the position of capital will strengthen as the process of development proceeds and that the state will suffer a commensurate decline in influence. However, it is a finding that accords with the arguments made throughout this study that neoliberal reform can be a powerful tool in the hands of the state. The rhetoric of reform was itself powerful, even if the effect of the reforms was to further limit the capacity of the state to intervene.

Thus it is through analysis of *power relations* – the politics of the developmental alliance – that the state's efforts to rein in the power of the *chaebols* become apparent. As the previous section noted, the bureaucracy was crucial to the state's adoption of the liberal agenda in the 1980s and 1990s. However, it was not until after the crisis that the liberal agenda could be used to the advantage of the state rather than the *chaebols*.

A final issue to emerge from the analysis is what the findings of this study indicate about the future direction of power dynamics within the developmental state. As the previous section noted, the majority of the contextual variables worked in favour of capital under Park, a period of eighteen years. Most of the variables also furthered the interests of capital within the developmental alliance from the 1980s until the financial crisis of 1997, another period of eighteen years. The study found that all five variables worked in favour of the state after the crisis.

It would be imprudent to suggest that the contextual variables will continue to act in favour of the state for another decade or as long as thirty years.

Indeed, there have been some indications that the position of strength that the state assumed in the immediate post-crisis period is weakening. More to the point, it appears that the *chaebols* are regaining some of the ground that they ceded following the financial crisis.

Chapter 6 noted that the state under Roh Moo-hyun appeared to reach a 'grand compromise' with the *chaebols* in 2004. This entailed an easing of regulations on the *chaebols* in return for promises of new investment. In any case, a renewed period of *chaebol* strength is certainly not difficult to imagine given the gradual depletion of the state's policy tools over the past two decades. Perhaps what is most likely to eventuate is a period of uneasy balance between the state and the *chaebols*, during which neither side is capable of asserting itself upon the other. The ascension of Lee Myung-bak to the presidency would seem to ensure a more sympathetic ear in government for the *chaebols*.

Still the developmental alliance?

Given the myriad changes that the alliance underwent during the process of development, do state–business relations in Korea still take the form of an alliance? Or have the positions of each actor, and the relationship between the two parties, changed too markedly in the decades since the founding of the alliance under Park Chung Hee? The case could be made that state–business interaction in Korea has traditionally been relatively intense. Thus any reduction in the intensity of the interaction between the state and capital may only represent an incremental change towards a new stage of the alliance. The intimate involvement of the state in the restructuring of the *chaebols* in the post-crisis period and also in discussions to bolster investment in the years after the crisis bear witness to the ongoing links between these two key parties to the alliance.

While close interaction between the state and capital will continue, it does not automatically follow that the *purpose* and *aims* of that interaction will replicate previous decades. The developmental alliance has involved the interaction of state infrastructural power and the structural power of capital. Both parties have been oriented towards economic development. The transition in the alliance over the past two decades appears to be diminishing the developmental capacities of both parties. The state used its infrastructural powers to secure the resources that the *chaebols* needed for economic develop-ment. As this chapter has mentioned, the state's adoption of the neoliberal agenda in the post-crisis period has made the pursuit of purely national goals, such as economic development, much more problematic. The promotion of national economic development is complicated by the fact that the *chaebols* are no longer exclusively concerned with their Korean operations, having diverted a part of their focus towards large-scale foreign investment from the late 1980s. This foreign investment was made more attractive for it dovetailed with the goal of the *chaebols* to escape the discipline of the Korean state.

Another distinctive element of the DA has been that each party has had a degree of leverage over the other. The state under Park controlled the allocation and distribution of credit, allowing it to have some input into investment decisions. Policy loans, while generous in quantity and repayment terms, were only made to projects that the state designated as being important to economic development. The *chaebols* meanwhile held a virtual veto over some aspects of economic policy by dint of the structural power that emanated from their pre-eminent position in the economy. They operated the most lucrative and strategic industries and also accounted for a significant degree of economic concentration.

Yet the leverage of both parties had been weakened by the post-crisis period. The state had retrenched its most potent policy tools in accordance with the advice of liberals both within the state apparatus and also in international institutions. It was also incumbent upon the state to cater to sectors of capital other than the *chaebols*. That is, the *chaebols*' pre-eminent position in the economy diminished as a result of the IMF reforms. The restructuring of the financial system resulted in easier access to credit for SMEs, and government programmes have also helped SMEs relocate offshore or establish joint ventures with foreign enterprises (especially in China). Of equally great significance has been the influx of foreign capital and enterprises to Korea.

Chapter 6 mentioned that foreign capital now controls some leading Korean enterprises, including well-known firms such as Samsung Electronics. Foreign ownership of shares listed on the Korean stock exchange is also nearing 50 per cent. It is thus somewhat problematic to speak of an alliance between the state and 'capital' in Korea, given the much-diminished structural position of the *chaebols*. It is the highly unified nature of *big* business that gives meaning to terms such as 'business power', and it is generally assumed that the capital involved will be *national*. So any predictions about the future of the developmental alliance in Korea will continue to refer to the state and the *chaebols*. However, these predictions must account for the changes wrought on the structure and position of Korean capital since the financial crisis. While the SMEs and foreign capital are of growing importance to the fate of economic development, it will chiefly be with the *chaebols* that the state will formulate future development strategies. Whether these strategies can be as successful as in the past is questionable, given the diminished position of the *chaebols*.

The alliance and the market

The Korean developmental alliance has accomplished economic development, a key component of the broader goal of modernity. This represents a significant achievement for the state and business. However, modernisation has proven to be a traumatic process for Korean society. It has wrought numerous changes, not least of which has been to expose Korean capitalism to the full force of the international economy.

The latter phases of economic development have witnessed the transition from a state-centric mode of governance to a market-centric one. The mode of state–business interaction most commonly associated with the developmental alliance changed significantly by the late 1990s. Both the state and the *chaebols* had shared an interest in formulating and implementing economic policies with little input from other parties during the early phases of development. With the maturation of the economy, the pursuit of economic development becomes more complex. As argued in the study, this is because the process of development is intimately linked with broader socio-political processes. The preferences of domestic actors such as labour and SMEs, along with external ones such as the United States, have increasingly influenced Korean development.

The study demonstrated the difficulty involved in governing even the initial stages of Korea's development. By the 1980s, the economy's degree of complexity was such that the state could not direct the process of development alone. Liberals called for the state to share the task of governance with the market, but attempts to reform the governance structure were half-hearted at best. The division of labour in the political economy was not clear-cut during the 1980s and 1990s. Previously, the state had assumed responsibility for supplying economic resources to, and guaranteeing the debts of, the *chaebols*. The transition to a market-based governance structure should have resulted in financial institutions subjecting the *chaebols* to market pressures. However, the market failed to discipline the *chaebols*.

Instead, the economy was caught in the awkward middle ground between a state-centric governance structure and a market-centric one. The *chaebols* enjoyed the benefits of state support without the commensurate sanctions. They also enjoyed unfettered access to a liberalised financial system without the discipline of prudential lending requirements. The state continued to offer an implicit guarantee for the *chaebols*. However, the state could not discipline the *chaebols* and thus ensure that they acted in accordance with the interests of economic development. Consequently, the economy was plunged into crisis when Korea endured liquidity shortages during the second half of 1997. International lenders recalled their loans rather than continuing to lend to the heavily indebted *chaebols*. The state proved to be incapable of fulfilling the task that international lenders assumed of it, which was to guarantee the debts of the *chaebols*. Lending only resumed when the state agreed to implement reforms that reduced the *chaebols'* proclivity for excessive borrowing.

The state thus implemented a raft of reforms following the crisis as a condition of the IMF's bailout. This expedited the transition from the governance structure of initial phases of development, which had previously favoured the concentration of economic resources in the *chaebols*. Reforms to corporate governance structures reduced the *chaebols'* capacity to transfer resources from one affiliate to another. The state's guarantee for the *chaebols'* debts also largely disappeared due to the introduction of more stringent limits to debt-equity ratios. The reforms thus forced the *chaebols* to act more in accordance with market principles. The net effect of the post-crisis reforms was that the intimacy of the affair between the state and the *chaebols* lessened markedly. That is, the mutual dependence between these two parties decreased. Thus Korean development has witnessed a fragmentation of the alliance between the state and capital. The transition to the market-centric mode of governance has exposed the developmental alliance more fully to forces of the market economy.

The transition to the market mode of governance has removed much of the intimacy that characterised the initial and intermediate phases of the developmental alliance. This is not to say that the market mode of governance has for the first time exposed the alliance to transnational capital. However, the state proved adept in limiting the scope of transnational capital's involvement in the Korean economy until the 1990s. This was because the state reasoned that non-Korean capital would not serve the end of national development. However, the state, as well as much of the public, perceived the behaviour of the *chaebols* in the 1990s to be reckless to the extent that it caused the catastrophic crisis of 1997. The crisis altered the understanding of the state elites about the relative merits of national as opposed to transnational capital.

The DA thus faces an identity crisis due to the globalisation of the Korean economy. The goals of economic development were initially closely aligned with the interests of national capital. However, this has not been the case since the 1990s due to the increasingly international nature of the economy and also the *chaebols*. If national capital does not serve the national interest, the state will instead attempt to co-opt transnational capital to that end. This involves the incorporation of transnational capital into key sectors of the industrial economy and also the financial system. Traditionally the state has preferred these sectors to use solely national capital.

The challenge for the state in the post-crisis period has been to redefine its role in economic development so that it reflects the transition to the market mode of governance. While foreign capital has become a vital component of the Korean economy in the post-crisis period, it has not as yet been fully incorporated into the Korean economy. This may not be possible, given the divergent interests between the national focus of economic development and the developmental alliance on the one hand, and global capital on the other.

The state has thus drawn on its power resources in order to devise a new developmental alliance. That is, instead of relying on dirigiste methods such as policy loans to discipline the *chaebols* and thus lead economic development, it has relied on market-based instruments to achieve that end. The outlines of this new system have been taking form in recent years. For example, a notable feature of the new mode of governance has been a better-functioning financial system. The *chaebols* remain the most important group of borrowers within the Korean financial system. However, lenders have subjected the *chaebols* to greater scrutiny in the use of their loans. One reason for this has been the involvement of foreign capital in the financial system. That is, non-Korean institutions have demanded higher standards of accountability from the *chaebols*. The state has thus encouraged a degree of non-Korean involvement in the economy because this has served the ends of economic development by disciplining the *chaebols*. National capital has been subjected to the state's use of market discipline rather than the traditional methods of industrial policy.

The new directives introduced as part of the IMF's reforms have also forced the *chaebols* to lower their debt levels. The state required the *chaebols* to reduce their debt-equity ratios to a maximum of 200 per cent in order to be eligible for new loans. The *chaebols* are thus now less prone to collapse. This in turn reduces the possibility of a systemic collapse and a renewed liquidity crisis. The state thus has less incentive to bail out indebted *chaebols*.

Further, Korea has amassed one of the highest stocks of foreign exchange reserves in the world in recent years. Reserves slumped to only a few billion dollars by the end of 1997, the peak of the financial crisis. Thereafter Korea's foreign currency reserves reached $52 billion by the end of 1998, $96 billion at the end of 2000, and $155 billion by late 2003 (National Statistical Office 2004). They stood at $206 billion in May 2005, the fourth largest in the world. The upsurge in Korea's foreign exchange reserves has stabilised the financial system, and effectively guarantees that there will be no repetition in the foreseeable future of the liquidity crisis that occurred in the second half of 1997. In this respect the position of the state is far stronger than in the 1990s, when the prospect of a liquidity crisis prevented it from disciplining the *chaebols*. Nonetheless, some commentators suggest that the accumulation of foreign exchange reserves may have passed the level where they serve a useful purpose, and that artificially supporting the Korean currency is now undermining the national industrial base (see for instance K.-H. Kim 2007).

Another noteworthy issue has been the emergence of Korea's vibrant democracy in the past two decades. Whereas the state clearly sided with the *chaebols* when the interests of the *chaebols* clashed with those of civil society during the initial stages of the DA, the state has had to acknowledge the interests of society in the latter stages. Thus the state has sought to address deleterious aspects of the *chaebol* model such as inattention to environmental degradation and health and safety standards. The outlines of a nascent social safety net also appeared in the wake of the financial crisis. The emergence of the Korean Democratic Labour Party has offered the possibility of a legitimate left–right political spectrum in South Korea for the first time since national division. This has placed issues on the public agenda such as the logic and objectives of the developmental alliance, and the role of labour within the alliance. Public policy has – at least to some degree – reflected this new plurality of interests.

This is not to say that the negative aspects of the DA have disappeared. Korea is still prone to cronyism, but this occurs on a far smaller scale than during the presidencies of Park Chung Hee, Chun Doo-hwan and Roh Tae-woo. The Korean Electoral Commission is far more stringent in monitoring contributions from the *chaebols* to political campaigns than in previous decades. Cronyism instead tends to take the form of payoffs for specific projects such as real estate developments.

Nonetheless, state–business relations in Korea appear to be markedly different compared to previous decades. The developmental alliance of the Park era has changed into a more fragmented relationship. Therein the loyalties and sense of shared interest that characterised the Park-era alliance appear to have evaporated to some extent. The end of the old affair, and the beginning of a new relationship between the state and the *chaebols*, may be a condition of Korea's transition to political and economic maturation.

Appendix 1

Key personages in the Korean developmental alliance

Chang Myon (張勉): Korea's first ambassador to United States; prime minister 1951–2 before joining parliamentary opposition during presidency of Syngman Rhee; elected vice-president in 1956 but wielded little power; prime minister again, 1960–1 (Second Republic); resigned in wake of Park Chung Hee's coup and ceased political activity.

Choi Kyu-hah (崔圭夏): bureaucrat and prime minister in the late 1970s; served as caretaker president from Park's assassination in 1979 until Chun Doo-hwan's assumption of power in 1980; influenced by liberals such as Kim Jae-ik; introduced a dose of 'shock therapy' while in office.

Chun Doo-hwan (全斗煥): professional soldier who was part of first group to pass through Korean Military Academy; assumed control of KCIA and then state in 1979–80 in conjunction with his colleague Roh Tae-woo; implicated in Gwangju massacre of May 1980; president 1981–8; sentenced to 23 years in jail along with Roh for involvement in the coup and acceptance of bribes; the former presidents served 18 months in jail until Kim Young-sam pardoned them, in 1997.

Chung Ju-yong (鄭周永): founder of Hyundai Group, beginning business career in areas of rice trading, auto repairs and contracts with American military; favoured by Park Chung Hee in the 1970s along with Daewoo's Kim Woo Choong; fell out of favour with Roh Tae-woo and Kim Young-sam for contesting the 1992 presidential election; regained favour during Kim Dae-jung's period in office; central to promotion of economic ties with North Korea.

Kang Bong-gyun (康奉均): mid-level bureaucrat in Ministry of Finance, 1970s; senior officer – including director – of EPB, 1985–9; various portfolios in early to mid-1990s; prime minister and EPB director, 1994–6; special economic advisor to Kim Dae-jung 1998–9; thereafter Minister for Finance and Economy; resigned from this post in early 2000 in order to pursue parliamentary career with Uri Party.

Kim Chung-yum (金正濂): economist and central bank official in the 1950s; bureaucrat and minister during 1960s, holding portfolios such as finance and commerce and industry; involved in issues such as currency reform, 1972 presidential decree, HCI drive and New Village Movement; chief of staff to Park Chung Hee 1969–78; ambassador to Japan 1979–81.

Kim Dae-jung (金大中): one of the 'three Kims' of modern Korean politics, along with Kim Jong-pil and Kim Young-sam; statesman and dissident from Jeolla province, surviving assassination, imprisonment and kidnapping; suffered numerous election defeats (several by dubious means); president, 1998–2003; oversaw implementation of IMF's reforms; won Nobel Peace Prize, in 2001, for efforts to improve inter-Korean relations.

Kim Jae-ik (金在益): received doctorate in economics from Stanford in 1973; returned to Korea and served in senior positions in EPB during Park Chung Hee era; disapproved of Park's development strategy but failed to change its course; influenced policies of Chun Doo-hwan, serving as his personal economic advisor; advocated 'stabilisation' policies in early 1980s; lost life in Rangoon bombing of 1983.

Kim Jong-pil (金鍾泌): nephew of Park Chung Hee; emerged from Korean Military Academy at same time as Park; masterminded coup and founded KCIA, 1961; chairman of ruling Democratic Republican Party for many years; nine terms as a parliamentarian over four decades; prime minister 1971–5; helped found three-party merger with Roh Tae-woo and Kim Young-sam before leaving party in 1995 due to falling out with Kim Young-sam; gained revenge by joining forces with Kim Dae-jung in 1997 to defeat ruling party candidate; prime minister again 1998–2000.

Kim Jong-rak (金鍾珞): elder brother of Kim Jong-pil; advisor to Park Chung Hee in the 1960s and 1970s; also worked in banking sector.

Kim Woo Choong (金宇中): Daewoo chairman and founder, having benefited from US military contracts after Korean War; close ties with Park Chung Hee regime saw Daewoo enter capital-intensive industries such as shipbuilding and automobiles; convicted for bribery during Chun Doo-hwan–Roh Tae-woo scandal, 1995–6, but not jailed; FKI chairman 1998–9; resigned this post upon collapse of Daewoo group; fled from Korea in 1999 and was a fugitive abroad until 2005; although convicted of embezzlement, was pardoned by outgoing President Roh Moo-hyun in late 2007.

Kim Yong Hwan (金龍煥): mid-level bureaucrat and junior minister in various portfolios 1966–72, with involvement in planning HCI; special economic advisor to Park Chung Hee 1973–4; Minister for Finance 1974–8; parliamentarian 1988–2004.

Kim Yong-tae (金龍泰): served as chief secretary to President Park; involved in promotion of industrial policy in the 1960s; office bearer in Park's Democratic Republican Party in 1960s and politically close to Kim Jong-pil.

Kim Young-sam (金泳三): long-time member of parliamentary opposition, vying with Kim Dae-jung for leadership of anti-regime forces; his arrest in late 1979 sparked demonstrations in Gyeongsang province that contributed to the assassination of Park Chung Hee; central to anti-state forces in 1980s; left main opposition groups to join Roh Tae-woo in 1990; president 1993–8; promoted 'globalisation' (*segyehwa*) policy to open Korea's markets; widely blamed for financial crisis.

Lee Byung-chul (李秉喆): entrepreneur who maintained close affinity with Japan, having attended university there during colonial period; began career in rice trading, trucking, real estate, noodles, sugar refining and brewing; founded what would become Samsung Group in 1938; profited from US military occupation and access to lucrative contracts under Syngman Rhee; considered Korea's richest man at the time of Park's coup; a key player in bargain struck with regime in 1961 whereby business leaders were pardoned for their crimes; father of Lee Kun-hee.

Lee Hun-jai (李憲宰): mid-level bureaucrat in Ministry of Finance and presidential secretariat in 1970s; chairman of Securities and Exchange Commission 1991–6; chairman of FSC 1998–2000; chairman of Restructuring and Reform Commission in late 1997; Minister for Finance and Economy, 2000; Roh Moo-hyun's Minister for Finance and Economy, 2004–5.

Lee Ki-ho (李起浩): completed education in US and returned to serve in EPB, 1977–95, gradually rising to highest ranks; served as minister in various portfolios thereafter, including prime minister for six months in 1997; economic advisor to Kim Dae-jung as well as holding various ministries since 1998.

Lee Kun-hee (李健熙): chairman and key shareholder of Samsung Group following his father's death in 1987; made Samsung Korea's most profitable *chaebol*, with electronics division being most impressive unit; assumed responsible for Samsung's ill-fated venture into automobile industry from 1994; member of International Olympic Committee from 1996.

Lee Kyu-seong (李揆成): mid-level bureaucrat in Ministry of Finance and presidential secretariat in the 1970s; prime minister 1983–8; Minister of Finance 1988–90; Minister for Finance and Economy 1998–9 in Kim Dae-jung government.

Lee Myung-bak (李明博): long-time employee of Hyundai Construction, serving 27 years in total, culminating in his rise to the position of CEO; resigned to pursue business and political career, making a small fortune from real estate speculation; resigned from parliament 1998; served as mayor of Seoul, 2002–6; elected president in December 2007 as candidate of Grand National Party.

O Wonchol (吳源哲): worked in automobile industry before joining Park Chung Hee regime in 1961 as an economic advisor; senior technocrat in MCI in 1960s; served as senior economic secretary to president 1971–9; influential in HCI project, 1970s; instigator of EOI approach.

Park Chung Hee (朴正熙): trained as school teacher before enlisting in military, late 1930s; served Japanese imperial army in Manchuria, early 1940s; lieutenant–general in Korean army, leading military coup, 1961; normalised relations with Japan, 1965; sent troops to Vietnam in same year; launched range of measures to modernise Korea including HCI and New Village Movement; prioritised exports as a means of creating national wealth; promulgated Yusin Constitution to extend his rule; president from 1961 until his assassination in 1979.

Park Tae-jun (朴泰俊): passed through Korean Military Academy with Park Chung Hee; Park's secretary after coup; primary responsibility for founding a Korean steel mill; subsequently chairman of POSCO, Korea's state-owned steel maker; Chung Ju-yong's running mate and confidante during campaign for presidency in 1992; forced to resign his post at POSCO following election.

Roh Moo-hyun (盧武鉉): democracy activist in the 1980s, working as human rights lawyer; served prison terms for these and related activities; used parliamentary position to pursue corruption charges against former presidents; president 2003–8; National Assembly voted to impeach Roh in 2004 but Constitutional Court failed to ratify charges against him.

Roh Tae-woo (盧泰愚): Chun Doo-hwan's military colleague; president 1988–93; in power during Seoul Olympics; oversaw Korea's transition to democracy, first by allowing reasonably fair ballot, 1988, and then manoeuvring Kim Young-sam into ruling party, 1990; pursued reform with mixed results, to consternation of *chaebols*; jailed for his involvement in events of 1979–80 and accepting bribes.

Syngman Rhee (李承晚): president of 'Korean government in exile'; campaigned for independence from Japan; president of ROK, 1948–60; Korea's war-time leader, retreating to Busan in first year of conflict; sought to unify Korea by force and thus opposed armistice, 1953; launched successful land reform program following Korean War; student uprising of 1960 forced him to leave Korea for exile in Hawaii.

Yun Bo-seon (尹潽善): member of parliamentary opposition during Rhee period; won the poll for office of vice-president in 1960; interim president after Rhee's demise; resigned from office after Park's coup in 1961; barred from political activity in the wake of the Yusin Constitution.

Appendix 2

Glossary of Korean terms used in the text

chaebol (財閥): family-owned conglomerates that monopolise Korean business; usually refers to only the biggest of these; rendered in Japanese as *zaibatsu*.

daema-bulsa (大馬不死): 'Too big to fail' mentality; expectation that state will guarantee loans of *chaebols*.

gwanchi gyeongje (官治 經濟): 'Rule by bureaucracy'; society characterised by authoritarian politics and bureaucratic leadership.

jeonggyeong yuchak (政經 癒着): close relations between government (*jeong*) and business (*gyeong*), often assumed to be improper or illegal in nature.

minjung (民衆): people, as in people's movement.

saeop poguk (事業 報國): 'Serving the country through entrepreneurial activities'; slogan of the *chaebols*.

saneop ipguk (産業 立國): 'Industrial development'; slogan of the *chaebols*.

sanonggongsang (士農工商): four traditional classes of East Asian society – scholars, farmers, artisans and tradesmen.

segyehwa (世界化): globalisation; eponymous policy of Kim Young-sam.

seondansik (船團式): convoy or flotilla system (of management).

silmyeongje (實名制): real-name financial transaction system, aimed at eliminating illegal political donations.

yangban (兩班): Korean aristocratic class.

Yusin (維新): reform, revitalisation; name of Park's 'reforms' in 1972; inspired by Meiji 'restoration' (*isshin*), Japan's 'self-strengthening' movement.

References

Ahn, Ki-seok (2002) 'Jeongchi-neun naega matgo gyeongje-neun Kim Hoejang-iya (I'll take care of politics and the economy [is the responsibility of] Chairman Kim)', *Shindonga*, February: 134–45.

Aghevli, Bijan B. and Marquez-Ruarte, Jorge R. (1985) *A case of successful adjustment: Korea's experience during 1980–84*, Washington DC: International Monetary Fund.

Alford, Peter (2007) 'Never mind ethical smudges, pragmatism flows through Seoul', *The Australian*, 22 December: 22.

Amsden, Alice H. (1990) 'Third World industrialization: "Global Fordism" or a new model?', *New Left Review*, no. 182: 5–31.

—— (1992) *Asia's next giant: South Korea and late industrialization*, revised ed., Oxford: Oxford University Press.

Baek, Ja-geon (1995) '4gaewol jinggye: Samsung–jeongbu naenggiryu jeonmal (Four months of punishment: Cold current expected between Samsung and the government)', *Shindonga,* September: 386–92.

Bell, Stephen (1994) 'Statist analysis', in A. Parkin, J. Summers and D. Woodward (eds) *Government, politics, power and policy in Australia*, Melbourne: Longman Cheshire.

Bellin, Eva (2000) 'Contingent democrats: industrialists, labour and democratisation in late-developing countries', *World Politics*, 52, no. 2: 175–205.

Bisley, Nick (2007) *Rethinking globalisation*, Basingstoke: Palgrave Macmillan.

Bleiker, Roland (2005) *Divided Korea: toward a culture of reconciliation*, Minneapolis MN: University of Minnesota Press.

Block, Fred (1977) 'The ruling class does not rule: Notes on the Marxist theory of the state', *Socialist Revolution,* no. 33: 6–28.

—— (1992) 'Capitalism without class power', *Politics & Society*, 20, no. 3: 277–303.

Boyd, Richard and Tak-Wing Ngo (2005) 'Emancipating the political economy of Asia from the growth paradigm', in R. Boyd and T.-W. Ngo (eds) *Asian states: beyond the developmental perspective*, London: Routledge/Curzon.

Brazinsky, Gregg A. (2005) 'From pupil to model: South Korea and American development policy during the early Park Chung Hee era', *Diplomatic History*, 29, no. 1: 83–115.

Burmeister, Larry L. (1986) 'Warfare, welfare and state autonomy: structural roots of the South Korean developmental state', *Pacific Focus*, 1, no. 2: 121–46.

Callon, Scott (1995) *Divided sun: MITI and the breakdown of the Japanese high-tech industrial policy, 1975–1993*, Stanford CA: Stanford University Press.

Chang, Dae-oup and Jun-Ho Chae (2004) 'The transformation of Korean labour relations since 1997', *Journal of Contemporary Asia*, 34, no. 4: 427–48.

Chang, Ha-Joon (1993) 'The political economy of industrial policy in Korea', *Cambridge Journal of Economics*, 17, no. 2: 131–57.

—— (1998) 'South Korea: Anatomy of a crisis', *Current History*, December: 437–41.

—— (2002) *Kicking away the ladder: development strategy in historical perspective*, London: Anthem.

Chang, Sea-Jin (2003) *Financial crisis and transformation of Korean business groups: the rise and fall of chaebols*, Cambridge: Cambridge University Press.

Cherry, Judith (2005) '"Big Deal" or big disappointment? The continuing evolution of the South Korean developmental state', *Pacific Review*, 18, no. 3: 327–54.

Chibber, Vivek (1999) 'Building a developmental state: The Korean case reconsidered', *Politics & Society*, 27, no. 3: 309–46.

—— (2002) 'Bureaucratic rationality and the developmental state', *American Journal of Sociology*, 107, no. 4: 951–89.

—— (2003) *Locked in place: state-building and late industrialization in India*, Princeton NJ: Princeton University Press.

—— (2005) 'The politics of a miracle: Class interests and state power in Korean developmentalism', in D. Coates (ed.) *Varieties of capitalism, varieties of approaches*, New York: Palgrave Macmillan.

Cho, Hee-Yoon and Jessop, Bob (2001) 'The listian warfare state and authoritarian developmental mobilization regime in the East Asian anticommunist regimented society: a study on the characteristics of the state and accumulation regime in South Korea and Taiwan', paper presented at 'In Search of East Asian Modes of Development: Regulationist Approaches', Tunghai University, Taichung, 19–20 April.

Cho, Yeong-cheol (2003) '*Chaebol* cheje-wa baljeon jibae yeonhap: minjujeok *chaebol* gaehyeokron-ui yeoksajeok geungeo (The *chaebol* system and the developmental control alliance: the historical bases of the democratic *chaebol* reform thesis)', in B. C. Lee (ed.) *Gaebal dokjae-wa Park Chung Hee sidae: uri sidae-ui jeongchi gyeongjejeok giwon (Developmental dictatorship and the Park Chung Hee era: the political–economic origins of our era)*, Seoul: Changbi Publishers.

Cho, Yoon-Je (1999) 'The political economy of the financial liberalization and crisis in Korea', paper presented at Conference on Comparative Study of Financial Liberalization in Asia, East–West Centre, Hawaii, 23–24 September.

Choi, Don Mee (2003) 'An interview with Ko Un', *Acta Koreana*, 6, no. 2: 139–51.

Choi, Sung Il (1983) 'South Korea under Park Chung Hee: Development or decay?', *Bulletin of Concerned Asian Scholars*, 15, no. 2: 67–72.

Choong, Yong Ahn (2001) 'Financial and corporate sector restructuring in South Korea: accomplishments and unfinished agenda', *Japanese Economic Review*, 52, no. 4: 452–70.

Chung, Un-Chan (1998) 'IMF guje geumyung-gwa geosi gyeongje jeongchaek (The IMF emergency loan and macroeconomic policy)', *Han-Eun Jeongbo*, April: 74–89.

Chung, Young-Iob (1985) '*Chaebol* entrepreneurs in the early stage of Korean economic development', *Journal of Modern Korean Studies*, no. 2: 15–29.

Clifford, Mark (1990) 'Seoul-mates again', *Far Eastern Economic Review*, 1 March: 46–7.

—— (1991) 'Biggest is best', *Far Eastern Economic Review*, 10 October: 59–60.

—— (1998) *Troubled tiger: businessmen, bureaucrats and generals in South Korea*, revised ed., Armonk NY: M. E. Sharpe.

Crotty, James and Lee, Kang-Kook (2002a) 'Is financial liberalization good for developing nations? The case of South Korea in the 1990s', *Review of Radical Political Economics*, 34, no. 3: 327–34.

—— (2002b) 'A political–economic analysis of the failure of neo-liberal restructuring in post-crisis Korea', *Cambridge Journal of Economics*, 26, no. 5: 667–78.

Cumings, Bruce (1981) *The origins of the Korean War: liberation and the emergence of separate regimes, 1945–1947*, vol. 1, Princeton NJ: Princeton University Press.

—— (1984) 'The origins and development of the Northeast Asian political economy: industrial sectors, product cycles and political consequences', *International Organisation*, 38, no. 1: 1–40.

—— (1989) 'The abortive abertura: South Korea in the light of Latin American experience', *New Left Review*, no. 173: 5–32.

—— (1990) *The origins of the Korean War: the roaring of the cataract, 1947–1950*, vol. 2, Princeton NJ: Princeton University Press.

—— (1997) *Korea's place in the sun: a modern history*, New York: W. W. Norton.

—— (1998) 'The Korean crisis and the end of "late" development', *New Left Review*, no. 231: 43–72.

—— (1999) 'Webs with no spiders, spiders with no webs: the genealogy of the developmental state', in M. Woo–Cumings (ed.) *The developmental state*, Ithaca NY: Cornell University Press.

Cumings, Bruce and Jacobsen, Kurt (2006) 'Prying open American political "science"', *post-autistic economics review*, no. 37: 55–8.

Department of Defense (2004) 'US, Republic of Korea reach agreement on troop redeployment', *US Department of Defense, Office of the Assistant Secretary of Defense (Public Affairs)*, 6 October.

Dodds, Klaus (2003) 'Cold War geopolitics', in J. A. Agnew, K. Mitchell and G. Toal (eds) *A companion to political geography*, Oxford: Blackwell Publishers.

Doner, Richard F. (1992) 'Limits of state strength: toward an institutionalist view of economic development', *World Politics*, 44, no. 3: 398–431.

Doner, Richard F., Ritchie, Bryan K. and Slater, Dan (2005) 'Systemic vulnerability and the origins of developmental states: Northeast and Southeast Asia in comparative perspective', *International Organisation*, 59, no. 2: 327–61.

Downs, Chuck (1999) *Over the line: North Korea's negotiating strategy*, Washington DC: AEI Press.

East Asia Analytical Unit (1999) *Korea rebuilds: from crisis to opportunity*, Canberra: Department of Foreign Affairs and Trade.

Eckert, Carter J. (1991) *Offspring of empire: the Koch'ang Kims and the colonial origins of Korean capitalism, 1876–1945*, Seattle WA: University of Washington Press.

—— (1996) 'Total war, industrialization and social change in late colonial Korea', in P. Duus, R. H. Myers and M. R. Peattie (eds) *The Japanese wartime empire, 1931–1945*, Princeton NJ: Princeton University Press.

Eckert, Carter J., Lee, Ki-Baik, Lew, Young Ick, Robinson, Michael and Wagner, Edward W. (1990) *Korea old and new: a history*, Seoul: Ilchokak Publishers.

Evans, Peter B. (1989) 'Predatory, developmental and other apparatuses: a comparative political economy perspective on the third world state', *Sociological Forum*, 4, no. 4: 561–87.

—— (1995) *Embedded autonomy: states and industrial transformation*, Princeton NJ: Princeton University Press.

—— (1998) 'Transferable lessons? Re-examining the institutional prerequisites of East Asian economic policies', *Journal of Development Studies*, 34, no. 6: 66–86.

Feldstein, Martin (1998) 'Refocusing the IMF', *Foreign Affairs*, 77, no. 2: 20–33.

Fifield, Anna (2007) 'Lone Star selling off Korean assets', *The Australian*, 26 June: 21.

Frieden, Jeff (1981) 'Third world indebted industrialization: International finance and state capitalism in Mexico, Brazil, Algeria and South Korea', *International Organization*, 35, no. 3: 407–31.

Friedland, Jonathon (1990) 'Roh's new ground rules', *Far Eastern Economic Review*, 24 May: 62–3.

Friedman, David (1988) *The misunderstood miracle: industrial development and political change in Japan*, Ithaca NY: Cornell University Press.

Garnaut, Ross (1998) 'The financial crisis: a watershed in economic thought about Asia', *Asian–Pacific Economic Literature*, 12, no. 1: 1–11.

Gatz, Karen L. and Patterson, David S. (eds) (1999) *Foreign Relations of the United States, 1964–1968: Korea*, vol. 29, Washington DC: United States Government Printing Office.

Gill, Stephen R. and Law, David (1989) 'Global hegemony and the structural power of capital', *International Studies Quarterly*, 33, no. 4: 475–99.

Grant, Wyn and Sargent, Jane (1987) *Business and politics in Britain*, London: Macmillan Education.

Haggard, Stephan (2000) *The political economy of the Asian financial crisis*, Washington DC: Institute of International Economics.

Haggard, Stephan, Lim, Wonhyuk and Kim, Euysung (2003a) 'Conclusion: whither the *chaebol*?', in S. Haggard, W. Lim and E. Kim (eds) *Economic crisis and corporate restructuring in Korea*, Cambridge: Cambridge University Press.

—— (eds) (2003b) *Economic crisis and corporate restructuring in Korea*, Cambridge: Cambridge University Press.

Hahm, Joon-Ho (2003) 'The government, the *chaebol* and financial institutions before the economic crisis', in S. Haggard, W. Lim and E. Kim (eds) *Economic crisis and corporate restructuring in Korea*, Cambridge: Cambridge University Press.

Han, Jongwoo and Ling, L. H. M. (1998) 'Authoritarianism in the hyper masculinized state: hybridity, patriarchy and capitalism in Korea', *International Studies Quarterly*, 42, no. 1: 53–78.

Heo, Yong-jeol (1999) 'Kim Jong-rak-i malhaneun dongsaeng Kim Jong-Pil-gwa Park Chung Hee-ui mimyohan gwangye bisa (Kim Jong-rak's version of the secret history of the close relationship between his younger brother Kim Jong-Pil and Park Chung Hee)', *Wolgan Chosun*, July: 406–20.

Higgott, Richard (1999) 'Economics, politics and (international) political economy: the need for a balanced diet in an era of globalisation', *New Political Economy*, 4, no. 1: 23–36.

Huff, W. G., Dewit, G. and Oughton, C. (2001) 'Credibility and reputation building in the developmental state: a model with East Asian applications', *World Development*, 29, no. 4: 711–24.

Hundt, David (2005) 'A legitimate paradox: neo-liberal reform and the return of the state in Korea', *Journal of Development Studies*, 41, no. 2: 242–60.

Ikenberry, G. John (2001) 'American power and the empire of capitalist democracy', *Review of International Studies*, 27, no. 5: 191–212.

Jayasuriya, Kanishka (2005) 'Beyond institutional fetishism: from the developmental to the regulatory state', *New Political Economy*, 10, no. 3: 381–7.

Jessop, Bob (2005) 'A regulationist and state-theoretical analysis', in R. Boyd and T.-W. Ngo (eds) *Asian states: beyond the developmental perspective*, London: Routledge/Curzon.

Joh, Sung Wook and Kim, Euysung (2003) 'Corporate governance and performance in the 1990s', in S. Haggard, W. Lim and E. Kim (eds) *Economic crisis and corporate restructuring in Korea*, Cambridge: Cambridge University Press.

Johnson, Chalmers (1982) *MITI and the Japanese miracle: the growth of industrial policy, 1925–75*, Stanford CA: Stanford University Press

—— (1984) 'Introduction: the idea of industrial policy', in C. Johnson (ed.) *The industrial policy debate*, San Francisco CA: Institute of Contemporary Studies.

—— (1999) 'The developmental state: Odyssey of a concept', in M. Woo–Cumings (ed.) *The developmental state*, Ithaca NY: Cornell University Press.

Jones, David Martin (1998) 'Democratization, civil society and illiberal middle class culture in Pacific Asia', *Comparative Politics*, 30, no. 2: 147–69.

Jung, Tae-hern (2000) 'Economic features of colonial modernity in modern Korea', *International Journal of Korean History*, 1: 39–62.

Jwa, Sung-Hee and Lee, In Kwon (eds) (2004) *Competition and corporate governance in Korea: reforming and restructuring the chaebol*, Cheltenham: Edward Elgar.

Kagan, Robert (1998) 'What Korea teaches', *New Republic*, 9 March: 38–47.

Kang, C. S. Eliot (2000) 'Segyehwa reform of the South Korean developmental state', in S. S. Kim (ed.) *Korea's globalisation*, Cambridge: Cambridge University Press.

Kang, David C. (1995a) 'South Korea and Taiwanese development and the new institutional economics', *International Organization*, 49, no. 3: 555–87.

—— (1995b) *Profits of doom: transaction costs, rent-seeking and development in South Korea and the Philippines*, PhD thesis, Berkeley CA: University of California.

Kang, Man-gil (2000) *Hanguk jabonjuui-ui yeoksa: bbae-atkin deul-e seoda (The history of Korean capitalism: standing in a plundered field)*, Seoul: Yeoksa Pipyeongsa.

Kay, Cristóbal (2002) 'Why East Asia overtook Latin America: agrarian reform, industrialisation and development', *Third World Quarterly*, 23, no. 6: 1073–102.

Keefer, Edward C., Mabon, David W., Schwar, Harriet Dashiell and LaFantasie, Glenn W. (eds) (1996) *Foreign Relations of the United States, 1961–1963: China, Korea, Japan*, vol. 22, Washington DC: United States Government Printing Office.

Kim, Byung-Kook (2003) 'The politics of *chaebol* reform, 1980–1997', in S. Haggard, W. Lim and E. Kim (eds) *Economic crisis and corporate restructuring in Korea*, Cambridge: Cambridge University Press.

Kim, Chung-yum (1994) *Policymaking on the front lines: Memoirs of a Korean practitioner 1945–79*, Washington DC: World Bank.

—— (1997) *Ah, Park Chung Hee*, Seoul: Choongang M&B.

Kim, Dae-jung (1997) *Kim Dae-jung daetongryeong gija hoegyeongmun yoji (Main points from press conference with President Kim Dae-jung)*, DJ Road website, 18 December. Available: www.djroad.com (accessed 16 March 2004).

Kim, Eun Mee (1997) *Big business, strong state: collusion and conflict in South Korean development, 1960–1990*, Albany NY: State University of New York Press.

—— (1999) 'Crisis of the developmental state in South Korea', *Asian Perspective*, 23, no. 2: 35–55.

Kim, Gwang-hyeon (1990) '"Heungdae" pan-e *chaebol*-i ddwinda (*Chaebols* run on "rising" field)', *Wolgan Observer*, April: 224–34.

Kim, Hong-ki (1998) 'Seogusik-eul ddaraya sanda (We must follow the Western style to survive)', *Wolgan Chosun*, August: 173–6.

Kim, Hyeong-sik (1999) 'Jeongchi nolli-ro taeeonatta gyeongje nolli-ro sarajineun Hanguk jadongcha saneob-ui bikeuk (The tragedy of the Korean car industry, born from political logic and dying from economic logic)', *Wolgan Chosun*, February: 296–312.

Kim, Hyuk-Rae (2000) 'Korea's economic governance in transition: Governance crisis and the future of Korean capitalism', *Korea Observer*, 31, no. 4: 553–77.

Kim, Jae-ho (2000) 'Jaemubu chulsin janggwan-ui deungjang-e Gihoekwon chulsin-deul ginjang (Former EPB officials concerned at rise of MOF minister)', *Wolgan Chosun*, April.

Kim, Jong-cheol (2004) 'Jabon-ui "pae-op"-e du son duen jeongbu (The government grapples with a capital "strike")', Available: www.ohmynews.com/articleview/article_view.asp?no=168764&rel_no=1 (accessed 28 May 2004).

Kim, Joo Hwan (1999) *Gaebal gugka-eseo-ui gugka–gieob gwangye-e gwanhan yeongu: hanguk-ui joseon saneob baljeon-gwa 'jiwon–gyuyul' teje-e daehan bipanjeok geomto (State–business relations in the developmental state: a critical study of industrialization in the Korean shipbuilding industry and the thesis of 'support–discipline')*, PhD thesis, Seoul: Seoul National University.

Kim, Key-hoon (1998) 'Jayuljeok sijang gineung-i pagoe-doen sanghwang (A case where the autonomous market mechanism has collapsed)', *Wolgan Chosun*, August: 169–72.

—— (2007) 'Gov't has exhausted potential of foreign exchange', *Chosun Ilbo*, 29 October.

Kim, Ki-man (1988) 'Jaegye-ui chongkyeok seoneon, deo isang "dongnebuk" ilsu eopda (Shock declaration of business world: we can no longer be a "punching bag")', *Shindonga*, November: 376–89.

Kim, Kyong-Dong (1976) 'Political factors in the formation of the entrepreneurial elite in South Korea', *Asian Survey*, 16, no. 5: 465–77.

Kim, Sang-jo (1998) 'IMF guje geumyung-gwa Hanguk gyeongje: Sinjayujuuijeok jaepyeon-e daehan dae-eung jeollyak (The IMF emergency loan and the Korean economy: Responses to neoliberal reforms)', *Gyeongje-wa Sahoe*, no. 37: 118–42.

Kim, Se-Jin (1971) *The politics of military revolution in Korea*, Chapel Hill NC: North Carolina University Press.

Kim, Su-gil (1989) 'Kim Jae-ik-gwa Moon Hee-gap (Kim Jae-ik and Moon Hee-gap)', *Wolgan Choongang*, September: 254–67.

Kim, Sungyoung (2006) 'Developmental states under the WTO: the shipbuilding industry in Korea', paper presented at the Second Oceanic Conference on International Studies, University of Melbourne, 5–7 July.

Kim, Yeon-gwang (1999) 'Komin-haneun *chaebol* (The worrying *chaebols*)', *Segye Ilbo*, 21 August: 4.

Kim, Yeon-gwang and Lee, Sang-heun (2002) '"Dumok" Kim Yong-tae, honsin-ui daseot sikan jeungeon ("The head" Kim Yong-tae, a full-blooded five-hour testimony)', *Wolgan Chosun*, April: 274–307.

Kim, Yong Bok (1996) *Gyeongje jayuhwa sidae-e isseoseo saneop jojeong-ui jeongchi: Hanguk-gwa Ilbon-ui saneop jeongchaek gwajeong bigyo bunseok (The politics of industrial adjustment in the period of economic liberalisation:*

a comparative study of industrial policy processes in Korea and Japan), PhD thesis, Seoul: Seoul National University.

Kim, Yong-gi (1991a) 'Dae-*chaebol* jeongchaek 9wolcho-e hwakjeongdoenda (*Chaebol* policy to be finalised by early September)', *Wolgan Observer*, September: 300–7.

—— (1991b) 'Gwan–jaegye-ui 6gong gyeongje jeongchaek pyeongga (Bureaucracy's and business world's evaluation of economic policy during the Sixth Republic)', *Wolgan Observer*, August: 224–41.

Kim, Yong Hwan (2002) *Imja, jane-ga saryeonggwan aninga (Aren't you an officer?)*, Seoul: Maeil Gyeongje Sinmunsa.

Kim, Yong-sam (1999) '*Chaebol* gujo gaehyeok-gwa chongsudeul-ui jeohang (The structural reform of the *chaebols* and the leaders' opposition)', *Wolgan Chosun*, July: 422–59.

Kim, Yun Tae (1999) 'Neo-liberalism and the decline of the developmental state', *Journal of Contemporary Asia*, 29, no. 4: 441–61.

Kohli, Atul (1999) 'Where do high-growth political economies come from? The Japanese lineage of Korea's "developmental state"', in M. Woo–Cumings (ed.) *The developmental state*, Ithaca NY: Cornell University Press.

Kong, Tat Yan (1995) 'From relative autonomy to consensual development: the case of South Korea', *Political Studies*, 43, no. 4: 630–44.

—— (2000) *The politics of economic reform in South Korea: a fragile miracle*, London: Routledge.

—— (2004) 'Neo-liberalization and incorporation in advanced newly industrialized countries: a view from South Korea', *Political Studies*, 52, no. 1: 19–42.

—— (2006) 'Labour and globalisation: locating the Northeast Asian newly industrializing countries', *Review of International Political Economy*, 13, no. 1: 103–28.

Koo, Hagen (1990) 'From farm to factory: proletarianization in Korea', *American Sociological Review*, 55, no. 5: 669–81.

—— (1999) 'Modernity in South Korea: an alternative narrative', *Thesis Eleven*, no. 57: 53–64.

—— (2001) *Korean workers: the culture and politics of class formation*, Ithaca NY: Cornell University Press.

Koo, Hagen and Kim, Eun Mee (1992) 'The developmental state and capital accumulation in South Korea', in R. P. Appelbaum and J. Henderson (eds) *States and development in the Pacific Rim*, London: Sage Publications.

Kuznets, Paul W. (1981) 'Growth and modernization in Korea', *Pacific Affairs*, 54, no. 2: 302–10.

Kwon, Hyeok-cheol (2006) 'Roh Moo-hyun Jeonggwon 3nyeon-ui gyeongje seongjeokpyo (An economic report card of three years of the Roh Moo-hyun government)', *Wolgan Chosun*, March: 262–71.

Kwon, Yeong-ki (2000) 'Kang Bong-Gyun, Jaejeong Gyeongjebu Jangkwan (Kang Bong-Gyun, Minister for Finance and Economy)', *Wolgan Chosun*, January: 64–77.

Lee, Baek-man (1993) 'YS-ui *chaebol* daesusul, sigi-man namattda (Only the timing remains for YS' major surgery on the *chaebols*)', *Shindonga*, June: 320–32.

Lee, Byoung-Hoon (2002) 'Restructuring and employment relations in the Korean auto industry', *Bulletin of Comparative Labour Relations*, no. 45: 59–94.

Lee, Charles S. (1998) 'Kim turns up the heat', *Far Eastern Economic Review*, 19 February: 61–2.

Lee, Cheol-hyeon (1999) '*Chaebol* vs ban-*chaebol* 10gaji haeksim jaengjeom (Ten main issues in the *chaebol* vs anti-*chaebol* debate)', *Shindonga*, September: 248–66.

Lee, Heung (1991) 'Chaeboldeul-ui bankyeok (The *chaebols*' counterattack)', *Wolgan Chosun*, July: 238–55.

Lee, Kwon-Hyung (1998) 'A misunderstood success: the impact of industrial policy on the Korean car industry', *Studies in Economic Development*, 2, no. 2.

Lee, Man-hui (1993) *EPB-neun gijeok-eul natneunga: Hanguk saneop jeongchaek-ui isang-gwa hyeonsil (Did the EPB produce the miracle? The ideals and reality of Korean industrial policy)*, Seoul: Haedodji.

Lee, Nam-gyu and Cho, Kab-Je (2003) 'Hanguk-ui moksumi pareureu ddeolko isseotdda (Korea's life was shaking)', *Wolgan Chosun*, October: 532–74.

Lee, Nari (2003) 'DJ jeongkwon, Big Deal yaksok an jikyeotdda (DJ government didn't keep promises about Big Deals)', *Shindonga*, March: 218–27.

Lee, Sam-Ho (1999) *1980nyeon-gwa 1997nyeon Hanguk-ui gyeongje wigi bigyo yeongu (A comparative study of two economic crises in Korea: 1980 vs 1997)*, MA thesis, Seoul: Seoul National University.

Lee, Su-kon and Woo, In-ho (2004) 'Goodbye Korea: nuga gieobin-eul jichige hana (Goodbye Korea: who's tiring out business leaders?)', *Herald Gyeongje*, 5 January.

Lee, Yeonho (2005) 'Participatory democracy and *chaebol* regulation in Korea: state–market relations under the MDP governments, 1997–2003', *Asian Survey*, 45, no. 2: 279–301.

Lee, Yeonho and Yoo-Jin Lim (2006) 'The rise of the Labour Party in South Korea: causes and limits', *Pacific Review*, 19, no. 3: 305–35.

Leftwich, Adrian (2000) *States of development: on the primacy of politics in development*, Cambridge: Polity.

Leung, Joan Y. H. (2003) 'State capacity and public sector reforms in post-crisis Korea', in A. B. L. Cheung and I. Scott (eds) *Governance and public sector reform in Asia: paradigm shifts or business as usual?*, New York: RoutledgeCurzon.

Lew, Seok-Jin (1992) *Bringing capital back in: a case study of the South Korean automobile industrialization*, PhD thesis, Newhaven CT: Yale University.

Lie, John (1998) *Han unbound: the political economy of South Korea*, Stanford CA: Stanford University Press.

Lim, Eun Mie (2002) *Big horses don't die: the chaebol dominance in the course of Korean industrialization*, PhD thesis, Seattle WA: University of Washington.

Lim, Gyu-jin (1999) 'DJ, neungnyeok eobneun *chaebol* chongsu toechul-sikinda (DJ says he'll remove incompetent *chaebol* leaders)', *Shindonga*, September: 218–26.

Lim, Hyun-Chin and Jang, Jin-Ho (2006) 'Neo-liberalism in post crisis South Korea: Social conditions and outcomes', *Journal of Contemporary Asia*, 36, no. 4: 442–63.

Lim, Timothy C. (1992) *Competition, markets and the politics of development in South Korea, 1945-1979*, PhD thesis, Hawaii: University of Hawaii.

—— (1998) 'Power, capitalism and the authoritarian state in South Korea', *Journal of Contemporary Asia*, 28, no. 4: 457–83.

—— (1999) 'The origins of societal power in South Korea: understanding the physical and human legacies of Japanese colonialism', *Modern Asian Studies*, 33, no. 3: 603–33.

—— (2001) 'Bringing competition in: capitalist development in South Korea and the limits of institutionalism', *Competition & Change*, 5, no. 2: 103–33.

Lim, Wonhyuk (2000) 'Path dependence in action: the rise and fall of the Korean model of economic development', paper presented at History Matters: Economic Growth, Technology and Population – A Conference in Honour of Paul A. David, Stanford University CA, 2–3 June.

—— (2003) 'The emergence of the *chaebol* and the origins of the *chaebol* problem', in S. Haggard, W. Lim and E. Kim (eds) *Economic crisis and corporate restructuring in Korea*, Cambridge: Cambridge University Press.

Lindblom, Charles E. (1977) *Politics and markets: the world's political–economic systems*, New York: Basic Books.

Luedde–Neurath, Richard (1986) *Import controls and export-oriented development: a reassessment of the South Korea case*, Boulder CO: Westview Press.

—— (1988) 'State intervention and export-oriented development in South Korea', in G. White and J. Gray (eds) *Developmental states in East Asia*, New York: St Martin's Press.

McNamara, Dennis L. (ed.) (1999) *Corporatism and Korean capitalism*, London: Routledge.

Mann, Michael (1984) 'The autonomous power of the state: its origins, mechanisms and results', *European Journal of Sociology*, 25, no. 2: 185–213.

—— (1986) *The sources of social power: a history of power from the beginning to AD 1760*, vol. 1, Cambridge: Cambridge University Press.

Mardon, Russell (1990) 'The state and the effective control of foreign capital: the case of South Korea', *World Politics*, 43, no. 1: 111–38.

Marsh, David (1983) 'Interest group activity and structural power: Lindblom's *Politics and markets*', in D. Marsh (ed.) *Capital and politics in Western Europe*, London: Frank Cass.

Mason, Edward S., Kim, Mahn Je, Perkins, Dwight H., Kim, Kwang Suk and Cole, David C. (1980) *The economic and social modernisation of the Republic of Korea*, Cambridge MA: Harvard University, Council on East Asian Studies.

Matray, James I. (1979) 'Truman's plan for victory: national self-determination and the thirty-eighth parallel decision in Korea', *Journal of American History*, 66, no. 2: 314–33.

Mo, Jongryn and Moon, Chung-In (2003) 'Business–government relations under Kim Dae-jung', in S. Haggard, W. Lim and E. Kim (eds) *Economic crisis and corporate restructuring in Korea*, Cambridge: Cambridge University Press.

Moon, Chung-In and Rashemi Prasad (1994) 'Beyond the developmental state: networks, politics and institutions', *Governance*, 7, no. 4: 360–86.

Moran, Jonathon (1998) 'Corruption and NIC development: a case study of South Korea', *Crime, Law and Social Change*, 29, nos. 2–3: 161–77.

Morriss, Peter (1997) 'Roh regrets: leadership, culture and politics in South Korea', *Crime, Law and Social Change*, 28, no. 1: 39–51.

National Statistical Office (2004) 'Tonghap jaejeong suji (Gross fiscal accounts)'. Available: http://kosis.nso.go.kr/cgi-bin/sws_999.cgi (accessed 6 December 2004).

Neary, Michael (2000) 'Hyundai Motors 1998–1999: the anatomy of a strike', *Capital & Class*, Spring: 1–7.

No, Chan-baek, Lee, Si-hyeong, Jeong, Ju-sin and Choe, Yong-seob (2002) *Hanguk jeongchi-ui ihae (Understanding Korean politics)*, Seoul: Hyungseul Publishing.

O, Wonchol (1996) *Hanguk-hyeong gyeongje geonseol: engineering approach (The Korean model of economic construction: the engineering approach)*, vol. 3, Seoul: Kia Economic Research Institute.

Oberdorfer, Don (1997) *The two Koreas: a contemporary history*, New York: Basic Books.

Oh, Ingyu and Varcin, Recep (2002) 'The mafioso state: state-led market bypassing in South Korea and Turkey', *Third World Quarterly*, 23, no. 4: 711–23.

Okimoto, Daniel I. (1989) *Between MITI and the market: Japanese industrial policy for high technology*, Stanford CA: Stanford University Press.

Onïs, Ziya (1991) 'The logic of the developmental state', *Comparative Politics*, 24, no. 1: 109–26.

Onishi, Norimitsu (2008) 'South Korean president pledges pragmatism', *New York Times*, 26 February.

Paisley, Ed (1993) 'Flight and fight', *Far Eastern Economic Review*, 14 January: 16.

Park, Chung Hee (1970) *The country, the revolution and I*, 2nd ed., Seoul: Hollym Corporation.

Park, Chung Hee and Shin, Bum Shik (1970) *Major speeches by Korea's Park Chung Hee*, Seoul: Hollym Corp.

Park, Hun Joo (2002) 'After dirigisme: globalisation, democratization, the still faulted state and its social discontent in Korea', *Pacific Review*, 15, no. 1: 63–88.

Park, Tae-Gyun (1991) *1945nyeon–1946nyeon Migunjeong-ui jeongchi seryeok jaepyeon gyehoek-gwa Namhan jeongchi kudo-ui byeonhwa (The US military government's plans for reorganizing politicians and changes in political aspects in South Korea from 1945 to 1946)*, MA thesis, Seoul: Seoul National University.

—— (1999) 'Change in US policy toward South Korea in the early 1960s', *Korean Studies*, no. 23: 94–120.

—— (2001) 'W. W. Rostow and economic discourse in South Korea in the 1960s', *Journal of International and Area Studies*, 8, no. 2: 55–66.

Park, Won-bae (1993) 'Chongwadae-ui milwol sidae *chaebol*-ui gyesan-gwa gomin (The *chaebols*' calculations and concerns in an era of close relations with the Blue House)', *Wolgan Mal*, November: 42–7.

Pempel, T. J. (1999) 'The developmental regime in a changing world economy', in M. Woo–Cumings (ed.) *The developmental state*, Ithaca NY: Cornell University Press.

Pirie, Iain (2005a) 'Better by design: Korea's neoliberal economy', *The Pacific Review*, 18, no. 3: 355–74.

—— (2005b) 'The new Korean state', *New Political Economy*, 10, no. 1: 25–42.

—— (2008) *The Korean developmental state: from dirigisme to neo-liberalism*, London: Routledge.

Polidano, Charles (2001) 'Don't discard state autonomy: revisiting the East Asian experience of development', *Political Studies*, 49, no. 3: 513–27.

Presidential Truth Commission (2004) *A hard journey to justice: first-term report by the Presidential Truth Commission on Suspicious Deaths of the Republic of Korea*, Seoul: Samin Books, Daetongnyeong Sosok Uimunsa Jinsang Gyumyeong Wiwonhoe.

Radelet, Steven and Sachs, Jeffrey (1998) *The onset of the East Asian financial crisis*, Cambridge MA: Harvard Institute for International Development.

Ravenhill, John (2001) *From national champions to global partnerships: the Korean auto industry, financial crisis and globalisation*, Boston MA: Centre for International Studies, Massachusetts Institute of Technology.

Samuels, Richard J. (1987) *The business of the Japanese state: energy markets in comparative and historical perspective*, Ithaca NY: Cornell University Press.

—— (1994) *'Rich nation, strong army': national security and the technological transformation of Japan*, Ithaca NY: Cornell University Press.

Scanlon, Charles (2004) 'S Korea's shock at US troop cuts', BBC, 8 June. Available: http://news.bbc.co.uk/1/hi/world/asia-pacific/3786811.stm (accessed 12 December 2004).

Schneider, Ben Ross (1998) 'Elusive synergy: business–government relations and development', *Comparative Politics*, 31, no. 1: 101–22.

Schopf, James C. (2001) 'An explanation for the end of political bank robbery in the Republic of Korea: the T + T model', *Asian Survey*, 41, no. 5: 693–715.

Seabrooke, Leonard (2002) *Bringing legitimacy back in to neo-Weberian state theory and international relations*, Canberra: Department of International Relations, Australian National University.

Seliger, Bernhard (2004) 'The European Union and North Korea: personal experience and possible development', *European and Intercultural Discourses Discussion Papers*, no. 1–4–05, May: 3.

Seo, Jee-yeon (2004) 'FKI eager to resolve anti-business sentiment', *Korea Times*, 5 April.

Shaw, Brendan and Hughes, Owen (2002) 'Economic governance and a coordination role for the state: the case of industry policy', in S. Bell (ed.) *Economic governance and institutional dynamics*, South Melbourne: Oxford University Press.

Shin, Dongyoub (2000) 'Dual sources of the South Korean economic crisis: institutional and organisational failures and the structural transformation of the economy', in F. J. Richter (ed.) *The East Asian development model: economic growth, institutional failure and the aftermath of the crisis*, New York: St Martin's Press.

Shin, Jang-Sup and Chang, Ha-Joon (2003) *Restructuring Korea Inc*, London: RoutledgeCurzon.

—— (2005) 'Economic reform after the financial crisis: a critical assessment of institutional transition and transition costs in South Korea', *Review of International Political Economy*, 12, no. 3: 409–33.

Shin, Wookhee (1992) *Security, economic growth and the state: dynamics of patron–client state relations in Northeast Asia*, PhD thesis, Newhaven CT: Yale University.

—— (1994) 'Geopolitical determinants of political economy: the Cold War and South Korean political economy', *Asian Perspective*, 18, no. 2: 119–40.

Smith, Heather (2000) 'The state, banking and corporate relationships in Korea and Taiwan', in P. Drysdale (ed.) *Reform and recovery in East Asia: the role of the state and economic enterprise*, New York: Routledge.

So, Alvin Y. and Chiu, Stephen W. K. (1995) *East Asian and the world economy*, Newbury Park CA: Sage Publications.

Song, Changzoo (2003) 'Business elite and the construction of national identity in Korea', *Acta Koreana*, 6, no. 2: 55–86.

Song, Yang-Min (1999) '10–20% gamwon-haeya modu sanda (10–20% [of jobs] must be cut to save all)', *Wolgan Chosun*, April: 88–97.

Strange, Susan (1994) *States and Markets*, London: Pinter Publishers.

Stubbs, Richard (1999) 'War and economic development: export-oriented industrialization in East and Southeast Asia', *Comparative Politics*, 31, no. 3: 337–55.

Thurbon, Elizabeth (2003) 'Ideational inconsistency and institutional incapacity: why financial liberalisation in South Korea went horribly wrong', *New Political Economy*, 8, no. 3: 341–61.

Tsai, Ming-Chang (1999) 'Geopolitics, the state and political economy of growth in Taiwan', *Review of Radical Political Economics*, 31, no. 3: 101–9.

Underhill, Geoffrey R. D., and Xiaoke Zhang (2005) 'The changing state–market condominium in East Asia: rethinking the political underpinnings of development', *New Political Economy*, 10, no. 1: 1–24.

Vogel, David (1989) *Fluctuating fortunes: the political power of business in America*, New York: Basic Books.

Wade, Robert (1990) *Governing the market: economic theory and the role of the government in East Asian industrialization*, Princeton NJ: Princeton University Press.

—— (1993) 'The visible hand: the state and East Asia's economic growth', *Current History*, December: 431–40.

Wade, Robert, and Veneroso, Frank (1998) 'The Asian crisis: the high debt model versus the Wall Street–Treasury–IMF complex', *New Left Review*, no. 228: 3–23.

Weiss, Linda (1998) *The myth of the powerless state: governing the economy in a global era*, Cambridge: Polity Press.

—— (2003) 'Guiding globalisation in East Asia: new roles for old developmental states', in L. Weiss (ed.) *States in the global economy: bringing domestic institutions back in*, New York: Cambridge University Press.

—— (2005) 'The state-augmenting effects of globalisation', *New Political Economy*, 10, no. 3: 345–53.

Weiss, Linda and Hobson, John M. (2000) 'State power and economic strength revisited: What's so special about the Asian crisis?', in R. Robison, M. Beeson, K. Jayasuriya and H.-R. Kim (eds) *Politics and markets in the wake of the Asian crisis*, New York: Routledge.

Wells, Kenneth M., ed. (1995) *South Korea's minjung movement: the culture and politics of dissidence*, Honolulu, Hawaii: University of Hawaii Press.

West, James W. (1987) 'The suboptimal "miracle" of South Korean state capitalism', *Bulletin of Concerned Asian Scholars*, 19, no. 3: 60–71.

Wilson, Graham K. (1990) *Business and politics: a comparative introduction*, London: Macmillan.

Woo, Jung-en (1991) *Race to the swift: state and finance in Korean industrialization*, New York: Columbia University Press.

Woo–Cumings, Meredith (1994) 'The "new authoritarianism" in East Asia', *Current History*, December: 13–16.

—— (1998a) 'All in the family: reforming corporate governance in East Asia', *Current History*, December: 426–30.

—— (1998b) 'National security and the rise of the developmental state in South Korea and Taiwan', in H. S. Rowen (ed.) *Behind East Asian growth: the political and social foundations of prosperity*, London: Routledge.

—— (1999) 'Introduction: Chalmers Johnson and the politics of nationalism and development', in M. Woo–Cumings (ed.) *The developmental state*, Ithaca NY: Cornell University Press.

World Bank (1993) *The East Asian miracle: economic growth and public policy*, New York: Oxford University Press.

Yoo, Young-eul (1999a) 'Gyeongyeong neungryeok eopnneun *chaebol* 2se twoechulsikyeoya (The *chaebols*' second-generation [leaders] who have no managerial abilities must be forced out)', *Shindonga*, January: 226–41.

—— (1999b) 'Samsung-Cha mollak-ui drama (The drama of Samsung Motor's collapse)', *Shindonga*, August: 248–59.

Yoon, Chang-Ho (1999) 'Entrepreneurial development in late industrialization: a comparative analysis', *International Economic Journal*, 13, no. 2: 1–20.

Yoon, Heo (2001) 'Development strategy in Korea re-examined: an interventionist perspective', *Social Science Journal*, 38, no. 2: 217–31.

Yoon, Hyoung-sup, Kim, Young-rae and Lee, Wan-bom (2003) *Hanguk jeongchi eotteoke pol keot inga (Understanding Korean politics)*, Seoul: Pakyoungsa Publishing Co.

Yoon, Yeong-ho (1999) 'Muneojin Daewoo sinhwa, haebeob-eun momtong palgi? (The collapsed Daewoo myth: is the solution to sell it outright?)', *Shindonga*, June: 264–77.

Yu, In-Ho (1972) 'Formation of modern economic relations in Korea', *Korea Journal*, 12, no. 11: 27–33.

—— (1980) '70nyeondae gyeongje seongjang-ui hoego: Banseong-gwa jeonmang (Retrospective on economic growth in the 1970s: Reflections and prospects)', *Changjak-kwa-Bipyong*, no. 55: 7–28.

Yun, Mikyung (2003) 'Foreign direct investment and corporate restructuring after the crisis', in S. Haggard, W. Lim and E. Kim (eds) *Economic crisis and corporate restructuring in Korea*, Cambridge: Cambridge University Press.

Zhai, Zhihai (1993) 'China's decision to enter the Korean War: history revisited', in C. B. Kim and J. I. Matray (eds) *Korea and the Cold War: division, destruction and disarmament*, Claremont CA: Regina Books.

Index

.